JUDGMENT

HOW WINNING LEADERS MAKE GREAT CALLS

NOEL M. TICHY

AND

WARREN G. BENNIS

PORTFOLIO

PORTFOLIO

Published by the Penguin Group

Penguin Group (USA) Inc., 375 Hudson Street, New York, New York 10014, U.S.A.
Penguin Group (Canada), 90 Eglinton Avenue East, Suite 700, Toronto, Ontario,
Canada M4P 2Y3 (a division of Pearson Penguin Canada Inc.)
Penguin Books Ltd, 80 Strand, London WC2R 0RL, England
Penguin Ireland, 25 St Stephen's Green, Dublin 2, Ireland
(a division of Penguin Books Ltd)
Penguin Group (Australia), 250 Camberwell Road, Camberwell, Victoria 3124,
Australia (a division of Pearson Australia Group Pty Ltd)
Penguin Books India Pvt Ltd, 11 Community Centre, Panchsheel Park,
New Delhi – 110 017, India
Penguin Group (NZ), 67 Apollo Drive, Rosedale, North Shore 0632, New Zealand
(a division of Pearson New Zealand Ltd)
Penguin Books (South Africa) (Pty) Ltd, 24 Sturdee Avenue, Rosebank,
Johannesburg 2196, South Africa

Penguin Books Ltd, Registered Offices: 80 Strand, London WC2R 0RL, England

First published in the United States of America by Portfolio,
a member of Penguin Group (USA) Inc. 2007
This paperback edition published 2009

1   3   5   7   9   10   8   6   4   2

"Handbook for Leadership Judgment" is based on *Judgment* by Noel M. Tichy and
Warren G. Bennis. Copyright © Chris DeRose and Noel M. Tichy, 2007

THE LIBRARY OF CONGRESS HAS CATALOGED THE HARDCOVER EDITION
AS FOLLOWS:
Tichy, Noel M.
Judgment : how winning leaders make great calls / Noel Tichy and Warren Bennis.
p. cm.
Includes bibliographical references and index.
ISBN 978-1-59184-153-1 (hc.)
ISBN 978-1-59184-293-4 (pbk.)
1. Leadership. I. Bennis, Warren G. II. Title.
HD57.7.T496 2007
658.4'095—dc22   2007027169

Printed in the United States of America

To General Wayne Downing, a key leader in this book who unexpectedly passed away on July 18, 2007. Wayne led the creation of the modern-day Special Operations Forces; served as national director and deputy national security advisor for Homeland Security; and developed, taught, and held the position of distinguished chair at the Combating Terrorism Center, West Point. He also taught with us at the University of Michigan. He was a great friend, teacher, and patriot.

Noel and Warren made judgment calls
on every page of this book.
Without the wisdom of our in-house,
all-star coaching staff of
Patricia Stacey and Grace Gabe,
our winning calls
would have tumbled.

Contents

1. Judgment and Leadership   1
2. Framework for Leadership Judgment   17
3. Having a Storyline   45
4. Character and Courage   67
5. People Judgment Calls   85
6. People Judgment: CEO Succession   105
7. Strategy Judgments   127
8. Strategy Judgments at GE   154
9. Crisis Judgments   178
10. Crisis as a Leadership Development Opportunity   211
11. Knowledge Creation   237
12. Judgment for Future Generations:
    The New York City Leadership Academy   263
13. Conclusion   283

Handbook for Leadership Judgment   285
Acknowledgments   371
Sources   375
Index   383

1

JUDGMENT AND LEADERSHIP

> JUDGMENT: the essence of effective leadership. It is a contextually informed decision-making process encompassing three domains: people, strategy, and crisis. Within each domain, leadership judgments follow a three-phase process: preparation, the call, and execution. Good leadership judgment is supported by contextual knowledge of one's self, social network, organization, and stakeholders.

■ **Making Judgment Calls Is the Essential Job of a Leader**
- With good judgment, little else matters.
- Without good judgment, nothing else matters.

■ **Long-Term Success Is the Sole Marker of Good Judgment**
- Good leaders sort the important from the trivial.
- They focus on getting the important calls right.

■ **Leaders Make the Calls and See to Their Execution**
- They manage relationships with key constituencies.
- They align and mobilize team members for support.

◆ ◆ ◆

On November 1, 1997, when Michael Armstrong became chief executive officer, AT&T was a $130 billion company. It wasn't the powerhouse it had been for much of its hundred-plus-year history, but it had a stockpile of cash and plenty of opportunity. For the next eight years nothing seemed to work for AT&T, and Armstrong's long string of poor strategic judgments finally caught up with him, bringing his career to an unenviable end. In 2005 a nearly dead-broke AT&T was acquired by its former subsidiary, SBC, for a paltry $16.9 billion. Only its name survived on the combined company.

In 1999, when Carly Fiorina joined Hewlett-Packard (HP), she was hailed as a transformational leader. She was going to kick-start the company after years of mediocre performance. For the next six years, she stayed in the headlines, but she never really settled in at HP. She had a mixed scorecard. She had the courage and character to drive change, but did not relate well to the informal, nonhierarchical culture of HP. The optics were not good, nor was her popularity in HP. To make matters worse, HP missed more than half of its earnings targets during her tenure. The share value of HP stock dropped a jaw-dropping 58 percent during her tenure. On May 7, 2002, the acquisition of Compaq was completed. It was a long, bitter fight for Fiorina to get the acquisition closed, a $24 billion stock deal intended to mark her triumph as CEO. Instead the strategic judgment went bad in execution and helped set the stage for the HP board's messy political firing of her in early 2005.

In 2000, when A. G. Lafley took the reins at Procter & Gamble (P&G), the 160-year-old consumer-products company was in trouble. Shortly before Lafley was named CEO the company announced it would not meet its projected first-quarter earnings. The stock tanked in a matter of two short months, falling from its lofty peak of $116 in January 2000 to $60 in March of the same year, a 52 percent free fall.

Like Carly Fiorina at HP, Lafley was faced with the challenge of finding new markets and new avenues for growth at a mature company with a tired business model and lackluster operations. Like Fiorina, whose "blockbuster" acquisition of Compaq did not turn out well for her, Lafley eventually made a big acquisition. But P&G's $57 billion purchase of Gillette was a much savvier business move and produced vastly superior results in its first few months as a P&G company.

Even before the acquisition, Lafley had succeeded in turning the company around, having taken the reins after the resignation of an unsuccessful seventeen-month CEO stint by Durk Jager. By the end of 2006, P&G was riding high. Its stock price was up an impressive 66 percent since 2000, versus a mere 10 percent for the Standard & Poor's 500 index during the same period.

Just a few months after Lafley took over at P&G, Jeff Immelt walked into a very different situation at General Electric. GE's stock had suffered in the wake of the stock market crash of 2001, but Immelt was succeeding Jack Welch, dubbed "manager of the century" by *Fortune* magazine[1] and *BusinessWeek*.[2]

Jack Welch had left GE after failing to complete the huge $47 billion acquisition of Honeywell in the final hours of his twenty-year reign. But the company was still a huge dynamo, and Immelt's job was to find a way to keep generating more power. With revenues of $130 billion in 2000, Immelt would have to come up with $3.5 billion in new revenue every quarter to maintain the torrid 10 percent annual growth pace set by Welch. To do that, he took bold steps to reinvent the company. He shifted the company's primary business model to capitalize on emerging technologies and emerging markets. By mid-2007 the stock market was rewarding his efforts. Immelt had succeeded in delivering average growth of some 8 percent per year, no small feat for a $100 billion-plus juggernaut.

Michael Armstrong, former AT&T CEO, and Carly Fiorina, former HP CEO, could not turn their companies around and in a short space of time lost significant shareholder value and ultimately lost their jobs as well.

A. G. Lafley at P&G and Jeff Immelt and Jack Welch at GE faced no easier challenges, yet they and their organizations ride from success to success. When they stumble they are able to recover quickly. Why is that?

It's a matter of judgment.

◆ ◆ ◆

Throughout our lives, each of us makes thousands of judgment calls. Some are trivial, for example, what kind of cereal to buy. Some are monumental: whom to marry, what career to pursue. The measure of our success in life is the sum of all of these judgment calls. How many good ones did we make? And more important, did we make good ones about the things that really mattered? Our ability to exercise good judgment determines the quality of our individual lives. And, as we rise to positions of leadership, the importance and consequences of our judgment calls are magnified exponentially by their increasing impact on the lives of others. The cumulative effect of leaders' judgment calls determines the success or failure of their organizations.

As the title of this book states, the essence of leadership is judgment. The single most important thing that leaders do is make good judgment calls. In the face of ambiguity, uncertainty, and conflicting demands, often under great time pressure, leaders must make decisions and take effective actions to assure the survival and success of their organizations. This is how leaders add value to their organizations. They lead them to success by exercising good judgment, by making smart calls and ensuring that they are well executed.

It is our hope in writing this book to demystify the leadership judgment process, to explore and understand why it is that some leaders have much greater success in exercising good judgment than others. We take up this challenge because we are convinced that a keen sense of judgment is what makes or breaks a leader. Without a deeper and more compelling understanding of how leaders exercise judgment, the study of leadership can never be complete. (For those who wonder why and how judgment has been missing in most leadership studies—the proverbial elephant on the dining room table that no one dares speak about—we'll address that later on. One hint: it's hard.)

TOUR DE JUDGMENT

As we leave the starting gate on our *tour de judgment*, we are aware that we are not going to have the last word on this important matter. Judgment is too complex a phenomenon, too dependent on luck and the vicissitudes of history, too influenced by personal style and countless other variables, to pin it down once and for all. Doubly doomed is the hope of creating an elegant theory of judgment. Whenever anyone comes close to formulating a final word about judgment, some unforeseen, history-changing event rewrites all that preceded it.

Today, even as we admire the best that is being thought and written in the emerging field of "judgment and decision making," we must keep in mind what John Keats wrote in a letter to his brothers in 1817. Keats observed, expressing his admiration for Shakespeare, that "he possessed so enormously, a 'negative capability,' capable of being in uncertainties, mysteries, doubts without any irritable reaching after fact and reason."[3] Even as we enter the complex territory of judgment, full of curiosity but without a reliable map, we are reminded that our most glittering insights could be negated in an instant.

Nonetheless, we do know a couple of things for sure about judgment.

1) First of all, judgment is the core, the nucleus, of leadership. With good judgment, little else matters. Without it, *nothing* else matters. Take any leader, a U.S. president, a *Fortune* 500 CEO, a big-league coach, wartime general, you name it. Chances are you remember them for their best or worst judgment call.

Can anyone forget that Harry Truman issued the order to drop an atom bomb? When Nixon comes to mind, so does Watergate. If you are thinking of Bill Clinton, there's the Monica episode. What about CEOs? Coca-Cola's Roberto Goizueta was demonized for New Coke and won back his corporate superstar status with Coke Classic. Michael Dell is "Mr. Direct." Carly Fiorina was a pioneer in the ranks of female executives. But what will she be remembered for? For "destroying HP's redoubtable culture."

Leadership is, at its marrow, the chronicle of judgment calls; this is the leader's biography. Good leadership requires good judgment.

2) In decision making, the only thing that counts is winning or losing: the results. Nothing else.

Long-term success is the sole marker of good judgment. It's not "The operation was a success, but the patient died." It's not "He acted brilliantly, but the outcome was poor." Judgment is successful only when the outcome achieves the espoused goals of the institution. Period. Enthusiasm, good intentions, and hard work may help, but without good results, they don't count. Management writer Peter Drucker got it right in 1954 in *The Practice of Management* when he wrote, "The ultimate test of management is business performance. Achievement, rather than knowledge, remains, of necessity, both proof and aim."

Grady Little, former manager of the Boston Red Sox, exemplifies both of the aforementioned points. In the seventh game of the American League pennant race against the New York Yankees in 2003, Pedro Martinez was on the mound for the Sox. For seven brilliant innings, he destroyed one Yankee batter after another. Then Martinez faltered. He walked a batter, gave up a long single, and was on the verge of walking another batter. At that point, Grady Little walked to the mound, obviously intent on yanking Martinez. Now, even casual fans knew that Martinez loses his stuff after a hundred pitches. He'd already thrown more than 115 and was clearly losing his edge. But Martinez had no intention of being replaced. On the mound, he persuaded Little that he still had his stuff and demanded that he be allowed to continue pitching. The Yankees went on to clobber Martinez, scoring four runs in the interrupted inning, and won the series. Grady Little was fired a short time later.

Grady Little may have relieved pitchers a hundred times before that fateful game with good results. However, when it mattered most, his judgment failed. Little's single call, made in the context of a pennant game with Boston's century-old rival, stained his reputation and indeed defined his entire career. A reasonably successful manager up to that point, he will always be remembered for that single poor judgment call.

In world affairs, think of John F. Kennedy and the Cuban missile crisis. Russian ships were steaming toward Cuba with nuclear missiles. Kennedy courageously and skillfully stared the Russians down, defusing the situation and avoiding a potentially catastrophic confrontation. Now that we understand what was really going on during those frightening days, we admire JFK even more for his courageous judgments. But had he gotten it wrong—if there was anyone left to do the remembering—he would not have emerged the hero that he remains to this day, more than four decades after his death. George Bush the elder, "Bush 41," probably did not have to promise "no new taxes" in order to get elected, but once he had implored us to "read my lips," his contrary and ill-fated decision made him a marked man.

And often the damning call is a failure to act. Where would Merck now be if it had held off marketing Vioxx, or if its CEO, Ray Gilmartin, had recalled Vioxx two to three years earlier, as evidence mounted that the drug might be risky for cardiac patients? We can answer that: Gilmartin might still be CEO and Merck would not be facing thousands of lawsuits.

Good judgment is the essence of good leadership.

THE LITERATURE ON JUDGMENT

So, if judgment is so important, why the "lacuna problem"? Why has judgment gotten so little attention in the ever-growing literature on leadership? Why have we, our colleagues, and the other longtime chroniclers of leadership ignored what we believe is the core of the complex phenomenon of leadership?

Part of the answer involves the vagaries and uncertainties of the decision-making process. Every situation unfolds in its own unique way at its own unique pace with its own unique cast of actors. Sir William Osler, one of the fathers of modern medicine, ruefully lamented in the middle of the nineteenth century: "If only all patients were identical, medicine would be a science, not an art." The same can be said about judgment. To paraphrase Sir William, if all problems were identical, judgment would be a science, not an art. In decision making, as Churchill said of war, "the terrible 'Ifs' accumulate."

Then there are also the personal, substantive, and stylistic variations in human nature. On January 9, 1961, eleven days before his inauguration as thirty-fifth president of the United States, John F. Kennedy addressed the Massachusetts Legislature for the last time as a senator. In the course of that landmark speech, Kennedy observed:

> When at some future date the high court of history sits in judgment on each one of us . . . our success or failure in whatever

office we hold will be measured by the answers to four
questions:

Were we truly men of courage . . . ?
Were we truly men of integrity . . . ?
Were we truly men of judgment . . . ?
Were we truly men of dedication . . . ?[4]

Thirty-eight years later, during a conference titled "Presidential
Decision Making" at Harvard's Kennedy School, Ted Sorenson, one
of JFK's closest advisers and speech writers, was asked to reflect on
his former boss's decision-making style. Sorenson answered: "I cannot emphasize enough how important that *elusive* quality is; far more
important than organization, structure, procedures, and machinery.
These are all important, yes, *but nothing compared to judgment*"
(emphasis added). Sorenson elaborated: "Judgment is more important
even than the political sense that he brought to these decisions; and I
am referring to political in the broad sense of the term: an understanding of Congress, an understanding of the country, an understanding
of what will be acceptable and what can be explained and defended."[5]

At that same conference, the decision-making styles of five other
former presidents were discussed by once-close members of their inner
circles. In looking back, each associate found a different key to the
former president's method of making decisions. There is no one-size-
fits-all manner of making a judgment.

At least on the surface, the variations and idiosyncrasies exposed at
that conference overshadowed the similarities. Dwight Eisenhower, a
formidable soldier and a man of battle-hardened experience, appreciated
the role that structure plays in successfully moving large organizations
(remember he reshaped the National Security Council to give him a coun-
terbalance to the State Department). Despite the rumors that his secretary
of state, John Foster Dulles, called the shots on foreign policy, Ike kept all
important decisions in his hands, although he was good at delegating less
important responsibilities. Lyndon Baines Johnson and Gerald Ford were
shaped by their Senate experiences and, thus, inclined to "build bridges."
They reflexively searched for trade-offs and formed alliances.

For the most part, we don't think of Gerald Ford as a decision maker, and with good reason. The only truly important decision Gerry Ford made, and the one he will always be remembered for, was pardoning Richard Nixon. That decision, he later admitted, was prompted less by principle than by a sense that he had to perform the expected service to the former president before the brief honeymoon period of his own presidency had passed.

Ronald Reagan was as ideologically motivated as Ford was pragmatic. If the twentieth century had one value-driven president, aside from Wilson in his first term, it was Reagan. His entire presidency was based on a single principle, that "the free individual is the creative principle in a society and an economy. . . . Democracies are best because they leave most people free."[6]

The first President Bush was collaborative, responsive, and accessible. Neither an ideologue nor impulse driven, he probably relied on his advisers more than any of the other presidents we've mentioned. His most important decision was made on the advice of his two most influential advisers, Brent Scowcroft and James Baker. Both men strongly urged him *not* to invade Baghdad and take out Saddam Hussein. The wisdom of that decision has not yet been vetted by time or history.

The second President Bush has also made a series of decisions that history has already judged and will haunt not only the remainder of his term in office but future presidents as well. What is clear is that his 2003 decision to invade Iraq, however well intentioned, was based on flawed information and a serious foreign-policy failure. What still remains unclear is what role the elder Bush has played in the decision making of his president son, although it is likely that the father is a factor in how the younger man views his office and his eventual role in history. Whatever else the story of the two Bush presidents can be said to be, it is a father/son tale of Shakespearean proportions, one whose playing will have a lasting effect on American history.

At that Harvard conference, Ted Sorenson told a resonant and time-honored tale that pretty accurately reflects the state of thinking about judgment until quite recently. It involves two generations of lawyers:

> A new associate happens to be seated at lunch next to a senior partner, and the younger man says to the veteran, "Tell me,

why is it you have this big reputation for judgment?" "Well," the great man replies, "there are people who seem to respect my judgment." "If you don't mind my asking another question, how is it you have this reputation for judgment?" "Well, I guess I've made the right decision enough times." "If you don't mind me bothering you, what was the basis on which you made the right decision?" "Oh," he said, "that comes from experience." "One last question, what's the experience based on?" "Wrong decisions," the elder statesman replies.

AN EMERGING DISCIPLINE

The relatively new discipline of Judgment and Decision Making that is just now beginning to show up in the curricula of better business schools still falls short of Vilfredo Pareto's 80/20 Rule; we haven't reached the 20 percent of understanding needed to predict 80 percent of the success or failure of judgments. But we are getting there.

Political scientist Herbert Simon, in 1957, laid the groundwork in his seminal work on the limits of rationality, his famous "bounded rationality." In addition to its blunt attack on the hyperrational exuberance of classical economics and game theory, Simon's work made clear the necessity of taking into account the messiness and irrationality of the real world when making decisions. Psychologist Daniel Kahneman gets credit for digging the grave of rational choice theories (including expected utility theory) when he wrote, "Research indicates that people are myopic in their decisions, may lack skill in predicting their future tastes, and can be led to erroneous choices by fallible memory and incorrect evaluation of past experiences."[7] Given all of the above—the abundance of "ifs," the messiness of reality, the newness of a true science of judgment, and the capriciousness of luck—it would be surprising if there was not a black hole in leadership studies where the appreciation of judgment should be.

One of the problematic realities is that, with good judgment, unlike pornography, you *don't* always recognize it when you see it. Can anyone yet say for certain whether former President Bush's 2003 invasion of Iraq achieved its aims or was one of the worst judgment calls of the new century? The poets always seem to do a better job at getting it right than the pundits. Consider Auden's cautionary words:

> The Inevitable is what will happen to you purely by chance.
> The Real is what will strike you as really absurd.[8]

Given Auden's achingly appropriate words, it might be easier to continue to ignore the question of judgment, however important, or even to question our own judgment in addressing it. But what gives us hope, call it unwarranted optimism if you will, is the potential and momentum of the work now taking place in the exploding field of Judgment and Decision Making.

We can say, without hyperbole, that the promise of this new field is astounding. One reason for optimism is the variety and richness of the roots of the current boom: the "choice" and "utility" theories of the classical economists; the logicomathematical work of Rudolf Carnap, W. V. Quine, and Ludwig Wittgenstein; the advances made by Norbert Weiner, Jay W. Forrester, and J.C.R. Licklider in computer and system sciences; the insights of the social psychologists, including Kurt Lewin, Leon Festinger, Edgar Schein, Irving Janis, and many others, who plumbed group dynamics and the effects of "groupthink" on decision making; and the contributions of the political scientists, such as Richard Neustadt, Ernest May, Fred Greenstein, Graham Allison, Alexander George, and others, whose focus of convenience was presidential decision making.

We must also include an ever-increasing number of biographers and historians. John Lukacs's brief narrative of Churchill's leadership, *Five Days in London: May 1940*,[9] is almost as grand in scope as Shakespeare's *Henry V*. Also important are the writings of reflective practitioners, decision makers themselves, who are contributing by their willingness to evaluate their own judgments. Self-serving or not, they are an invaluable source of wisdom, full of cautionary tales.

One of the most critical contributions toward the development of any persuasive theory of judgment is the groundbreaking work of psychologists Daniel Kahneman and Amos Tversky. Their pioneering work on what has come to be called behavioral economics is, above all, the study of decision making. Closely related is the wide-ranging and brilliant work of the cognitive neuroscientists and positive psychologists.

Among the most important are Robert Sternberg, Antonio Damasio, Daniel Gilbert, Peter Whybrow, Mihaly Csikszentmihalyi, George Loewenstein, Karl Weick, and Gary Klein. The latter two are of special interest for us because they study leaders and teams in their *natural* settings and try to *make sense* of how real leaders make real decisions under pressure. They take judgment out of the laboratory, where highly controlled experiments offer fascinating insights that may or may not provide guidance that leaders can use. Instead, they explore judgment in the messy, ever-changing context in which decisions are actually being made.

Their work is especially resonant for us because our own "make it up as we go along" methodology has a lot in common with theirs. We have come at judgment in a less systematic way than most of these researchers, mainly by "hanging out" with leaders and their teams while they are acting and immediately afterward. *It is this real-world experience that convinced us that no study of leadership is complete without an understanding of judgment.*

OUR FOCUS OF CONVENIENCE

Everyone makes judgment calls. Throughout our lives each of us makes thousands of them. In our personal lives, these range from the trivial choices of route to work each day to the monumental decisions about picking spouses and careers. But we want, as much as possible in this book, to avoid the platitudinous generalities that might fit all occasions. So we will focus our lens. We will discuss the things we care and know most about. We will talk about leaders and how the good ones make important judgment calls.

The Leader
The leader is the central figure in our complex firmament of judgment. He or she is not only the protagonist but the architect of the action.

Some of the examples of good and bad judgment that we studied were the work of a more or less autonomous actor. But most are not. We will focus on the principal actor most of the time, because, as Harry Truman put it, the proverbial buck stops there. At the same time, however, we are exquisitely aware that judgment calls usually involve a host of complicit individuals. We continue to recognize the importance of the supporting cast.

The play is called *Othello,* but would it work without Iago? Or take the mythic shift in Intel's strategy. For years, Intel dominated the memory chip business. Then one day in 1984, as the Japanese gained ground with copycat commodity chips, Andy Grove, Intel's number two at the time, turned to number one, Gordon Moore, and asked the question, "If we got kicked out and the board brought in a new CEO, what do you think he would do?" Moore responded, "He'd probably get us out of memories." Then, said Grove, "Why shouldn't you and I walk out the door, come back and do it ourselves?"[10] The rest is history. Without Grove's probing and insistence on assuming an outsider's perspective, would Intel be a failing "memory company" or the microprocessor powerhouse it is today?

Make no mistake: the leader is the Copernican pivot at the center of the decision-making process. All the satellites, other players, and surprising walk-ons revolve around the leader. Jeff Immelt, who makes decisions affecting hundreds of thousands of people weekly, if not daily, describes the process: "I make every decision, but get lots of advice. I don't delegate. It's 'What do you think? What do you think? What do you think?' Then boom. I decide." The responsibility and the accountability is his alone.

The Team/Social Network

While we focus on the leader, we take into account the leader's relationship to others. Without that supporting cast, there would be no leader or need for one. We wouldn't need teams or organizations if it were possible for one person to do the job, and, as we all know, we need teams now more than ever.

In all industrial societies, solo acts have become rare to the point of nonexistent. And don't even *think* Lance Armstrong. There is a reason his team rides that victory lap with him and passes round the bright yellow victory shirt. So, to look at a leader in operation, we will have on the screen *all* the significant others, the allies, critics, and all those whose lives are affected, even shaped, by the leader's judgments. Those stakeholders, from investors to employees, from customers to the broader public, are the ultimate winners and losers whenever judgments are made.

In our byline culture, the leader gets the glory whenever he makes the right call. When *Fortune* named former GE CEO Jack Welch Manager of the Century, they cited his mantra of speed, his famous rallying call, "Who wants to be *slow?*" But Jack only set the pace. He accomplished nothing without his team and supporting staff, those he called his "A" players, the purveyors of needed information and the executors of his decisions.

So, engaging and aligning stakeholders will be key elements in our judgment framework. Like a master pianist, a gifted leader knows which chords to strike hard and how to strike them, at certain times fortissimo, at others a subtle pianissimo. That's called *touch*. Master leaders learn that, but it takes time. Engaging and aligning are crucial if good judgments are to become successful actions: crucial so that the board won't be surprised, crucial so that the customers will be primed, crucial so that the staff has the will and the resources to make the plan work.

There is a brilliant scene in arguably Shakespeare's best leadership play, one that should be required reading for anyone who cares about leadership, *Henry IV, Part I*. In it, the Welsh seer, Glendower, boasts to Hotspur, "I can call spirits from the vasty deep!" Hotspur deflates him with a quick retort: "Why, so can I, or so can any man; But will they come when you do call for them?"[11]

These are the questions leaders must ask themselves: Will the followers come when you call them? Can you as a leader engage and align them? Without those abilities, leaders inevitably fail, no matter how bright their promise. Recall how Cato once compared the two famous orators of his age. "When Cicero spoke, people marveled. When Caesar spoke, people marched." Leadership is not simply speech. It is speech that makes people march. Good judgment without action is worthless.

GETTING THE IMPORTANT ONES RIGHT

When we first began to think about this book, the question we framed was: Why do some people make a better percentage of good judgment calls than others? Nobody is brilliant all of the time. Each of us makes mistakes and misjudgments. But some people have much better track records than others. Then, as we got into discussing it, we realized that we didn't have the question quite right.

The thing that really matters is not *how many* calls a leader gets right, or even what *percentage* of calls a leader gets right. Rather, it is how many of the *important* ones he or she gets right. Good leaders, we observed, not only make better calls, but they are able to discern the really important ones and get a higher percentage of them right. They are better at a whole process that runs from seeing the need for a call, to framing issues, to figuring out what is critical, to mobilizing and energizing the troops.

Good leaders are able to triage their time and energy, and focus on the consequential. Jack Welch used to say at GE that if he wasn't careful with his time, he could spend days at the company's headquarters knee deep in bureaucratic crap and add no value to the company. Peter Drucker wrote in *The Effective Executive* that "the executive's time tends to belong to everybody else . . . [that he or she is] captive of the organization."[12] All too many leaders let Rome burn while attending to the trivial.

WHAT DO WE KNOW?

Earlier we mentioned our "methodology"; methodolog*ies* would be more accurate. We've used about every social science method in our quiver, from formal surveys and structured interviews to "hanging out" and schmoozing with leaders and their teams.

If you counted each of our encounters with leaders, they would number in the thousands. In this book, we look at relatively few cases and focus on "representative anecdotes" to make our points. We also draw on history and literature for illustrations. Whatever our sources, *our primary purpose is to develop a useful framework that will help leaders make better judgments and help shape the next generation to do the same.*

In order to do that, we address the most vexing questions and conundrums leaders confront when making their most important judgments.

2

FRAMEWORK FOR

LEADERSHIP JUDGMENT

▌ Good Judgment Calls Are a Process, Not an Event
- It starts with the leader recognizing a need and framing the call.
- It continues through execution and adjustment.

▌ Leaders Must Make Calls in Three Critical Domains
- Calls about people are the most difficult, and the most critical.
- Other key domains are strategy and crisis.

▌ Exercising Good Judgment Requires Self-Knowledge
- It isn't a solo performance; support teams are vital.
- Engaging others leads to success.

◆ ◆ ◆

Fingerspitzengefühl.

It's a word our late friend Wayne Downing used with us one day. Downing was the former head of the U.S. military's Special Operations Forces and a retired four-star general.

"You have to have a sense for the situation . . . know when to act, and know what to do. You need *fingerspitzengefühl*," he told us.

Fingerspitzengefühl. It's a German term that is often translated as "sure instinct." More literally, it's about feeling through the tips of one's fingers. You get it, Downing told us, from experience. He's right. Experience is very important in developing judgment.

One of the reasons that we and other students of leadership haven't written a lot about judgment is that it is a hard subject. It's easier—and therefore tempting—to toss it off as one of those important but ineffable qualities. Downing wasn't doing that. His comment came in the midst of a long, thoughtful conversation. But it brought to mind how often we do hear, and sometimes even think to ourselves, that judgment is largely about intuition. It's about the je ne sais quoi of just sensing, having good antennae. There are things you know in your gut. Or you "blink" and have a wondrous, instantaneous epiphany.

These statements of nonrational "thinking" certainly do *feel* true, and it might be that in a sense they even are true. There is the moment, as Jeff Immelt puts it, when "Boom, I decide." But to the extent that that is true, it is a shorthand description for a complex web of other thoughts and activity. It's like saying that Duke beat Michigan at basketball because the Blue Devils scored more points. It may be true, but it is not very helpful to understanding how the Blue Devils came to outscore the Wolverines. What about the strategy, the practice, the timing, the training, and even the recruiting? As sports fans know, there's a lot more to it.

And, as all of us know, there is a lot more to exercising good judgment as well. Good judgment is not one terrific aha moment after another. In the real world, good judgment, at least on the big issues that make a difference, is usually an incremental process. Quantum theory, the polio vaccine, cubism, the double helix, the iPod—all these landmark breakthroughs in business, science, engineering, and the arts came about only after years of trying and "trialing," of mistakes and missteps, of correcting, refining, and, yes, trying again. Intuition helps; so does blinking, but it is rarely sufficient. As the Talmud says, expect miracles, but don't count on them.

So, here goes. Having come face-to-face with our belief that good judgment is the essential genome of good leadership, we have tackled it head-on. We have come up with a framework for understanding how good leaders go about making good judgment calls.

All the usual caveats are present. We don't pretend to have all the answers. We don't even presume that we have asked *all* of the possible questions. But we have been around and watched hundreds of leaders making thousands of judgment calls. We have seen good calls and bad ones. We have seen leaders make so-so initial calls and then manage and retune them midair to produce brilliant results. And we have seen leaders make spot-on, inspired decisions and then end up in the ditch because they didn't follow through on execution, or looked away at a key moment and missed a critical context change. We have seen, and learned, a lot. And, putting our brains and experience together, we have come up with our framework.

We offer it with two goals in mind. One is to help leaders working in the field not only to improve their own judgment-making faculties, but also to do a better, more intentional job of developing good judgment in others. The second goal is to encourage and influence a more vigorous public conversation about judgment. We need more leaders with better judgment. In the terms used in the process we describe below, we have "sensed and identified" the need for a keener focus on judgment. Now we are "naming and framing" the issue.

THE FRAMEWORK

Despite the implications of the word *call,* the judgment calls that leaders make cannot be viewed as single, point-in-time events. Like umpires and referees, leaders do, at some moment, make a call. They make a determination about how things should proceed. But unlike umpires and referees, they cannot—without risking total failure—quickly forget them and move ahead to the next play. Rather, for a leader, the moment of making the call comes in the middle of a process.

That process begins with the leader recognizing the need for a judgment and continues through successful execution. A leader is said to have "good judgment" when he or she repeatedly makes judgment calls that turn out well. These calls frequently turn out well because the leader has mastered a complex, constantly morphing process that unfolds in several dimensions. We have identified three phases to the process.

TIME

Pre: What happens before the leader makes the decision

The Call: What the leader does as he or she makes the decision that helps it turn out to be the right one

Execution: What the leader must oversee to make sure the call produces the desired results

DOMAIN

The elements of the process, the attention that must be paid to each of them, and the time over which the judgment unfolds varies with its subject matter. We have identified three critical domains in which most of the most important calls are found:

judgments about *people*

judgments about *strategy*

judgments in time of *crisis*

CONSTITUENCIES

Leaders make the calls, but they do it in relation to the world around them. A leader's relationships are the sources of the information needed to make a successful call. They also provide the means for executing the call and represent the various interests that must be attended to throughout the process. A leader must interact with these different constituencies and manage the relationships to make successful calls.

In addition, to improve judgment-making throughout the organization, the leader must use these interactions to help others learn to make successful calls. We have identified four different types of knowledge needed to do this.

SELF-KNOWLEDGE

How do you learn? Do you face reality? Do you watch and listen? Are you willing to improve?

SOCIAL NETWORK KNOWLEDGE

Do you know how to build a strong team? How do you teach your team to make better judgments?

ORGANIZATIONAL KNOWLEDGE
Do you know how to draw on the strengths of others through-out the organization? Can you create broad-scale processes for teaching them to make smart judgments?

CONTEXTUAL KNOWLEDGE
Do you know how to create smart interactions with the myriad other stakeholders, such as customers, suppliers, government, stockholders, competitors, and interest groups?

The Judgment Calls Matrix

JUDGMENT: the essence of effective leadership. It is a contextually informed decision-making process encompassing three domains: people, strategy, and crisis. Within each domain, leadership judgments follow a three-phase process: preparation, the call, and execution. Good leadership judgment is supported by contextual knowledge of one's self, social network, organization, and stakeholders.

Domains

Knowledge Creation		People pre-call-execution	Strategy pre-call-execution	Crisis pre-call-execution
	Self Knowledge			
	Social Network Knowledge			
	Organizational Knowledge			
	Contextual Knowledge			

THE THREE JUDGMENT DOMAINS:
PEOPLE, STRATEGY, AND CRISIS

These are the three domains that make the most difference to the survival and well-being of any institution. If they are unattended to or if bad calls are made in these domains, it can be fatal to an organization.

1. People Judgment Calls

While misjudgments in any of the three domains have the potential to be fatal, the one with the most potential is people. If leaders don't make smart judgment calls about the people on their teams, or if they manage them poorly, then there is no way they can set a sound direction and strategy for the enterprise, nor can they effectively deal with crises. The first priority is getting the right people on the team, and then setting the strategy and being ready for the inevitable crises.

The selection of Mark Hurd to succeed Carly Fiorina as CEO of Hewlett-Packard made all the difference. Almost without changing Fiorina's strategic portfolio at all or changing her team, he turned her dismal failure into a roaring success. When Fiorina was fired in early 2005, her $19 billion acquisition of Compaq was considered a bad strategic judgment. The company was in disarray. HP's stock price had declined 15 percent during a period when rival Dell's shares had surged a remarkable 90 percent. Morale was terrible.

When Hurd walked in the door two months later, he immediately turned his attention to "rebuilding the foundation," as he put it. Undoing the Compaq merger was not an option. But there was a rising clamor on Wall Street for a strategic shift. Spinning off the company's marginally profitable PC business from its very profitable printer business was one often-discussed scenario. But Hurd judged that after years of turmoil, the people at HP didn't need yet another new vision. What they needed was to buckle down and solve the thorny problems in the existing businesses.

Hurd's philosophy of leadership and his personality couldn't have been more different from Fiorina's. She was a celebrity who viewed her role as being the highly visible poster girl for HP. She talked about her grand vision for the company in an interconnected world and jetted around the globe attending conferences and making speeches. But her look-at-me style and failure to deliver results alienated both employees and investors.

Hurd, who had previously been CEO of NCR, was a hands-on operations guy. He was immediately welcomed within HP because he seemed to be the "anti-Carly." Unlike her, he avoided the limelight and focused all of his attention on fixing internal problems and pleasing customers. His unflashy style and no-nonsense approach were what allowed him to succeed where Fiorina failed. He laid off an additional fifteen thousand workers, on top of the twenty-six thousand that were let go after the Compaq merger. He reached outside the organization to bring in a few key executives and he made cost cutting a top priority. Under another leader, these could have been unpopular moves. But Hurd dug in and went to work alongside his new colleagues. He focused on the fundamentals and delivered on Fiorina's promises where she could not. To be fair to Fiorina, Hurd got the benefit of her strategic judgments, including the company acquisition that finally started paying off.

At Merck, there were several serious failures in the people judgment category. One very questionable judgment was the hiring of Ray Gilmartin as CEO. He appears to have delayed and avoided facing up to the problems with the company's Vioxx drug until a rising tide of evidence tying the drug to heart problems forced a multi-billion-dollar recall. There were over 86 million people using Vioxx in eighty countries. In planning for his anticipated retirement, Roy Vagelos, Merck CEO, who preceded Gilmartin as CEO, had begun grooming a successor, and in 1993 had named Richard Markham, chief operating officer, the heir apparent. But just months before Vagelos was to retire, Markham abruptly left for "personal reasons" and the Merck board began a frantic search for a successor.

Driven by the urgent need to replace Vagelos, who was approaching the mandatory retirement age, the board made a poor judgment call in Gilmartin. His background and job as CEO of Becton Dickinson, a much smaller company in the medical technology business, *had not* prepared him to lead a company of the size and complexity of Merck, nor did he have any experience in big pharma, a vastly different industry than medical technology.

Mark Hurd also joined Hewlett-Packard from a much smaller company, but NCR's business was much more similar to HP's than Becton Dickinson's was to Merck's. In fact, an HP board member said that the reason Hurd was chosen was that he demonstrated in his interviews that he had a deep understanding of HP and how it made money.

Once Gilmartin arrived, he was unable to build the sort of high-performance team he sorely needed. The deck was stacked against him in part because Vagelos, as a longtime Merck insider, a medical doctor, and former head of research at Merck, had been comfortable dealing with the scientific side of the business. Because he had expertise of his own, he was less dependent on his scientists and was able to make better judgments about their work. But Ray Gilmartin, who was not a research scientist, had to depend on others. And, as things turned out, he depended on the wrong people. He didn't put together a team that gave him good information and wise counsel.

Carly Fiorina was similarly unprepared to head HP. Her previous career had been as a sales and marketing executive manager at AT&T and then Lucent Technologies, where she rose to group president of Lucent's Global Service Provider business. She lacked the experience to lead a complex, multibusiness, high-tech multinational firm. Both Fiorina and Gilmartin did not exercise good judgment in people and did not put together strong collaborative teams to augment their own competencies.

People calls are often more complex and difficult to get right than other types of calls. They are more likely to be affected by the emotional attachments or dislikes of the leader, and they evoke emotional reactions in the people affected by the calls. People calls must be made while the actors in the drama are reacting to and shaping the judgment process as it is under way.

People calls are often viewed as win-lose decisions for various players in the organization, and as such they unleash the most powerful of political forces in an organization. In order to make good judgment calls, a leader must effectively manage these forces.

2. Strategy Judgment Calls

The Vioxx crisis was not the only problem at Merck on Gilmartin's watch. He also made strategic mistakes that could, again, be traced back to people judgment. Before Gilmartin arrived, Merck had a history of going it alone and relying on its scientists to come up with big new drugs. It was a strategy that had served Merck well. But in the mid-nineties, as several promising products didn't work out, the new-drug pipeline was nearly dry. Faced with a historically go-it-alone culture and without good guidance, Gilmartin didn't recognize the severity of the problem, nor did he make the necessary changes to the company's strategy.

The role of the leader is to lead the organization to success, so when the current strategic road isn't leading toward success, it is his or her job to find a new path. How well a leader makes strategic judgment calls is a function of both (a) his or her own ability to look over the horizon and frame the right question and (b) the people with whom he or she chooses to interact.

In the case of Jack Welch, interactions with Peter Drucker had a powerful impact on his strategic thinking. Soon after he became CEO of General Electric, Welch had a meeting with Drucker. As they discussed GE's various businesses, Drucker, Welch recounts, asked him at one point: "If you weren't already in this business today, would you go into it?" It was a question that crystallized Welch's thinking and ultimately resulted in his famous "#1, #2, fix, close, or sell strategy."

It took Welch a while to arrive at the conclusion that the way GE was going to succeed was by having only businesses that were number one or number two in their industries. Other businesses that couldn't be raised to one of those positions would be sold or closed. One prominent example was the sale of GE Housewares in 1984. The press derided Welch for selling off one of GE's most visible businesses, but as a division increasingly under pressure from knockoffs coming from Asia, it was unquestionably the right move at the right time. Welch's consultation with Peter Drucker started the process that helped him frame his strategic thinking in a new way. This judgment call radically altered the history of GE.

Over the course of his twenty-year tenure, Welch changed the content of his strategy for GE several times. But he never forgot

Drucker's fundamental question. In the late 1990s, a group of mid-level students at GE's Crotonville leadership institute challenged him, saying that the "#1, #2, fix, close, or sell" strategy was hurting the company because executives were gaming the system.

They were deliberately defining their markets narrowly so that they could be number one or number two, and as a result, the company was missing opportunities. In response, Welch ordered that all business heads redefine their markets so that they had no more than a 10 percent share. And in the mid-1990s he redefined GE from a company that sold products to be a company that delivered services. It still manufactured many kinds of equipment and electrical machinery, but Welch's new business model was, for example, to provide a hospital with an efficient radiology department, rather than just a good CAT scan or MRI. The machinery was only part of a package that included software and support to help the hospital get and remain operationally effective.

When Jeff Immelt succeeded Welch, he made judgment calls of his own about the strategy of GE. He decided it was time to transform the company into a technology growth company. He selected ten key technologies, such as nanotechnology and molecular imaging, and has made several acquisitions to execute this strategy, including the $10 billion Amersham acquisition.

Immelt says he believes making strategic judgment calls is how he adds value to the company. In the fall of 2004, he told a group of Michigan MBAs: "There's more importance today on strategy, on picking businesses than ever before. . . . When you're Chairman of GE, you spend a lot of time thinking about which businesses to pick, investing in health care, or investing in entertainment. . . . In the environment we're in, good execution and good operations aren't enough to fix a business with a flawed strategy. So you need to spend time understanding what businesses you think are going to work, what business models seem to make sense. Strategy is more important than ever before."[1]

3. Crisis Judgment Calls

It's obviously important for leaders to make good judgment calls in crisis situations because crises are by definition very dangerous moments. But errors at these times aren't actually any more likely to be fatal than errors in judgment regarding people and strategy. The big difference is that they are usually time pressured and, as a result, any disastrous consequences brought on by bad calls at these moments often come very quickly.

It's instructive to look at crisis calls, not only because getting them right is so important, but also because they compress and highlight so many of the important elements of making judgment calls. They require that a leader have clear values and know his or her ultimate goal. There must be open and effective communication among members of the senior team and throughout the ranks. There must be a good process for gathering and analyzing data. And there must be effective execution. These are the fundamental elements for making good judgment calls under any circumstances, but the added pressure of a crisis brings them more clearly into focus.

One organization that paradoxically handles crises as part of its regular routine is the military when it is at war. The leaders at all levels in the military deal with crises as a regular part of their role. The stakes are clearly different in business than in the military, but the urgency, the unpredictability, and the serious nature of the situations are the same. There are important lessons for business leaders to be found in reflecting on how the military handles crises.

Wayne Downing pointed out that the first thing you need to do in a crisis is keep your wits about you. Understand, as best you can, what you are facing, and then come up with the best strategy you can for accomplishing your ultimate goal in the given circumstances. First of all, you need to know what your strategic goal is. "It's amazing to me how in crisis, sometimes people forget that one," he said. "They will come up with a great solution but they will find that it has nothing to do with accomplishing what it is they are supposed to be doing. If you don't stay focused on the mission, you drift into activity that is wasted."

Crises are not restricted to military organizations. All organizations face crises at one time or another. Some are life-threatening to the institution, if not to human life. Crises not handled well, where good judgment calls were not made, can lead to the demise of an institution. The organizational crisis most taught to business students is the Johnson & Johnson (J&J) Tylenol case, where poison was found in bottles of the product on store shelves. The CEO at the time, Jim Burke, did a masterful job of pulling the product, assuring all employees and consumers that they were taking quick action to deal with the crisis, and ultimately won the consumers back to the product. Burke made great on-the-fly judgment calls in that crisis. They were guided by the J&J credo that puts the customer first.

CHAMBERS AT CISCO

A much more complex crisis than Tylenol, one that threatened the total organization's future, was the stock-price crash Cisco faced in early 2001. Cisco, led by CEO John Chambers, was at the top, literally. For a couple of days its market cap was number one in the world, bigger than GE at $531 billion (GE was $520 in March 2000). Then in early 2001 the crash occurred in the industry and the near-death Cisco crisis. As Chambers said, "If somebody would've told me that we'd go from 70 percent growth to minus 30 percent growth in forty-five days, I'd have said it was mathematically impossible. The company was in a free fall."[2]

At its peak in 2000 its stock was over $80 a share. When it finally bottomed out, it hit $9.42 in late 2002 (at its peak it was performing 250% above the S&P average, at its lowest it was 50% below). Never in the history of business has a company gone from number one to such depths and then had a comeback, all under the leadership of the same CEO. In mid-2007 the stock had rebounded and was around $28 per share with a market capitalization of $170 billion. In contrast, the IBM crisis under John Akers in the early 1990s was triggered by the market capitalization going from close to $100 billion to below $38 billion. In the IBM case it resulted in Akers being fired and the board going outside for the turnaround CEO, namely, Lou Gerstner.

Chambers's crisis judgments set the stage for one of the most unique turnaround stories in business history, made even more amazing because the leader who was at the helm when the company went off the cliff is the same one who made the judgments to transform and revitalize the company.

He can be faulted for not originally sensing and identifying the need for dealing with the crisis earlier, because there were those inside the company and outside who saw some of the signals. Once the crisis hit, Chambers was quick on the trigger to frame and name the judgments that had to be made. The result: deep staff cuts, 8,500 or 18 percent of the workforce, stopping all acquisitions, changing how the company worked together, breaking down silos, stopping the free-spending culture, and setting the stage for a new strategic direction for the company. Chambers says that "after fifty-one days we were already focused on the upside."[3] This was when all the IR [information retrieval] competitors, such as Lucent, Nortel, and 3Com, floundered for several years.

Unlike Burke's Tylenol crisis, a great example of crisis judgment to save a brand and the reputation of J&J, Chambers's crisis judgment was about saving a company and resulted in major people judgments for who would lead various elements of the company. New strategy judgments were also required to get out of the crisis. There has been a totally new Cisco created out of the crisis. Cisco was not only freshly imagined but re-created. J&J got one of its many brands and its sterling reputation.

THE PROCESS OF JUDGMENT CALLS: PREPARATION, CALL, EXECUTION

In all three of our domains, people, strategy, and crisis, good judgment calls always involve a process that starts with recognizing the need for the call and continues through to successful execution.

Understanding that a judgment call is a complex flow of events rather than a single, one-point event leads to the inevitable recognition that adjustments can be made throughout the process. There are points when irrevocable actions are taken. A bomb is dropped. A business is sold. A key leader is fired. An opportunity is missed.

Once JPMorgan closed the deal acquiring Bank One, there was no turning back. But there were myriad opportunities along the way to make adjustments to the execution. The merger decision turned out to be a good judgment call over time due to the continuous improvements made during the execution phase. The judgment calls made by Jamie Dimon and the team at JPMorgan Chase included changing key people, setting the strategy, and navigating the organization through the global financial crisis in 2008 and 2009.

Another implication of viewing judgment calls as flows rather than single events is that there are also myriad opportunities to mess it up. Carly Fiorina may have made a good strategy judgment when she decided that HP should acquire Compaq in 2001. But her efforts were doomed by flaws in the execution phase. By failing in the execution part of the process, she wasn't able to implement the merger effectively and reap the benefits. So by our definition, Fiorina's acquisition of Compaq was a bad judgment call. The fact that Mark Hurd, Fiorina's successor as CEO of HP, was able to make a success of the merger doesn't change the fact that Fiorina's judgment call didn't work out. Hurd simply made some new and better judgment calls after he took over.

Unlike Fiorina, who recognized the need to make a call but messed up the execution, the leaders at the old AT&T, Westinghouse, and GM (General Motors) failed at the beginning of the process. They succumbed to the boiled frog phenomenon. Like the frog that sits in the pan and doesn't jump out if the water is heated slowly enough, they didn't react quickly or aggressively enough to changes in their competitive environments. They saw the ongoing changes in their industries as only incremental, so they waited until their companies were nearly dead before they took action.

Andy Grove, whose career is a record of great judgment calls, illustrates the opposite of the boiled frog phenomenon. Like many people who are known for their good judgment, he is always scanning the horizon and looking for important change. In his book *Only the Paranoid Survive: How to Identify and Exploit the Crisis Points That Challenge Every Business,*[4] the former CEO who led Intel through the tumultuous early years of the computer industry focuses on what he calls strategic inflection points. A SIP is a ten-times force—a change of such magnitude that it is at least ten times stronger than any that preceded it. He explains that leaders must recognize the moments when fundamental changes are occurring and act swiftly and decisively. Framing the issue and mobilizing the troops when there are only the slightest bits of change in the air are what has kept Intel at the top of its game.

Good judgment depends on how you think as much as what you know. It requires intelligence and values. It depends on the ability to gather information and to process it. It draws on experience and knowledge. The ability to shape and guide the judgment process plays out in the context of a lifetime of learning. But when things go wrong, it is often because the leader has stumbled on the fundamentals.

The Preparation Phase

SENSING AND IDENTIFYING THE NEED FOR A JUDGMENT CALL

As simple as this one seems, as Barbara Tuchman pointed out in *The March of Folly: From Troy to Vietnam*,[5] failure to face reality and see the need to change has often had disastrous consequences. In the business world the demise of U.S. steel companies and of high-tech firms like Digital Equipment Corporation (DEC) and Compaq, as well as the disastrous decline of the U.S. auto companies, attest to the difficulty of recognizing the need to make tough judgment calls. This was Andy Grove's great strength and Ken Olsen's great weakness. Olsen, as head of the Digital team, could have led the transformation of the computer and information technology industry, but instead allowed Digital to be lolled into complacency.

Sensing the need for a judgment call varies in each of the domains. For people judgment calls, identifying the need for a call isn't really about *whether* something is going to happen, but rather when. Every CEO, every person in every job is going to leave it some day. Replacements *will* be needed. Nevertheless, an incredible number of otherwise highly regarded companies aren't ready when it comes time to name a new CEO.

There is nothing more important to an institution than who is going to be its leader. Good people judgment calls require that it be the most important agenda. Yet the last decade has seen Merck, HP, 3M, Boeing, Kodak, Motorola, AT&T (sold to SBC, which salvaged the brand to rename SBC to AT&T), Merrill Lynch (which outsider CEO John Thain ended up selling to Bank of America), and many others having to bring in outsiders as CEO. What were these companies' leaders doing ten years before the CEO crisis? One of the things they were not doing was identifying the need to develop strong leaders.

The companies that have developed internal CEO candidates and done well, such as GE, Pepsi, Intel, and P&G, have developed leadership pipelines, which, among other things, support making good judgment calls.

The other side of people judgment calls is letting go of the people who shouldn't be around. This weeding-out test is one that many leaders fail, and often the failure starts with an emotional unwillingness to see the need. Facing reality around difficult issues is one of the hardest things a leader has to do. And the reality of having to fire people, especially ones who you know, and perhaps like, is one of the hardest-to-face realities of all.

This is because leaders are human. We all have blinders. We get attached to people. We distort the facts. We look the other way. Our experience is that contrary to what you might expect, the more senior-level leaders seem to have a tougher time with this than people lower down in the organization. How could the late Ken Lay not have fired Jeff Skilling and Andy Fastow at Enron? If we assume that Ken was not an out-and-out crook, which we can't, then he made a very bad judgment call leaving these people on his team. As extreme as the Enron example is, it is not all that rare.

For strategy judgments, as we have already noted, scanning the horizon and identifying the need to make a judgment early are extremely helpful. The best prescription for helping leaders recognize the need for strategic judgment calls is captured by Andy Grove's view that you must look over the horizon at tomorrow's environment, be paranoid, and reinvent the organization. It's hard to do this all the time. It requires discipline and a constant searching. There have been all kinds of examples throughout history of leaders not recognizing the need for strategic judgment calls. The legendary economist Joseph Schumpeter (1883–1950) pointed out that most new industries do not grow organically from those in the industry because they can't see the need for change. Think the telegraph to telephones, railroads to automobiles, IBM hardware to Microsoft software.

Great leaders are always asking Peter Drucker's questions about what businesses are good for today and which ones will be good for tomorrow. Drucker was all about "purposeful abandonment," leaving behind what no longer worked while developing the breadwinners of tomorrow. A new environment often requires a new business theory. As the saying goes: "What brought you here won't get you there." Good strategy judgments usually start well before the need becomes obvious.

Many crises present themselves with such alarm-clanging ferocity that it is impossible to miss them. But others are more subtle. Sensing and identifying the need for a judgment call is what leadership at Merck did poorly. The leaders at Merck had plenty of data to have identified the Vioxx crisis long before its recall and the lawsuits started to pile up.

Two processes are required by the leader. One is cognitive: the ability to distinguish the important signals from the unimportant. The other is emotional: having the guts to face that something is indeed a crisis. Jack Welch always looked for leaders who had both qualities, but particularly the latter—the ability to make the really tough calls. Those who did not shy away from the most difficult decisions had what he called "edge." They knew when to say yes or no and avoid the maybes.

FRAMING AND NAMING THE JUDGMENT CALL

Once there is recognition that a judgment call is required, a leader has to frame it and name it. Framing can drive the whole process. The "power of the first draft" is a phrase Noel picked up from a CEO in the 1970s. The point he was making is that there is tremendous power in framing issues, and then giving them a name. For Jack Welch and GE, in the 1990s Welch wanted to get his business leaders to grow more services to offset the pressures on product pricing. He framed and named the GE strategy as "We are a service company with competitive products, not a product company with services on the side."

Best Buy had succeeded historically as a product-centric, big-box consumer electronics retailer selling the same products in all 675-plus stores regardless of the demographics of the location. Former CEO

Brad Anderson, who took the reins in 2002, and his leadership team framed and named the judgment as becoming "customer-centric," that is, understanding the value propositions for segments of customers and then being able to tailor product and service offerings to fit their individual needs.

There is a vast social psychology literature on "framing" and how people's cognitive maps make sense of the world around them. These are often referred to as mental models, and creative leaders use them to get people thinking about problems in ways that will be productive.

At Hewlett-Packard Mark Hurd framed the judgment he had to make when he arrived as "how to make the current portfolio of businesses succeed." "Our portfolio of businesses has yet to prove its full value—not due to issues with the strategy, but rather due to the execution of the strategy,"[6] he told investors in his first annual report letter. As a result, he focused on improving performance in those businesses. Had he framed the problem differently, as "What businesses do we want to be in?" he would have set about gathering data differently, and the answer would almost certainly have resulted in a realignment of the portfolio.

When Lou Gerstner took over IBM in the early 1990s, Big Blue was in big trouble, about to report its biggest loss ever, $8.1 billion. The company had missed the personal computer revolution, and arrogance and insularity had taken its toll on the once vaunted computer maker. Gerstner framed the judgment he had to make as follows: "In the spring of 1993, a big part of what I had to do was get the company refocused on the marketplace as the only valid measure of success. I started telling virtually every audience . . . that there was a customer running IBM, and that we are going to rebuild the company from the customer back."[7] Gerstner of course executed one of the great turnaround stories of modern-day business, turning an $8 billion-plus loss into a $5 billion gain in five years.

The mistake that most people make in framing crisis judgments is being too short-term. Almost by definition, there is great time pressure in a crisis, but a short-term fix uses up resources and is often not productive in getting toward the ultimate goal. "What should drive you in a crisis is your mission," General Downing said. "In business that mission is carrying out your business strategy. You've got to accomplish the mission. You can drift off into activity that is gonna make you feel good, but if that activity is not ultimately accomplishing what your mission is, then it's wasted and you're going to have to go back and do it anyway."

Ray Gilmartin never framed the Vioxx crisis appropriately. This failing compounded the series of failed judgment calls that threatens the survival of Merck.

MOBILIZING AND ALIGNING THE RIGHT PEOPLE

It is essential to get the people who have something to contribute on your team and into the game at the right moment while keeping all others out. Sometimes it means skipping over layers of the organization. Sometimes it means reaching out to unexpected places. It's a tricky art to figure out how many people you need and who they are. You need to engage the right brains and experience, but also the right personalities and dynamics. You don't want groupthink, but carpers, complainers, and footdraggers are no help either.

A poignant example of how bad judgments happen took place in GE Appliances's business. It resulted in a $1 billion compressor fiasco in the 1980s.

In the early 1980s Appliances borrowed an idea previously used in small air conditioners. GE Appliances' engineers designed an advanced rotary compressor to cool its refrigerators. Compared to GE's existing compressors, it would require one-third the parts, half the manufacturing cost, and far less energy to operate. There were many risks: the technology required parts manufactured to tolerances of as little as one one-hundredth the width of a human hair, and the cost included a $120 million investment in a new automated factory. After much agonizing with executives from Appliances, Jack Welch approved the plan to make the new compressors instead of buying them. This turned out to be a bad judgment.

When the new refrigerators appeared in 1986, people bought so many that GE's market share rose two percentage points. The rotary compressors represented breakthrough engineering. Then, in 1987, rotary-compressor refrigerators began to break down. The

GE engineers found that certain critical parts were far less durable than expected and very difficult to repair. Welch made another judgment call: replace all of them with conventional compressors purchased from other manufacturers. In his 1988 annual report letter to shareholders he wrote, "Our aim is to come out of this situation with our reputation for customer support and satisfaction not only intact but—if anything—enhanced."

In hindsight, the judgment process was flawed. The right people, whose mobilization and alignment could have changed the judgment, were left out of the loop. There were engineers who wanted to express their concerns. The layers of bureaucracy stifled these voices from being heard. Welch reflected on why that type of bad judgment happened and concluded, "With all the layers of approval we had then, no one had ownership of the decision. Ownership is essential." That judgment cost the organization's finances and reputation. This lesson and other, similar lessons strongly influenced Welch's maniacal attack on hierarchy in GE so that, in his words, the organization should be "ventilated and free" of oppressive layers. Getting the right people influencing key judgments with firsthand knowledge was the goal.

The aligning part of the equation means getting on board not only the people who can help you make a smart decision and get it executed, but also the people who can derail it. One of the biggest mistakes we have seen leaders make time and time again is to underestimate the power of resisters and ambitious plotters. At Ford this cost Jac Nasser his job. When the Firestone tire crisis hit, there were Ford Explorer rollovers causing accidents and deaths. Nasser, quite rightly, spent the majority of his time personally leading the response to the crisis. By not having a trustworthy team, several formed a coalition to plot against him while he was dealing with the crisis. Leaders should always consider the opposition and manage the politics.

The Call Phase: Making the Judgment Call

Jeff Immelt's "Boom, I make the decision" comes after he has gotten all the input. There is a moment when, based on his view of the time horizon for the judgment and sufficiency of input and involvement, the leader makes the call. Wayne Downing described a similar process when he was leading troops in battle. The judgment call for strategic direction of the company is often embedded in a stream of activity, such as Jeff Immelt's GE strategy, which took several years to work through. The seeds were in his mind and part of the conversation among senior leaders at GE as early as 2001. Since then a series of judgment calls have resulted in shaping the strategic direction of GE.

The Execution Phase: Action—Make It Happen

Larry Bossidy, the retired CEO of Honeywell who coauthored a book called *Execution: The Discipline of Getting Things Done*,[8] says that "thinking does not matter if nothing happens. There are too many people with bumble bee mentality who can't make things happen." Execution is a critical part of the exercise of good judgment. Once a clear call is made, then resources, people, capital, information, and technology must mobilized to support it. If they aren't, the decision doesn't get carried out and any good preparation and decision making simply goes down the tubes. By our definition, good judgment calls always produce good results.

When Brad Anderson and his leadership team at Best Buy made the judgment call in 2002 that Best Buy needed to be transformed into a customer-centric enterprise, he began a process that would take years of focus and effort. Once the call was made, he mobilized several senior-level action learning task forces to spend six months finding the segments in the Best Buy customer base that the company would cultivate. Next came selecting from among those leaders the people who would head up the segments, selecting the stores to be transformed, and mobilizing all the support functions to execute the new strategy. The whole execution process continues to play out in 2009 and will probably never be over.

Learn and Adjust: Continuous Adjustment

Because judgment calls are determined to be good or bad by their results, there is almost always time to make adjustments. Leadership judgment is a process; the final outcome can sometimes be dramatically altered in the execution phase. One example is Jack Welch's judgment call to acquire Honeywell for $41 billion in October 2000.

At the time this was seen as a brilliant move and a capstone to Welch's twenty-year run at GE. The call was vintage Welch. GE and Welch knew Honeywell (AlliedSignal had acquired Honeywell and taken the name) and its businesses in depth and had them on GE's acquisition radar screen for years. Welch exercised what we call "planful opportunism." The planning work ("our preparation phase") of judgment, of understanding Honeywell, was done in depth at GE. The opportunism part was Welch jumping on the "opportunity" when he saw that GE's competitor, United Technology, was also going after Honeywell. He made the call and made it fast. There were two important reasons to make the call. One was to prevent United Technology from getting the acquisition, the other was acquiring the businesses of Honeywell for GE's benefit. Both were strategically important. He made another call as well: he requested the GE board delay his retirement date so that the new CEO would not be burdened and potentially overwhelmed with the acquisition challenges.

As the judgment process unfolded in the execution phase, Welch had an opportunity to exercise one of his leadership precepts, to "face reality as it is, not as it was, or as you wish it were." Following the U.S. Justice Department giving its blessing to this huge deal, GE and Honeywell notified the European Commission (ruling on antitrust issues) for its clearance. This left the final part of Welch's judgment ("our execution phase") in the hands of the European Commission. The new reality for Welch and GE occurred in June and July of 2001, when GE was told that the European Commission rejected the proposed acquisition. The European competition commissioner, Mario Monti, said at the time, "I regret that the companies were not able to agree on a solution that would have met the Commission's competition concerns. . . . The European Commission and the U.S. Department of Justice have worked in close cooperation during this investigation. It is unfortunate that, in the end, we reached different conclusions."[9]

In June 2001 GE made a number of proposals to the Commission to deal with the competition problems they had identified. The packages that GE proposed were all rejected because the Commission did not view them as resolving the problems they had identified. On July 3 the European Commission formally rejected the merger. The new reality, a rejection from the Commission, plus a greater risk due to an economic downturn, led to a good judgment by Welch, backed by new CEO Jeff Immelt, to walk away from the deal.

Was the attempted Honeywell acquisition a good or a bad call? This is an interesting question, as it can be looked at as both. The preparation phase of going after Honeywell qualifies as a good judgment, given all the information at hand. Where there is room for argument around good or bad judgment is in the execution phase. Should Welch and his team have done a better job of anticipating the EC resistance? We will never know that answer. But given twenty-twenty hindsight, we can say that the final Honeywell judgment was a good one. For one thing, GE could walk away without having to pay Honeywell a huge merger breakup penalty. For another, Immelt did not have to deal with a huge merger deal on top of filling Welch's sizable shoes. All things considered, the outcome was good for the organization.

RESOURCES AND CONSTITUENCIES

The quality of a person's judgment depends to a large degree on his or her ability to marshal resources and to interact well with the appropriate constituencies. Most of the time the resources and the interested constituencies overlap. A good leader uses four types of knowledge to make judgment calls.

Self-knowledge
Do you know who you are? Do you have clear values about what you are trying to accomplish? Do you have clear values about what you will and will not do to achieve your goals? Do you know what you know and what you don't know? Can you empathize with others and anticipate their possible responses? Can you draw on your own experiences for future guidance? Are you willing to learn? Leaders who exercise good judgment calls are able to listen, reframe their thinking, and give up old paradigms. Jeff Immelt says, "It is an intense journey into

yourself."[10] You are always looking for ways of doing it better, willing to break it and make it better.

Social Network Knowledge

In the language of social psychology, a person's social network is a map of all of the relevant ties between the nodes being studied. The network can also be used to determine the social capital of individual actors. These concepts are often displayed in a social network diagram, where nodes are the points and ties are the lines. But we are using it here to mean the people you interact with and rely on most to help you achieve your corporate goals. Leadership is a team sport; there must be alignment of the leader's team, the organization, and critical stakeholders to create the ongoing capacity for good judgment calls. The leader must consciously work to encourage teamwork, draw on the best resources of each individual, and help them learn to make better judgments in their own areas of responsibility.

Organizational Knowledge

Good leaders work hard to continuously enhance the team, organizational, and stakeholder capacity at all levels to make good judgment calls. Brad Anderson, former CEO of Best Buy, his successor Brian Dunn and their leadership team are building a customer-centric organization at all levels. The effort is designed to enable store-level associates to participate in strategic judgment calls, as they go from a product-centric, one-size-fits-all business model to one that differentiates store merchandise and marketing according to the customer demographics in the area. It is not a static model; the store personnel are trained to continuously adjust the strategy based on day-to-day learning and teaching. The process not only keeps strategy on target, but also keeps improving the capacity of store associates to make good judgment calls. One example of the many we will explore later involved a twenty-year-old associate in the Westminster store in California. He spoke with us about his area of the store, plasma televisions. He told us: "I have really good news. I made the judgment call to change the physical display, widening the aisles, making the products stand out more. It has been great, my sales are significantly improving as measured by the store's daily P&L, but I also made a mistake that I have to fix real fast. I have too much inventory stacked up in the store. My ROIC [return on invested capital] is going down; I need to get rid of the inventory fast."

Reflect on this for a moment. In the old Best Buy the associate would never have been given the freedom or the tools to make the judgment call about the plasma TV area. Those decisions were centralized, all dictated by standardization from headquarters. All Best Buy stores looked the same and had the same products. The associate also would not have had any training to understand the financials and customer centricity. The Westminster associate has been equipped to make good judgment calls and to continuously adjust them based on data and commitment to the judgment call Brad Anderson and his top team made to implement a customer-centric strategy.

Stakeholder Knowledge

Engaging customers, suppliers, the community, and boards in generating knowledge to support better judgments is the final category. When GE started running Work-Out sessions with suppliers, it was a way to engage them in the generation of knowledge to feed better judgments. Work-Out was the name GE had given to the town hall meetings it began to implement with all of its employees and many of its suppliers, in which problems were literally "worked out" of the company. One such session in Medical Systems focused around building better MRI and CAT scan products, and included low-level teams from GE, low-tech metal cabinet producers, Kodak, and 3M as imaging materials producers, as well as small high-tech component makers.

In one workshop we had six supplier teams of six or seven members along with about twenty GE Medical Systems managers. The focus was on how to improve quality and productivity together in order to make better strategic judgments around the products. By spending three days in a workshop, the groups developed a common Teachable Point of View regarding their collective work and also worked out a lot of the human dynamic problems, conflicts, and unnecessary secrecy, thus building a stakeholder team that improved performance.

Engaging customers with the organization is another way to generate new stakeholder knowledge. At Intuit, the call centers work with customers—accountants who pay a fee for help in using the Intuit tax software with the accountants' clients. The role of the Intuit call center associate is to support the accountant in making better judgments for their clients. A database has been developed at Intuit to capture and share best practices and generate new customer knowledge to support better and better judgments.

A FRAMEWORK FOR GOOD AND BAD JUDGMENTS

The chart "Leadership Judgment Process" lays out the phases of a judgment with the leadership behaviors, good and bad, that impact the outcome of judgments. No leader is perfect in all of the behaviors.

Leadership Judgment Process

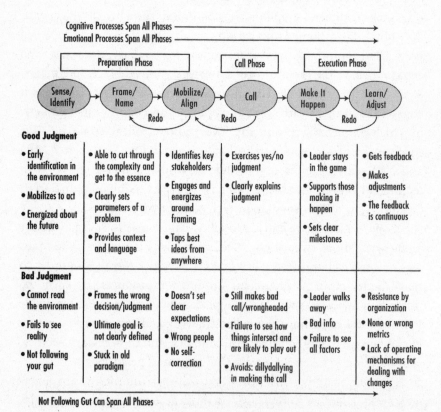

	Preparation Phase			Call Phase	Execution Phase	
Sense/Identify	Frame/Name	Mobilize/Align		Call	Make It Happen	Learn/Adjust
Good Judgment						
• Early identification in the environment	• Able to cut through the complexity and get to the essence	• Identifies key stakeholders		• Exercises yes/no judgment	• Leader stays in the game	• Gets feedback
• Mobilizes to act	• Clearly sets parameters of a problem	• Engages and energizes around framing		• Clearly explains judgment	• Supports those making it happen	• Makes adjustments
• Energized about the future	• Provides context and language	• Taps best ideas from anywhere			• Sets clear milestones	• The feedback is continuous
Bad Judgment						
• Cannot read the environment	• Frames the wrong decision/judgment	• Doesn't set clear expectations		• Still makes bad call/wrongheaded	• Leader walks away	• Resistance by organization
• Fails to see reality	• Ultimate goal is not clearly defined	• Wrong people		• Failure to see how things intersect and are likely to play out	• Bad info	• None or wrong metrics
• Not following your gut	• Stuck in old paradigm	• No self-correction		• Avoids: dillydallying in making the call	• Failure to see all factors	• Lack of operating mechanisms for dealing with changes

Not Following Gut Can Span All Phases

When mistakes are made due to bypassing a step, good leaders recover by looping back. A. G. Lafley, CEO of P&G, for example, once left out a good mobilizing and aligning process and had to loop back with his top team to get them aligned, even though he had made an initial judgment call. David Novak, CEO of Yum! Brands, had to go back in the process after he launched the multibranding strategy, having two stores in one store, for example, half KFC (Kentucky Fried Chicken) and half Taco Bell. He made the judgment, but his team was not at all aligned and not fully supportive of executing the strategic judgment.

REDO LOOP

The judgment process is not simply a linear process; the leader is managing a process that can include mistakes and facts gleaned along the way, with plenty of opportunities to recover. In programming there are "redo loops"; in Perl and other computer languages, redo "starts this loop iteration over again." We are using the term to underscore the importance of leaders self-correcting when they see a need to revisit and revise parts of the process.

Later in the book we will see how A. G. Lafley, CEO of P&G, created a "redo loop" in naming a CEO for one of the businesses because he did not have his vice chairmen and other senior executives mobilized and aligned. He did a redo that set the stage for a good judgment. David Novak had to do a redo in the execution of his multibranding of stores strategy judgment, which would have failed had he not slowed down the process, learned, and adjusted to make sure the judgment got executed. Welch's Honeywell judgment process included a big redo loop during the execution phase, one that dramatically altered the outcome that started out as an acquisition of Honeywell but ended up as walking away from the deal. GE did not acquire Honeywell, but neither did United Technology.

◆ ◆ ◆

We have begun to lay out our framework for leadership judgment calls. It is based on our premise that there is nothing more important in leadership than having the right people on the team who are able to set and execute the strategy and are capable of handling crises as they occur.

Great leaders not only make more important good judgment calls; they also take on the responsibility to develop the next generation of leaders with the capacity to make good judgment calls. They win today while very consciously building the team for tomorrow.

Furthermore, judgment is a process, not a "blink," as Malcolm Gladwell argues in his book *Blink: The Power of Thinking Without Thinking*[11] where he postulates, "When experts make decisions they don't logically compare all the options. They size up a situation immediately and act." We are more aligned with Jerome Groopman's *How Doctors Think*[12] analysis, which takes a counter position, namely, "Relying too heavily on intuition has its perils. Cogent medical judgments meld first impressions with deliberate analysis."

Blink and *How Doctors Think* both wrestle with judgment by "experts," not leaders, making organizational judgments. The judgments we are dealing with are ones that impact the total institution and involve others both in making the judgment and in executing it.

When Jeff Immelt, CEO of GE, makes a strategic judgment to invest billions in new technologies, he does not make a "blink" judgment. When he describes the process, he says that he "wallows" in the preparation phase, which for some strategic judgments can be more than a year. At the point he feels he has done sufficient framing/naming, mobilizing, and aligning, he does take that existential and intuitive leap, making the judgment call.

He then spends years ensuring that the judgment execution occurs. Otherwise, as a leader, his good "call" could turn into a bad judgment in the execution phase. Immelt is able to use the "redo loop" to ensure the success of the judgment process.

3

HAVING A STORYLINE

■ **Winning Leaders Use Mental Frameworks to Guide Good Judgment**
- Teachable Points of View set direction and behavioral values.
- Narrative storylines animate the future scenario.

■ **The Most Successful Storylines Are Compelling and Practical**
- They connect disparate elements in an unfolding stream of events.
- They enable leaders to deal with scale, complexity, and uncertainty.

■ **Storylines Are Organic: They Evolve in Response to Changing Circumstances**
- Leaders plug in options to test possible outcomes.
- Storylines provide the platform for subplots at all levels of the organization.

◆ ◆ ◆

One year after being named CEO of Boeing, Jim McNerney was in front of the world testifying to the Senate's Armed Services Committee about

Boeing's settlement with the Justice Department of serious legal allegations. He told the committee and the world at large:

> I hope to discuss why, going forward, the Congress and the taxpayers of this country can place their trust in Boeing. Companies doing business with the U.S. government are expected to adhere to the highest legal and ethical standards. I acknowledge that Boeing did not live up to those expectations.[1]

This framed one of McNerney's biggest leadership judgments since taking over as CEO of Boeing in July 2005. Boeing's 2006 agreement to pay $615 million put an end to three years of Justice Department investigations into alleged improper behavior on the part of several Boeing employees, including two senior executives. Boeing's settlement with the Justice Department allowed the company to avoid criminal charges or admission of wrongdoing. It was the largest financial settlement agreed to by a defense contractor for alleged wrongdoing. *The Wall Street Journal* summarized the story, saying that Boeing was charged with:

> [I]mproperly acquiring thousands of pages of rival Lockheed Martin Corp's proprietary documents in the late 1990s, using some of them to help win a competition for government rocket-launching business.
>
> Years later, Boeing illegally recruited a senior Air Force procurement official while she still had authority over billions of dollars in other Boeing contracts. She also championed company efforts to skirt normal procurement procedures in offering to provide refueling takers to the Air Force through a controversial $20 billion leasing program.
>
> The uproar led to the firing of Boeing Chief Financial Officer Michael Sears in 2003 and the resignation of Chairman Phil Condit. The flurry of Justice Department and congressional investigations expose the most sweeping Pentagon procurement scandal since the end of the Cold War.
>
> Mr. Sears, as well as Darleen Druyun, the former Air Force official served time in federal prisons.[2]

This was pretty tough stuff for the new CEO to take on during his first year. Weeks later, on August 1, McNerney went before the public in a Senate committee hearing to defend Boeing and his first high-profile crisis judgments at the company's helm. Senator John Warner opened the Armed Services Committee hearing on the Boeing Company's Global Settlement Agreement with the following statement:

> We meet today to discuss the results of two Department of Justice investigations of the Boeing Company, both begun three years ago, into the allegations of improper use of proprietary information obtained from a competitor to compete for launch services contracts under the Air Force's Evolved Expendable Launch Vehicle Program and an investigation of the circumstances surrounding the hiring of Ms. Darlene Druyan, a senior Air Force official, by Boeing.[3]

McNerney joined a once proud company with a very tarnished image facing very serious allegations. He was a board member prior to becoming CEO, so he was fully aware of the crisis he was inheriting. Three important leadership judgments at Boeing led up to his personal role in moving the crisis to a conclusion. The first two were people judgments by the board: the first was forcing the resignation of the previous CEO, Harry Stonecipher; the second was to appoint Jim McNerney, then CEO of 3M, to be the new CEO.

The third leadership judgment was for McNerney to involve himself deeply and directly in resolving the crisis that he inherited. He could have fought the allegations and dragged out the discussions; he could have underplayed the importance of the matter and blamed former leaders. Instead, he made a judgment that turned the crisis into an opportunity to transform Boeing's internal culture and leadership behaviors so that the new DNA was one that supported his strategy for Boeing to be a world-class model of competitiveness and ethical leadership. He also saw an important opportunity with the settlement to further the restoration of Boeing's tarnished public image and brand. He described the crisis in the following terms:

> [T]he events, themselves, have caused an immense amount of introspection at Boeing. How could a company with a history of reliability and self-image of unquestioned integrity have made

these mistakes? This introspection set a course of building one of the most robust ethics and compliance programs in corporate America. That is the lasting legacy—and silver lining—of this dark cloud in our history.[4]

McNerney Becomes Boeing's Third CEO in Three Years

McNerney had been one of three finalists to succeed Jack Welch as CEO of General Electric in 2001. When that job went to Jeffrey Immelt, McNerney had gone to become chairman of 3M in Minneapolis. When first mentioned for the Boeing job in early 2005, McNerney had taken himself out of the running. He had been at 3M only four years. He had brought new energy and fiscal discipline to the struggling manufacturer. The company's earnings and stock performance had rebounded for a gain of 45 percent, and he had begun developing new strong leaders to take the company into the future. He said he liked his work at 3M and he didn't want to leave.

But aerospace was too exciting for McNerney to turn down. In the late 1990s he had headed GE's Aircraft Engines business and helped it grow into the leading force in the industry. He had worked with Boeing as a supplier selling engines to customers buying Boeing planes. He had joined the Boeing board in 2001. So he knew a lot of people in the company and the industry, as well as a lot about its business. He had a passion for it, and when he thought of where he would like to end his career he realized that he had to seriously consider Boeing. He changed his mind and made a crucial judgment call to accept the job as Boeing CEO, he said, because the opportunity probably wouldn't come around again, and he really wanted to do it.

After Condit's sudden departure, the board had called Harry Stonecipher back from retirement. Stonecipher, a widely respected former Boeing president, stepped into the crisis and began to make good progress toward cleaning house. Then embarrassing e-mails surfaced, internally related to an affair with a female Boeing executive. At a time when Boeing was desperately trying to clean up its ethical act, the board made the difficult choice to request and accept his resignation, which it did in March 2005.

Even in good times, managing a company of the size and complexity of Boeing would be a major leadership challenge. But these were not good times for Boeing. Phil Condit had been forced out as CEO, after nearly forty years with the company, in late 2003. Condit himself had not been personally accused of any wrongdoing, but there were serious ethical violations associated with Boeing's government business under his stewardship. The violations occurred at senior levels of the company, so the board held him accountable for not exercising good judgment regarding controls and ethical standards.

When McNerney arrived, Boeing's senior ranks were demoralized, and employees throughout the organization were frustrated and embarrassed. The reputation of Boeing had been seriously tarnished by its top leaders twice in less than two years. Stonecipher had already been working on repairing the company's reputation and was working to build an internal culture of enhanced integrity and accountability. His removal as CEO created a fresh round of self-doubt, confusion, and consternation among many Boeing employees. It was a clear bump in the road in the transformation of the culture.

Having seen the crisis unfold from his seat on the company's board of directors, McNerney understood the legal, political, and business dynamics that surrounded the Boeing scandals and the company's efforts up to that point to reach a resolution. And he had developed a sense of timing and a framework for the judgments he would ultimately need to make to put the past issues to rest and focus his team on the future. McNerney also was acutely aware that how he handled this crisis would be a watershed in his leadership, affording him the opportunity to reenergize the transformation of the Boeing culture around ethics and integrity.

Anyone who knew Jim McNerney would have known that he was not the type to leave the crucial judgments of something as important as the Global Settlement to others. McNerney is a world-class team player. Others, including his board and legal team, played key roles. McNerney relied on them for their insights and judgment. But the course of events was profoundly shaped by Jim McNerney. He had a plan for restoring Boeing to the top tier of worldwide industry, and that plan called for a quick and amicable settlement with the Department of Justice and a sincere and dedicated effort to restore Boeing's reputation and relationships with both internal and external stakeholders.

TEACHABLE POINT OF VIEW AND JUDGMENT CALLS

In the second chapter, we laid out our framework for how successful leaders go about making good judgment calls. In the rest of this book, we will delve into the judgment matrix we described there. We will talk about how the good leaders we have observed go about marshaling their resources to make wise decisions and take effective action. We believe that this framework will help other leaders think about their own judgment-making processes. It will also help them build organizations that promote good judgment and develop the judgment-making abilities of others. But before we do that, we first need to take a couple of chapters to talk about some resources and attributes that good leaders bring to bear when working through the judgment matrix.

How a leader works the judgment process depends to a great extent on *who* the leader is. Winning leaders, the ones who continually make the best judgment calls, have clear mental frameworks to guide their thinking. They have stories running in their heads about how the world works and how they want things to turn out. And they have the all-important qualities of character and courage. They have the internal discipline and the guts to make the right calls and to follow through.

The personal resources that judgment leaders bring to the table are critical factors in their repeated success. The matrix is a valuable tool. It works. But to make good judgments, leaders must know to what aim they are using the matrix. They must know what they are trying to accomplish, where they are headed, and how they will get there. And they must have the courage to make tough calls and execute them. Any leader who follows the matrix can improve his or her judgment batting average, but without mental and moral rigor, they will never achieve consistency.

In our earlier work, we have both written extensively about transformational leadership, and about those who creatively destroy and remake their organizations for success in tomorrow's world. We have devoted our careers to studying how leaders build companies that succeed in the marketplace and other organizations that accomplish their missions. We have been particularly interested in how leaders transform their organizations to maintain success in changing environments. We have talked about how winning leaders are teachers. They drive their organizations through teaching, and they develop others to be leader/teachers.

Noel has written that winning leaders are good at this because they have made the effort and spent the time to develop Teachable Points of View (TPOVs).[5] TPOVs are what enable leaders to take the valuable knowledge and experiences that they have stored up inside their heads and teach them to others. Winning leader/teachers use their TPOVs to convey ideas and values to energize others and to help them make clear, decisive decisions.

While TPOVs are essential to transformational leadership and to developing others as leaders, TPOVs have an equally crucial role to play in guiding leaders' own decisions and actions. Roger Enrico, the former head of Pepsico who is a world-class teacher, has remarked that "having a point of view is worth 50 IQ points."[6] If that is the case, which we think it is, then having a TPOV is worth at least another fifty points when it comes to making judgment calls.

The TPOV comes alive and is most valuable when a leader weaves it into a storyline for the future success of the organization. As a living story, it both helps the leader make the judgment calls that will make the story become a reality and enlists and energizes others to make it happen.

As Noel wrote in *The Leadership Engine: How Winning Companies Build Leaders at Every Level,* the story and the TPOV must be inextricably linked.

> These points of view set the direction and provide the guiding principles for the organization. But these "points of view" can't be just dry intellectual concepts. To be effective, leaders must bring them alive, so that followers can and will act on

them. This means that they must make them understood not just rationally, but emotionally. And they do this by weaving them into personal stories. The stories and the points of view are intertwined. Without the stories, the points of view are often just arid concepts. However, the stories must be solidly based in the leader's points of view. Otherwise, they are just idle entertainment that amuses and engages, but doesn't lead anyone anywhere.[7]

A key factor in Jim McNerney's judgment calls surrounding the settlement with the Justice Department was that he had a TPOV about how Boeing was going to succeed in the future. He had clear ideas about what would drive success for Boeing. He knew what kind of culture and values he needed to cultivate to make those ideas work. And he had a strong sense for how to reenergize workers to help bring this vision to reality. Furthermore, he had begun crafting those elements into a storyline for Boeing's future success.

McNerney had a scenario that he was developing in his head about how the elements would interplay as the future unfolded. This meant that as issues came up and each judgment call needed to be made, McNerney could plug options into the mental scenario he had developed and foresee likely outcomes. The storyline, with its comprehensive scope, made it easier for him to keep an eye on the whole picture of what needed to happen at Boeing, rather than getting too narrowly focused on the specific issue at hand.

A leader's TPOV guides the development of the narrative. But it is the leader's capacity for writing his/her future story for the organization that provides the platform for making the key people, strategy, and crisis judgments. The larger and more complex the organization, the more the story looks like Tolstoy's *War and Peace* written as a look forward, not backward.

All of us have the capacity to mobilize action through vision and stories. We do it when we plan a vacation. We create a vision of the future, a future story with real events, people, drama, and so on. We try to envision what our trip to Grand Cayman will be like, the vision of the hotel on the beach, the scuba-diving trip, the dinner at the restaurant on the beach. The story may be totally out of touch with reality when it turns out that we get booked in a crummy hotel with bad food and the scuba trip turns out to be a disaster. The story, however, got us motivated to make the trip. The more competent we are at crafting not only compelling stories but ones based in practicality, the more effective we are at making things happen in our own lives.

This is truer for a leader. Leaders play the complex role of playwright, producer, and director. They draft the dramas in their minds. They take them "off Broadway" and test them out with a few trusted friends and colleagues. They revise and rewrite in response to the criticism. Then they put them onstage for the wider organization, continuing to revise and adjust even through the execution phase. The basic storyline is the platform for subplots and stories throughout all levels of leadership.

Leaders' storylines are always organic. They evolve in response to changing circumstances. Nonetheless, they are solid and concrete enough that they give good leaders solid foundations that enable them to deal with scale and complexity and uncertainty. Leaders who have storylines running in their heads are much better equipped to deal with unexpected events.

Clear storylines give leaders the critical ability to engage in "planful opportunism" when it comes to judgment calls. The "planful" part is the leader's storyline for the future, built on a solid TPOV. The "opportunistic" parts are the unpredictable moments when the need or opportunity arises for a judgment call. Storylines help leaders make good calls regarding people and strategy, and they are absolutely essential for successfully handling crises.

JIM MCNERNEY'S STORYLINE FOR BOEING

Jim McNerney's storyline for Boeing was a strong theme of high ethical standards that meant a new partnership with all of Boeing's stakeholders, both internal and external. This theme was a key element in making that scenario play out as he wished. That understanding directly guided his judgment calls about how to move Boeing beyond the ethical and legal issues that had dogged its recent past.

Even before his arrival as CEO at Boeing, McNerney had been at work developing his TPOV and crafting its elements into a storyline that he could follow in his head and use to teach and lead others. As he gained knowledge and experience on the inside, including adapting and incorporating many positive aspects of the existing Boeing culture and business plan, he would refine and reshape elements of it. Here are the elements of McNerney's TPOV for Boeing:

Ideas: About How to Make the Organization Successful in the Marketplace

McNerney inherited a focused set of core competencies, which Boeing leadership had defined several years prior, that were used to guide strategic decision making.

CORE COMPETENCIES
- Detailed customer knowledge and focus
- Large-scale systems integration
- Lean enterprise

Boeing Management Model

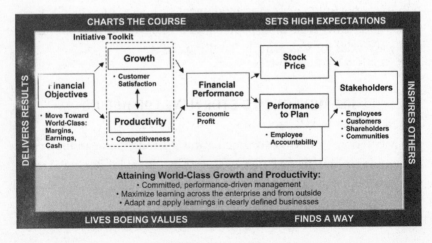

McNerney added a management model to align and integrate the company through common, disciplined approaches to leadership development, integrity, and values, and to work growth and productivity simultaneously to drive better business performance.

Values: About How We Behave and What Good Leadership Is at Boeing

McNerney inherited a strong set of values to which all employees aspired: leadership, integrity, quality, customer satisfaction, people working together, a diverse and involved team, good corporate citizenship, and enhancing shareholder value. He added a comprehensive model of leadership that not only defined the attributes Boeing would expect of good leaders but described how to animate leadership development throughout the ranks.

DEFINE IT: A BOEING LEADER
- Charts the course
- Sets high expectations
- Inspires others
- Finds a way
- Lives Boeing's values
- Delivers results

MODEL IT: IN ALL WE DO
- Action/words
- Every day
- Leaders leading leaders

EXPECT IT/MEASURE IT/REWARD IT
- Reinforce in HR processes

TEACH IT: THE BOEING LEADERSHIP CENTER
- Candor/openness
- Leaders teaching leaders
- Step function impact

Energy: How to Generate the Positive Emotional Energy to Get Things Done

- Tie pay to performance on values as well as financials
- Help people to grow
- Free people to act
- Maintain high standards

In previous writings, Noel has included a fourth TPOV element: edge, which is the willingness to face reality and make tough decisions. In the context of leadership judgment calls, exercising edge is the central phase of the judgment-making process. Leaders exercise edge when they make clear yes-or-no decisions.

The TPOV is framed in the chart "Teachable Point of View and Storylines" as three interrelated components—ideas, values, and emotional energy—that interact in the mind of the leader to guide the exercising of edge and the making of judgment calls.

Using these elements of his TPOV for Boeing, McNerney began developing his storyline. That storyline, which significantly guided his judgment calls in handling the Justice Department settlement, follows, and fully reflects his management model and other TPOV elements. It

Teachable Point of View and Storylines

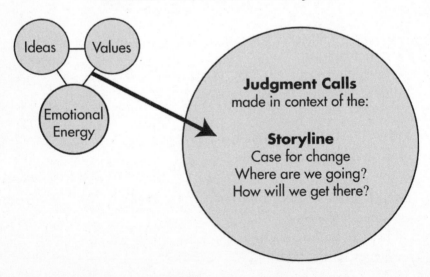

is drawn from comments McNerney made to Wall Street analysts and to Boeing shareholders:

> The Boeing Company aspires to deliver financial results that match the quality of our people and our technology—which is a meaningful improvement from where we are today. In short, we expect to meet a significantly higher standard of overall financial performance. We intend to get there by finding ways to make Boeing bigger and better than the sum of its parts.
>
> The foundation for this framework will be driving and nurturing a culture of leadership and accountability. We have started by setting challenging but attainable financial objectives and more strongly linking them to our own pay and career development. An intense but equal pursuit of productivity and growth will be the building blocks of our improved financial performance. We must have both growth and productivity—simultaneously—since they fuel each other. We will always remember that growth, our future, begins and ends with our customers. I am pleased that Boeing's teams have made significant strides in living at our customer's place and at our customer's pace.
>
> And we won't stop there. Further, we will strive to address growth as a disciplined process, not as a series of intermittent opportunities. Through this approach, we hope to anticipate our customers' needs better and earlier than our competitors do, respond faster, and solidify our standing as the preferred supplier for our customers around the world.[8]

> By tapping into the creativity of both our own people and those of our partners and suppliers . . . there is no end of opportunity for adding value and taking out cost in the wonderful products we build and the valuable services we provide.

> Our growth will be customer-inspired and customer-driven. In one of our principal businesses, our customers include the world's airlines and the traveling public; in the other, they include the armed services of the United States and allied governments. These are terrific customers to have. Without a doubt, if we do a great job of listening to them and finding the best way to satisfy their needs, Boeing will continue to grow . . . year after year.[9]

It's all there. All of the points of his TPOV about how Boeing is going to succeed in the future are in that short narrative. With this storyline running in his head, it was clear to McNerney that Boeing would be in a far better position to settle with the Justice Department

---

TPOV and Storylines

Martin Luther King Jr.'s "I Have a Dream" speech, delivered at the Lincoln Memorial in 1963, is one of the most famous and compelling examples of a leader transforming a clear, logical Teachable Point of View into a vivid and inspirational storyline. The goal of achieving it drove both King's decisions and the success of the civil rights movement. The elements of King's TPOV were powerful.

Here's the TPOV:

- Ideas: King was driven by the belief that America would one day fulfill its own Declaration of Independence: "We hold these truths to be self-evident; that all men are created equal."
- Values: His speech championed dignified nonviolent protest.
- Energy (teamwork and urgency): He also stressed the life-or-death urgency of immediate action.
- Edge: "There will be neither rest nor tranquility in America until the Negro is granted his citizenship rights."

But the narrative story he created brought it alive and made it even more powerful. It was the plot line that he played in his head to guide his own judgments and that he used to effectively mobilize millions of others in the civil rights struggle:

- Ideas: The dream that his children would "one day live in a nation where they will not be judged by the color of their skin but by the content of their character."
- Values: An emphasis on the power of faith to end conflict and advance justice and brotherhood.
- Energy and Edge: "With this faith we will be able to work together, pray together; to struggle together, to go to jail together, to stand up for freedom together, knowing that we will be free one day."[10]

sooner rather than later, even if it cost the company more in the short term in the form of a larger settlement payment.

Where Are We Going?—How Will We Get There?

While including all the elements of their TPOVs, winning leaders' storylines aren't dry narratives that can only be summoned up with the help of PowerPoint reminders. Rather, they are active, engaging stories that start in the present and lead toward a rewarding future.

Winning leaders create these powerful visions and stories for where their organization is going and how it is going to get there. Then, they use them as "self-talk." They tailor them to their situations and their audiences. They can tell the two-minute elevator version or give the eight-hour Fidel Castro oration. But no matter what the level of detail, these future stories provide the context for leaders to make judgments about people and strategy, and handle the crises that inevitably occur.

Winning leaders' storylines specifically address three areas of questions:

1. Where are we now? What is the hand we have been dealt? The storylines precisely describe and diagnose the current situation. This is the starting point for the journey. It often includes the strongest elements for motivating the drive to change.
2. Where are we going? What are we trying to accomplish? What are the benchmarks of success? How will things look and feel when we get there? The inspirational storyline here adds to the motivation for change, but more important, it sets the beacon. It defines the goal, and thus helps both the leader and the people in the organization to make judgments about whether a decision or action will get them closer to it or farther away.
3. How are we going to get there? This is part road map and part defining of roles. The road map part charts a path toward the goal and suggests some steps along the way. The role-defining part describes the kinds of behaviors and the contributions that people will have to make to execute the plan.

The version of his story that McNerney shared with his senior team in early 2006 was a more detailed rendering of the story than the one he laid out for the analysts and shareholders.

1. WHERE ARE WE NOW?

He had his case for change. Where was Boeing now, and where did it need to be?

> I want it to be more global than it is. We resist global pressures in some cases. They're not always immediate, but over time we're going to have to become a more global company. That's where the talent is, in many respects; and where the training is, in many respects. That's where the markets are. The fact is we've got a big competitor to BCA in Europe that has half the market. And we've got to know how to do business globally as well as they do, if not a whole lot better. They're going to start doing some things globally. So more global.

2. WHERE ARE WE GOING?

How would the company have to operate in the future to make itself a strong global competitor?

Over the years, Boeing had grown through some major mergers and acquisitions, the largest of which was the 1997 merger with McDonnell Douglas. And when McNerney arrived, it was largely operating as separate commercial and defense companies under a loose corporate umbrella. Part of his vision was to unify the company around common values and processes, and also to share best practices and eliminate the duplication of efforts.

> The theme in my mind is it's still one company, multiple businesses . . . each with separate, well-defined roles, with the sum being greater than the parts, and the financial results to prove it. I come back to that theme. That's my vision of this company. We're not there yet, but you can see that at least we aspire to some of that as we try to get leverage.

3. HOW WERE THEY GOING TO GET THERE? WHAT WOULD IT TAKE?

Now, what else? Sure, in five to ten years I'd like to see a step-function change in financial results. Sure, I'd like to see the market shares we're beginning to get in (Boeing Commercial Airplanes) and some key (Integrated Defense Systems) programs to stay and even improve. So I'd like to see business results better than historically. I think every management team in the world wants that, and I want that because I'm like you: I want to win. I don't want to lose. I want the other guys to lose.

But even more importantly, what I want is better, more excited leaders. That's what sustains companies. We've got great leaders. We've got great people. . . . We've got a pretty good group of people, not only in this room but also a year or two behind them, that are going to be better than us. I want to help create that. I want to help create a generation of leaders that are better than us and that are even more excited about this company and about this business than we are.

Ultimately, he said, he envisioned a company that would prosper because it was filled with people who were able and excited.

I want Boeing to be the best place to work. It is, in many respects, now. I want it to still be that way, even more so.

I want Boeing to be the most admired company not only in aerospace but in the country. That's what I want. That's an aspirational goal for me. . . but at the end of the day, I still have this fundamental belief that if we can create an environment where our people grow, our company will grow. It's that simple. Because we know what to do, if we're excited about it.

The chart "Storylines and Judgment" identifies what makes for good storylines and how they guide the judgment process.

MCNERNEY'S PLANFUL OPPORTUNISM IN A CRISIS

We interviewed Jim McNerney about his decision to settle quickly with the Justice Department and his other early judgment calls at Boeing. He talked to us in terms of where the company had been and where it needed to get. One hallmark of great leaders is their capacity for what we call "planful opportunism." This is the ability to turn an unexpected crisis or event into a way to drive a very thoughtful

STORYLINES AND JUDGMENT

THE KEY ELEMENTS OF THE LEADER'S STORYLINE
- It interprets the present and shapes the future.
- It is both rational and emotional.
- Building a storyline for a company is an organic, ongoing process.
- The storyline creates a sense that the organization is embarked on an ongoing journey.
- The storyline is constantly updated as circumstances change.
- The storyline defines the beliefs, attitudes, and values that the company holds and that its employees share.
- The storyline creates a sense of purpose for the business.
- The story comes from the heart and engages people emotionally and personally.

JUDGMENT
- Good judgments further the future story.
- Bad judgments disrupt and hinder the story.
- Leaders at all levels need storylines that are tied to the larger story to guide their judgments.

---

and planful agenda. This is exactly what McNerney did: he took the scandal and resulting crisis and turned it into a driving force for the cultural change he wanted to foster at Boeing.

Over the years, as Boeing worked to integrate its merged and acquired businesses, it struggled to create a common culture and the operating disciplines that go along with it. "We had patterns there that were not healthy," McNerney told us. The culture apparently was not strong enough to prevent the improper acts of some key people who put the whole company at risk. People were allowed to hide in the company's bureaucracy, and the culture lacked comprehensive functional checks and balances on individuals' behaviors. Nor was it a place where individuals felt it was their responsibility to stand up and be heard when something just didn't seem right to them.

So McNerney made a determined judgment to preserve the many positive elements of the Boeing culture but to challenge those he felt were dysfunctional. First, he stood strongly behind the efforts begun before his arrival to gain the commitment and alignment of all 155,000 employees. McNerney told us, "Every employee each year personally recommits to ethical and compliant behavior three ways: by going through a thorough training regimen, re-signing the Boeing Code of Conduct, and participating in one of our Ethics Recommitment stand-downs with his or her business or function." In addition there is an Office of Internal Governance, created under Stonecipher to consolidate investigative audits, and oversight resources, that reports to McNerney and has regular and routine visibility with the board of directors. This office monitors potential conflicts of interest in hiring, overseeing specific ethical and compliance concerns and cases for our top leaders.

Second, he put his personal imprint on the company's efforts to open up the culture. He is creating a work environment that encourages people to talk about the tough issues and to make the right judgments when they find themselves at the crossroads between meeting a tough business commitment and doing what is ethically right. McNerney says:

> There simply can be no tradeoffs between Boeing's values and Boeing's performance. We want people to know that it's OK to question what happens around them because that's what surfaces problems early. Silence that ignores the misconduct of fellow workers is not acceptable. . . . Ethics and compliance are core to our leadership development, not off to the side. At the end of the day, the character of an organization—its culture— comes down to the behavior of its leaders and must be seen to be a central part of the whole system of training and developing leaders, and the whole process of evaluating, paying, and promoting people.

McNerney's approach to the crisis—to get a reasonable settlement for both sides sooner rather than later and put Boeing on a new course— did work, and it created a new set of expectations for how McNerney and his team will conduct itself internally and externally for years to come. The judgments he made during this crisis clearly further the story he is creating for the future of Boeing.

Senator John McCain was Boeing's toughest critic during the Druyun scandal. At the Senate hearing, McCain credited Jim McNerney's judgment for a key decision that followed the settlement itself: a decision not to take a tax deduction for the huge cost of settling with the Justice Department. Senator McCain told the packed hearing room, "The fact is that Boeing did not have to make the decision it made on deductibility. But it did. And when coupled with the internal changes the company has made, what Boeing did here conveys to me how serious the company is to truly reforming and starting fresh."

McCain's comments were a testament to the leadership of Jim McNerney, who makes all of his judgments in the flow of his future story for Boeing. When he is faced with a key people decision, he places it in his mind in his storyline; he pictures how this person will interact with others to further the story. The strategy decisions, likewise, are done in the larger context of his story. And he faces crises not as one-off "put out a fire" situations, but in the larger context with a view to leveraging his longer-term storyline.

McNerney also seized an opportunity at the Senate hearing to further his leadership agenda by summing up his testimony with:

> Mr. Chairman and members of the Committee, in my fourteen months as the company's chairman, president, and CEO, I have made it my mission to understand the root causes of what went wrong in years past. And I can attest that those former employees referred to in the settlement do not represent the people at Boeing, who are devoted to conducting their work ethically and in the best interests of our customers and our country.
>
> Boeing is fully committed to operating at the highest standards of ethics and compliance. I will continue to do everything in my power to ensure that the company never finds itself in a situation like this in the future.[11]

Throughout the remainder of the book we will meet other leaders who are making judgments on the platform of their future storylines.

THE MAJOR WRITERS AND PRODUCERS
IN THE JUDGMENT DRAMA

There are many leaders who were interviewed and studied for this book. They are the ones who are producing, writing, and directing their organizational stories into the future, figuring out when to make the big judgments about casting (people), plots (strategy), and crises. Here are the major ones.

Company	Leader	Key Lessons for Others
Best Buy	Brad Anderson	• Building judgment capacity into frontline store associates
		• Building judgment into senior leadership through action learning
Boeing	Jim McNerney	• Global transformation for growth platform
Caterpillar	Jim Owens	• Judgments for growth
Grupo Salinas	Ricardo Salinas	• Strategy judgments during global economic downturn
Focus: HOPE	Eleanor Josaitis	• Judgment to transform lives through "practical solutions to racism and poverty"
GE	Jeff Immelt	• New GE strategy—judgment for technological growth and Global Research
HP	Mark Hurd	• Strategy execution
Intuit	Steve Bennett	• Judgment capability building at the front line/customers
New York City schools	Joel Klein/ Bob Knowling	• People judgment to invest in principals leadership academy
Polaris	Tom Tiller	• Strategic judgments
Procter & Gamble	A. G. Lafley	• Key people judgments to transform the business

(*continued*)

Company	Leader	Key Lessons for Others
Special Operations Forces	Wayne Downing	• Crisis judgments
Steelcase	Jim Hackett	• Character and courage
Trilogy	Joe Liemandt	• People and strategy judgment to move TU to India and China
Yum! Brands	David Novak	• Multibranding strategy judgment

◆ ◆ ◆

Leaders make important judgments on the platform of their Teachable Points of View and the storylines they have for the future of their organizations. Much as Martin Luther King Jr. used his "I have a dream" narrative to guide his judgments about people, strategy, and crisis, CEOs like Jim McNerney use their own corporate storylines to lead them to sound judgments.

The storyline is never complete and always being modified by the judgments the leader makes. However, without a solid storyline, the leader's judgments are disconnected acts that may or may not move the organization forward.

4

CHARACTER AND COURAGE

■ **To Sustain Good Judgment, a Leader Must Have Character and Courage**
- Character provides the moral compass.
- Courage produces the results.

■ **People with Character Have Clear Standards**
- They take responsibility and hold themselves accountable.
- They value self-respect over public esteem.

■ **Maintaining Standards in the Face of Obstacles Requires Courage**
- Character without courage is meaningless.
- Courage without character is dangerous.

◆ ◆ ◆

Eleanor Josaitis was a homemaker with five children living in white, suburban Detroit in July 1967 when the city erupted into five days of racial rioting. On the day after the bullets stopped flying, she walked through the downtown streets with her friend and pastor, Father William Cunningham. As they surveyed the horrifying scene of army tanks and still-blazing buildings, they turned to each other and agreed: "We have to do something."

In the following months, Father Cunningham quit his job as an English teacher at Sacred Heart seminary and began working in an inner-city parish. Eleanor and her husband sold their comfortable home in the suburbs and moved their young family to a neighborhood near the epicenter of the rioting. Together, Father Cunningham and Eleanor Josaitis began building an organization that they aptly named Focus: HOPE. They dedicated it to providing "intelligent and practical solutions to racism and poverty."[1]

From a tiny feeding program for women and children, the two of them grew Focus: HOPE, over the succeeding three decades, into a complex social services and educational institution. The feeding program came first because scientific evidence showed that hunger and malnutrition affected the critical early development of children, thus limiting their abilities from infancy. Without equal ability, there could be no equal opportunity, reasoned Josaitis and Cunningham. The children had to get better nourishment to become better learners. So that's where they started.

The feeding program, however, was never intended to be Focus: HOPE's primary vehicle for change. The long-term Focus: HOPE objective was to eliminate the need for supplemental food programs by providing opportunities for people to enter the economic mainstream and support themselves. Economic opportunity became Eleanor and Father Bill's working definition of civil rights.

Through years of setbacks and harassment, they pursued their goal of leveling the playing field for the people of inner-city Detroit. They lobbied Congress for better food programs for the elderly. They filed lawsuits to fight high, discriminatory grocery prices in low-income neighborhoods. Their avowed philosophy of taking a practical, intelligent approach to solving problems led them to understand that they needed to provide people with skills as well as nutrition.

As a result, in 1981 Focus: HOPE opened a school, the Machinist Training Institute (MTI), to teach precision machining and metalworking. Although there were few black machinists employed in Detroit at the time, their skills were in high demand. Josaitis and Cunningham were determined to produce workers whose abilities were so clearly superior that employers would not be able to resist them.

To support its students and help them succeed, Focus: HOPE also opened a Montessori preschool where students and other members of the community could bring their children while they were in class and at work. In 1989 it added a FAST TRACK program to help students improve their reading and math skills in order to qualify for the other training programs, or just to get better jobs in the community. In 1997 it began another, even more basic, First Step reading and math program to help students qualify for FAST TRACK.

By 2009, Focus: HOPE had achieved remarkable results; it had trained more than twenty-seven hundred qualified machinists and graduated nearly six thousand people from FAST TRACK and First Step. Its state-of-the-art Center for Advanced Technologies had graduated more than one hundred manufacturing engineers with associate or bachelor degrees issued by three neighboring universities. Its Information Technologies Center, a partnership with Cisco, Microsoft, and the Computing Technology Industry Association, had graduated nearly six hundred students who had embarked on careers in industry. Meanwhile, it is continuing to feed forty-three thousand low-income elderly, mothers, and children each month.

For the first thirty years, Father Cunningham and Eleanor Josaitis worked together as a team. Since Father Cunningham's death in 1997, Eleanor has continued as CEO of the organization, pushing it ahead as vigorously as before. In 1997, the very week that Father Cunningham died, a tornado all but destroyed the Focus: HOPE campus. Within twelve months Josaitis was back in operation and had rebuilt the campus.

At first blush, the Focus: HOPE story is one of action, hard work, and amazing results. But it is also a story of excellent judgment. A consistent track record of success does not occur without leaders consistently exercising good judgment on important issues. The judgment to start the Machinists Training Institute was a risky one. Focus: HOPE was running one of the most successful feeding programs in the country, and Josaitis and Cunningham knew that they would be putting it at risk if they undertook such a huge diversification. But they made the judgment that it had to be done, and they made it happen. Likewise, when they did the engineering program it was a tough judgment call. At many points along the way, especially in the early years, a misstep could have sent the whole endeavor spiraling down the tubes.

Two qualities are essential to exercising good judgment: *character* and *courage*. No matter what processes you follow, no matter how hard you try, no matter how closely you follow our framework, without character and courage no one can clear the high bar on judgment. You may luck into making some good decisions and sometimes obtain good results, but without character and courage you cannot sustain it. You will falter on the most difficult, and most important, judgments.

CHARACTER

What does it mean to have character? It means having values. It means having a moral compass that sets clear parameters for what one will, and will not do. Character is all about knowing right from wrong and having worked these issues out long before facing tough judgment calls. It is about knowing what your goals and standards are and sticking with them.

We often use the word *integrity* to describe a person of character, a person whose values and principles are above reproach. Psychiatry speaks of such people as integrated. Character plays the guiding role in how honest personal feedback and coaching are in the organization, how internal competition and politics are handled, and how suppliers and customers are treated. The CEO's character sets the stage for all the important judgment calls.

For us, character also means putting the greater good of the organization, or of society, ahead of self-interest. As Peter Drucker put it, it is about worrying about "what is right" rather than "who is right."[2] There is a kind of rigid linear logic that might lead some people to argue that Hitler must have made a lot of good judgment calls because he succeeded as well as he did in achieving the evil results he was seeking.

Using this same kind of logic, you could also argue that the Dennis Kozlowskis (Tyco), the Bernie Ebberses (WorldCom), the Andy Fastows

(Enron), and all the other corporate crooks caught up in recent years' scandals attained their goals of amassing vast amounts of power and money. They just messed up on the final judgment call, the one that would have told them when to quit. But we aren't going there. We are absolutely convinced that good judgment requires good values. Evil outcomes, even if they are the intended outcomes, can never be considered successes, and immoral judgments are never good ones.

Character is that distinctive, unfiltered personal voice that cannot be faked or imitated. It is the core essence of who we are. And perhaps in today's world, it is more powerful than ever before in shaping our actions. Chaos isn't just a theory, it is the current reality; learning to live with it, even love it, is an essential element of success today. As Jack Welch told us, "If you're not confused, you don't know what's going on." The pace of everything is accelerated. There is less time for thinking, less time for our intellectual brains to override our baser instincts. In a way, the difference between life in the old-style organization and in the new is the difference between golf and surfing. These days, you need to be able to ride the breaking wave of constant change. There is no stopping to change your equipment. Even when they have time to wallow in making a judgment, leaders never have *all* the facts, and the situation is constantly evolving. You are always making judgments on the fly.

Jim Hackett, CEO of Steelcase, told us the story of meeting Bill Marriott. Hackett was a young thirty-something president of Steelcase. Marriott was the seventy-something-year-old founder of the Marriott hotel empire. It was the early 1990s and a consultant had put them together because, as Hackett put it, "I was younger, trying to change an old family business and he was older, trying to change an old family business." He was running his business by his values.

Despite their differences in age and experience, the two men hit it off and spent a lot of time talking about values. Hackett recalled the plane trip home from Washington to Grand Rapids, Michigan. "I thought of the peace that this man had, in knowing what he needed to do. How could he make so many of the important decisions at Marriott grounded in his strong set of values? He was at total peace. Now being thirty-nine years old, maybe six months in the job, you do not have a lot of peace as a CEO. And it occurred to me that I wanted that peace. I wanted the opportunity to be able to make decisions and have the comfort of knowing that I had made the right decision."

Over the coming months, Jim Hackett kept thinking about values. Later that year, he gave a talk to his management team. "I talked about when a plane flies it has what's called an altitude and attitude indicator. It tells you whether it's at the right height and whether it's level. And so I was looking for the metaphorical attitude indicator inside me. What would tell me that as I was pointing the company in the right direction, that I was still on the right plane, like Mr. Marriott had understood. What is that inside people that gives you peace?"

At the end of the day, he reasoned, "there will be a list of things I didn't do right, because that's the human condition. We're not going to be able to design that out. But you can be at peace knowing that you have values and know what they are."

Jeff Immelt of GE calls leadership judgment "an intense journey into yourself. It's a commitment and an intense journey into your soul." But while you need to have rock-solid values, you also need to keep working on them, and on yourself. "Are you willing to take those journeys," he asks, "to explore how you can become better, and do it every day? How much can you learn? Can you look in the mirror every day and say, 'Geez, I wish I had done that differently, boy I think we have to, I have to do better here.' A commitment to lead change to make the organization better it starts with having the courage to be a constituency of one."[3]

Speaking to a group of first-year business students in 2002, Jim Hackett chose the importance of having clear values as the topic for his talk. "Navigating through your life, in business, is something that you have to start with today," he told them. "You have the benefit of great teachers, people who can share with you as you navigate, but [at some point] you are going to find yourself faced with a decision that calls your core values into play. Bill Marriott's conversation kept coming back to me regarding the peace of mind you can achieve by having strong values to guide the paths you take.

"I said to myself, you know on that airplane, I need to know right now how I'm going to think when I'm posed with the biggest dilemma that I might face. No one around, I've got to know right now how am I going to act?"[4]

Ten years after that meeting with Bill Marriott, and just a couple of years before that talk with the students, Jim Hackett was faced with a business judgment that had far greater implications than he could have known at the time.

The issue was fire retardants. Steelcase had begun selling a new line of products, with surfaces designed to be exchangeable between office cubicles and floor-to-ceiling walls. The advantage of this was that building managers would have to store only one kind of surface. But then Steelcase, which had a lot of experience in the cubicle business but not in the wall business, discovered that the material was not up to fire standards when used for floor-to-ceiling walls.

When they discovered the problem, Hackett said, "We had not had one damaged installation. Our customers even called us and said 'Oh, don't worry about it. What you're worried about, no one will ever have a problem.' We even had people inside the company say maybe it'll never be exchanged. You see, it was sold as exchangeable, but how often people would do it, we didn't know."[5]

The picture was further befogged by the fact that there is no one universal fire code. The standards vary by municipality. So just how fire-retardant would fire-retardant enough be? How far off the mark were they?

This is where Jim Hackett's character determined the answer. Steelcase recalled all the panels, replaced them with ones that met stricter fire codes, and took a $40 million write-off. Along the way Jim and all of Steelcase's executives lost their bonuses.

Going back to his airplane analogy, he explains: "I already have to know how I'm going act before I get there, because when all the pressure's on you to perform, the last thing you want to do is be searching for that attitude indicator. That pilot's looking for stability as they're coming in with the zero visibility and the thunderstorms and so forth, so you don't want to be experimenting with stability at the time you're making tough decisions. . . . You have to develop these points of view. How are we going to act when we get in trouble, because I can guarantee you in business, you will."[6]

For Jim Hackett, the day of reckoning came on September 11, 2001. When the airplane hit the Pentagon that morning, the product that was behind that wall was the new Steelcase fire-code material. "It was determined," Hackett said later, "with all the jet fuel and fire, if the new Steelcase material was not there, the fire would have spread in a far more disastrous outcome."[7]

This is a spine-chilling story of the sort that most leaders don't have to tell. Often, doing the right thing averts disaster, so there is no story to tell. What if someone somewhere along the line had drawn a hard line and insisted that the levees in New Orleans be strengthened? Or if someone at NASA had resisted the pressure to launch the shuttle *Challenger* because there were questions about whether the O-rings would work after sitting on the pad in unusually cold weather. Would we have heard about it? We guess probably not.

Katrina would still have been a horrific hurricane, but the most severe damage and disruption came from the flooding. If it hadn't happened, some people might have said, "Thank God the levees held." But it isn't likely that they would have noticed enough to put a name on the person who acted as God's agent in making the good judgment call. And the *Challenger,* well, it probably would have been launched at a later date and made an uneventful flight.

But recognition is not the important thing. People with character are more concerned with self-respect than public esteem. They have clear standards, they know what those standards are, and they hold themselves accountable. It's taking responsibility, in knowing that judgments have enormous, life-and-death consequences.

Having character as a leader is, if nothing else, the acceptance of consequence and responsibility.

COURAGE

Character and internal standards to calibrate one's decisions and keep them on "the right plane,"[8] as Jim Hackett puts it, is a fundamental requirement for building a track record of good judgment. Without good character, without strong moral fiber and a sincere desire to put the greater good above personal gain, a leader's judgment will stray too often to the pragmatic and expedient. The hard choices that good judgment often requires will not get made.

But judgment in our definition is about more than decision making. It is not only about coming up with the right solution to the right problem, but it is also about producing results, delivering the goods. And this is where courage comes in. Noel has, from time to time, made it a practice in his workshops with both client companies and business students at the University of Michigan to ask them to write about good and bad judgment calls that they have made. Discouragingly often, the bad judgment stories include a statement to the effect: "I really knew in my gut what I should do, but I didn't do it."

Having the courage to act on your standards is an integral part of the bundle of what it takes to exercise good judgment. The standards by themselves aren't enough. In fact, if you don't act on your "standards," there is some question as to whether they really are your standards.

Over twenty years ago, Tom Peters and Robert Waterman contrasted two types of stupid action (or inaction):

Ready . . . **Fire** . . . Aim
Ready . . . **Aim** . . . Aim . . . Aim . . . Aim . . . aim. . . .[9]

Shakespeare's Hamlet was always "aiming," never firing, except at the wrong time and at the wrong victim. One reason for the lasting significance of the play is Hamlet's *inability to act*. Virtually every thoughtful person, and surely every thoughtful leader, has experienced that excruciating state. Despite Hamlet's knowing everything he had to know, despite his awareness that killing Claudius was the only honorable thing to do, his fits and starts mesmerize us through five long acts. "This uncoupling, this sense of inward thoughts and feelings painfully cut off from the world around him, haunts virtually all of his relationships."[10] This "uncoupling" reinforces the imperative of action. Character, without courage, is meaningless, except in tragedy.

The courage required to exercise good judgment comes in many forms. Sometimes it is standing up to open direct threats. In the late

1960s, when Eleanor Josaitis decided to move her family into inner-city Detroit, her mother hired an attorney to take her five children from her. Her father-in-law disowned her, and her brother-in-law asked her to use her maiden name so no one would know they were related. Her mother came around to her side pretty quickly, but her father-in-law never did, and it was thirty-five years before her brother-in-law apologized.

Over the years, Eleanor Josaitis has also received a steady stream of threats and hate mail. She has been called every name in the book by racists and other people who are threatened by Focus: HOPE's success. Through it all, she has persisted. She even has a collection of hate letters that she has saved. She keeps and appreciates the touching letters of thanks from admirers and people that Focus: HOPE has helped. But, she says, it's the hate mail that reminds her what she is fighting and gives her the energy to carry on the good fight.

And well into her seventies, she is still going strong, doggedly and defiantly standing up for her values. On 9/11, as fears were mounting about a possible violent backlash against Detroit's large Arab-American community, Eleanor called together all six hundred people who were on the Focus: HOPE campus that day. They talked about what had already happened in New York, Washington, and Pennsylvania, and then they all signed a copy of Focus: HOPE's mission statement. The statement, adopted in 1968, reads:

> Recognizing the dignity and beauty of every person, we pledge intelligent and practical action to overcome racism, poverty and injustice. And to build a metropolitan community where all people may live in freedom, harmony, trust and affection. Black and white, yellow, brown and red from Detroit and its suburbs of every economic status, national origin and religious persuasion we join in this covenant.[11]

After the meeting, the *Detroit Free Press* asked Eleanor to write an editorial, which she did. Drawing on her and Focus: HOPE's core principles, she wrote one that ran under the headline "Strive to Build a World that Embraces Diversity."[12] A couple of days later, she received one of her favorite letters. It simply said: "Shove diversity up you ass, bitch." She carries it around with her to this day.

Like Eleanor Josaitis, Harry Truman was not flagged in his youth as the extraordinary leader he later became. According to a number of biographers, Harry Truman's leadership was defined by his experience in World War I.

David Gergen writes:

> The course of his life changed forever when, at the age of 33, he signed up for the Army to fight in World War I. . . . His initial test came on a rainy night in the Vosges Mountains. The Germans had dropped an artillery barrage close by, and his troops, panicked that they were being gassed, ran for it. In the frenzy, Truman's horse fell over on him and he was nearly crushed. Writes [David] McCullough: "Out from under, seeing the others all running, he just stood there, locked in place, and called them back using every form of profanity he'd ever heard . . . shaming his men back to do what they were supposed to do." They regrouped, got through the night. . . . Throughout the rest of their lives were loyal to Harry Truman.[13]

The historians tell us that this unexpected stand and its results surprised Truman as much as anyone on the field. But once he had this experience under his belt, he was set on a life of courageous living.

Unlike Eleanor Josaitis and Harry Truman, most of us are rarely, if ever, called on to exhibit physical courage and defiant courage in the face of open hostility. More often, it's quiet courage that is demanded of us. It's the courage to make the intense inner journey and to recognize and embrace what is right.

It's the courage that P&G showed in closing down plants in Africa for a year, rather than pay bribes. It is the courage that Jim Hackett showed in recalling the panels and taking the $40 million write-off despite pressure to make his earnings numbers. It is the courage to take the hard road, despite all the obstacles, because you *should*.

And, obstacles there will be. There will be obstacles within the organization. Resources are always limited, so you need the courage to make the hard budgeting decisions. Then there is the courage needed to do whatever else it takes to get the judgment carried out successfully. Maybe it's laying off people whose talent or temperament won't fit with the new plan. Or maybe it's hiring ten thousand new people. Or, maybe it's getting old antagonists to work together.

In any difficult judgment, there will always be people who disagree with it. A wise leader is exquisitely aware of where all the interested parties sit, and works to keep them on the team. But even in a group where most of the dissenters fall in behind the decision once it is made, there are almost always at least a few who will fight it. The leader then must have the courage to throw them out if they get in the way.

There will be obstacles—call them challenges if you like—that are beyond one's control. These are the external forces, often with gale-force winds. Sometimes the important climate is political. Often it's competitive and social as well. These are forces one cannot control, but one must have the courage to persevere despite the uncertainty and lack of control.

In important judgment calls, there are always stakes. There is always something big at risk. Otherwise, the judgment wouldn't be an important one. This is where a lot of leaders fall down. They avoid making calls because they don't have the courage to take the risks. Think of Ray Gilmartin. Even though the failure to make a courageous judgment and take a stand is ultimately what kills them, they can't bring themselves to act. Andy Grove, on the other hand, who named his book about Intel *Only the Paranoid Survive,*[14] got his courage from his fear about what would happen if he didn't step up to the helm and sail boldly out into the storm.

Perhaps the biggest obstacles leaders face are the ones they set up for themselves. They shy away because of self-doubts. Or, doing the right thing is just going to mean a lot of very hard work, and they are afraid that they can't do it. So they make compromises.

Joe Liemandt, the founder and CEO of Trilogy, an enterprise software company that he founded with four friends while they were students at Stanford in 1989, talks about a judgment he made in 2000. It was the era of e-commerce and whirlwind product development. Like many other high-tech companies, Trilogy had a habit of over-promising and underdelivering to customers. Trilogy's practice, as he explained, was to deliver software that would perform exactly as the salespeople said it would, but often it did not produce the positive results anticipated by the customers. Sometimes the software wasn't really the appropriate solution to the customer's problem. Sometimes the customer just never figured out how to make the software work. But, in any event, Trilogy would deliver the software, collect its money, and then move on to the next customer.

"The business model was one where you sell it, it works according to spec, and then—a couple years later—the customers say, 'I didn't get anything for this.' We'd respond, 'Well, it works, the product works. . . . If you look at the contract, it says here are the specifications that the software will do, this is how fast it will operate. These are all the various aspects of it. And it completely meets those specifications. If it doesn't meet spec, we'll give you your money back. But it absolutely meets specification.' "

This was a common practice in the industry and in the era. Trilogy was not alone in this. In the enterprise software business, an estimated 50–80 percent of *Fortune* 500 global projects failed. *The Wall Street Journal* was full of articles about companies taking big write-offs because an enterprise software project failed. One year, Hershey committed the unthinkable sin of not having enough chocolate for Halloween because they were putting in a big system and it simply didn't work.

But in 2000, says Liemandt, "we woke up as a company and realized that we couldn't keep acting like this entrepreneurial startup. . . . We had to change everything about how we looked at the world. We also needed to change how we measured our success—from building great products and shipping them, to measuring our success based on our customer's success."

Liemandt, who is an energetic and enthusiastic person, began in his signature manner to talk up the new idea around the company. A lot of people in the company agreed, but when he went to the head of his consulting unit, he got a firm push back. "Joe," the consulting head said, "there's no chance we're going to make our customers successful. You know, it's just too hard and we've known it's been too hard for ten years and that's why we haven't done it for ten years, Joe. What makes you think everything's going to change tomorrow?"

Liemandt describes this as a pivotal moment. "That's when I started to be able to sort out what was good vision, or what I felt was good vision, but superhard to execute versus bad vision but that you could execute. Then once I started to realize that this set of objections isn't that the vision's bad, or the strategy is bad. It's just so hard you just can't get over it. You're caught up in making bad decisions just because it's too hard. You're saying to yourself: 'I think this is a great idea. It's too hard to do. Let's discard it. Or I think this is a great idea but emotionally, I don't want to deal with the fallout.'"

As a result of this insight, Liemandt says he went on an inner journey of the type that Jeff Immelt described. "I realized that I needed to change my thinking 180 degrees and my viewpoint of the world and my mental model," Liemandt says. "That took time and conversations and me just thinking about it and talking through it. And over time it became clearer and I was able to project into the future, and describe this future company that we were going to be. Once I could project and paint the future picture, all my objections moved from being these reasons I wasn't going to make the decision to just obstacles to overcome to get to this good goal."

Another type of self-imposed obstacle comes from the pressure to succeed. Bill George, the former CEO of Medtronic, talks about how this pressure can

> pull us away from our core values, just as we are reinforced by our "success" in the market. Some people refer to this as "CEO-itis." The irony is that the more successful we are, the more tempted we are to take shortcuts to keep it going. And the rewards—compensation increases, stock option gains, the myriads of executive perks, positive stories in the media, admiring comments from our peers—all reinforce our actions and drive us to keep it going.[15]

George goes on to say in his book, *Authentic Leadership: Rediscovering the Secrets to Creating Lasting Values*,[16] that leaders have to resist those pressures while continuing to perform, especially when things aren't going well. That's exactly when character is essential. Thomas Carlyle, the nineteenth-century Scottish social philosopher, wrote: "The ideal is in thyself; the impediment, too, is in thyself."[17] The leaders in our study, like George, seemed to have overcome whatever impediments stood in their way. Most of those impediments were dissolved by a regular, ruthless self-scrutiny. They seem to have a built-in moral compass, a vigilant superego that constantly evaluates their motives and monitors for right and wrong.

Another leader with unusual strength of character is Novartis's CEO, Daniel Vasella. He discussed pressures, almost identical to George's, in an interview with *Fortune*:

> Once you get the domination of making the quarter—even unwittingly—you start to compromise in the gray areas of your business that cut across the wide swath of terrain between the top and the bottom. Perhaps you'll begin to sacrifice things that are important and may be vital for your company over the long term. . . . The culprit that drives this cycle isn't the fear of failure so much as it is the craving for success. For the tyranny of quarterly earnings is a tyranny imposed from within . . . the idea of being a successful manager is an intoxicating one. It is a pattern of celebration leading to belief, leading to distortion. When you achieve good results, you are typically celebrated, and you begin to believe that the center of all that champagne toasting is yourself. You are idealized by the outside world, and there is a natural tendency to believe that what is written is true.[18]

One of the most common impediments to making wise judgments is the isolation of the leader. Vasella alerts us to a form of isolation to which successful leaders are vulnerable. This is the form, often pernicious, related to a lifetime spent striving, driven by its almost palpable intoxication of success. Many of the most celebrated and gifted leaders are constantly struggling to find a balance between their constant hunger for success and the other attributes of a meaningful life.

Warren recalls a talk he had with the late John Gardner in August 2001. Gardner was in his eighty-seventh year. He had had a long and storied career: a former cabinet secretary under Lyndon Johnson, founder of Common Cause, and an important public intellectual. He had also been a marine officer in World War II, honored for his bravery in combat. The previous day Warren had interviewed the two cofounders of Embark.com, Steve Chen and Young Shin, both in their early thirties. That week, due to the dot-com crash, they were forced to lay off twenty-five of their one hundred employees, some of them close friends. So he asked Gardner, "What's more courageous, firing your best friends or risking your life at Iwo Jima?" Gardner thought, and slowly answered. "I don't know . . . I can't possibly answer that question."

Some might not agree with Truman, that saying no to a friend is more courageous than facing a duel. Former chief of staff of the U.S. Army, General Eric Shinseki, who was badly wounded in Vietnam, publicly disagreed with his superior, Donald Rumsfeld, about troop requirements for the Iraq operation. Was that more or less courageous than facing enemy mortar shells? Dr. Susan Wood quit the FDA (Food and Drug Administration) because her boss, Commissioner Lester Crawford, delayed approval of a drug.

In 1943, Jesse Bernard, a Roman Catholic priest from Luxembourg, was imprisoned at Dachau with some three thousand other priests, pastors, and bishops for opposing the Nazis' religious "reforms." The Nazi commandant of the death camp offered to free the priest if he would return to Luxembourg, to convince the archbishop there to accept Nazism. Instead, Father Bernard chose to die.

A friend drove off to Mississippi, one day after Katrina hit, to help rescue those who were stranded and to recover the bodies of the dead. A former student took leave from his doctoral work and re-upped in the National Guard to join his buddies in Iraq.

Whether a decision is popular or not often doesn't count for much in the long run. Truman claims that his most unpopular decision, firing General MacArthur, was one of his best. He said that ordering the atomic bomb to be dropped on Hiroshima, his most controversial decision, was also relatively easy; he concluded it was the only way to keep America's butcher's bill from continuing to grow.

These two decisions by Truman bring us to another very important point. The courage of a wise person is close-knit with his or her character. While good character without courage can be worthless, courage without good character can be, and often is, dangerous.

Courage without character gives you the Wall Street swindlers who brashly and brazenly push worthless goods on an unsuspecting public. It gives you "Chainsaw Al" Dunlap, who in the 1990s was first heralded as a successful turnaround leader as CEO of Scott Paper for his slash-and-burn strategy, but ended up being demonized as the destroyer of Sunbeam. In each case, he came in and started slashing jobs and operations. This produced mountains of cash, for which Dunlap earned tens of millions, but it also destroyed not only the jobs and lives of thousands of workers but, ultimately, the strength of Sunbeam. The problem with Dunlap was not that he laid off workers and cut operations; many wise and brave leaders have been forced to make huge layoffs to reposition foundering companies and get them on solid footing. The problem with Dunlap was that the cuts did not help Sunbeam thrive and be a contributing member of the community. Rather, his primary motivation appeared to be personal greed. That led him to make judgments that were not in the greater interest of the company and its broader constituency of stakeholders. The board at Sunbeam ultimately fired him in June 1998 after the stock went from a high in March of that year of $52 down to a low in June of $8.

A leader who has exhibited character and courage throughout his career is Bob Knowling, currently CEO of the private company Telwares, former senior executive at Ameritech, U.S. West, and Covad, and CEO of the New York City Leadership Academy (training school principals). Knowling's character and courage were shaped growing up poor and having to face racial discrimination of one sort or another just about every day of his life.

Being black challenges him to this day, ranging from the corporate jet staff who did not know he was an executive at Ameritech and telling him that the chauffeurs are to wait in the cars, to the police in Atherton, California, hassling him because a black guy was driving a Jaguar XK8 convertible. He channels his energy to make the world a better place and is a strong supporter of Eleanor Josaitis at Focus: HOPE and is on his own journey to join her with "practical solutions to racisms and poverty."[19]

Knowling took two and a half years off from the business CEO track and invested it in giving back to society. He took the job of founding CEO of the New York City Leadership Academy, which was set up to provide leadership development for New York City school principals, all twelve hundred, as well as ninety aspiring principals each year. Bob dedicated these years as a way to give back to the community. He worked with Joel Klein, the New York City chancellor, to help in the massive school transformation going on in New York. Along with help from CEO board members Jack Welch; Dick Parsons, CEO of AOL Time Warner; Walter Shipley, the former chairman/CEO of JPMorgan Chase; David Coulter from JP Morgan; and Sy Sternberg, CEO of New York Life, they raised close to $100 million and provided leadership development workshops and mentoring for all twelve hundred principals.

◆ ◆ ◆

This is a book about leadership judgment. We are not interested in leaders who cross the line by compromising on values of integrity and decency. We are only interested in leaders whose character and courage are exhibited when no one is looking.

Trust is the emotional glue that holds teams together. As Jim Hackett told us: "You can't lead if you don't have trust and you can't have trust if you don't have integrity." Hackett went on to tell us: "I was getting the crap beaten out of me by the analysts. But my mentor at Steelcase said don't listen to them, just do what's right. He was right."

Leading with character gives the wise leader clear-cut advantages. They are easier to trust and follow; they honor commitments and promises; their words and behavior match; they are always engaged in and by the world; they are open to "reflective backtalk"; they can admit errors and learn from their mistakes. They can speak with conviction because they believe in what they're saying. They are comfortable in their own skin. They feel at ease in the spotlight and they enjoy it there. They tend to be more open to opportunity and risk.

5

PEOPLE JUDGMENT CALLS

■ People Judgments Are the Platform for Good Strategic and Crisis Judgments
- Who-is-on-the-team-or-off-the-team judgments.
- Building a team at the top to support good judgment.

■ P&G CEO Lafley Making a Critical People Judgment to Head Up Baby Care
- Framing and naming the judgment.
- Making the call but failing to mobilize and align his team.
- Creating a redo loop to get alignment.

■ Team First, Strategy Second
- McNerney's Teachable Point of View.

◆ ◆ ◆

On the morning of June 6, 2000, A. G. Lafley was in San Francisco. As the fifty-two-year-old president of Procter & Gamble's global beauty care business walked into a nine A.M. meeting, his cell phone rang. The call was from P&G headquarters in Cincinnati. The caller was John Pepper, now retired P&G chairman. The message to Lafley was brief: come home. Immediately.

The last thing Lafley had done the previous day, just before leaving Cincinnati, was to meet with P&G's chairman and CEO Durk Jager. The meeting between the two top executives had been routine. They met often. Lafley got along well with the brusque Dutch-born leader and was seen as a likely successor to him. But Jager was only fifty-seven years old and had held the top job for just seventeen months.

So when Pepper asked Lafley if he was prepared to accept the job as P&G's president and CEO—immediately, Lafley was stunned. After a moment he said yes and Pepper told him to get on a plane. The two would talk later. As he flew back across the country, trying to behave normally with the other P&G executives on his flight, Lafley didn't know if he had been offered the job or if the board was just considering him. And why exactly was the job open? What had happened to Durk Jager?

The board officially voted to name A. G. Lafley president and CEO of Procter & Gamble the next day, and the following morning, June 8, the change at the top was announced to the public. Durk Jager had resigned and was leaving the company.

As Lafley took the reins, the company was in turmoil. Jager's aggressive plans to grow the company by launching new products and acquiring other successful businesses hadn't worked. In an effort to make its management structure more global, he had drastically reorganized the company and in the process succeeded in confusing and demoralizing thousands of workers. As a result, in recent months Jager had had to reduce two P&G earning projections. And on June 5 it became apparent that another downward revision would be necessary.

P&G's stock was in a tailspin. On March 7, the day the spring quarter's earnings projection had been reduced, P&G shares had tumbled 30 percent. The total drop from a January peak to the day that Jager left five months later was 50 percent. The company was in crisis. The biggest crisis, Lafley would later tell us in 2005, "was not the loss of $85 billion in market capitalization. The far bigger crisis was the crisis in confidence . . . particularly leadership confidence." As Lafley recalled: "P&G business leaders (had) retreated to their bunkers. Leaders were lying low. Heads were down. . . . Business units around the world were blaming headquarters for their problems. Headquarters was blaming line business units. Employees were calling for heads to roll." Meanwhile, analysts and investors were irate. Retirees, whose retirement plans were built on P&G stock, were distraught. In short, as the new CEO saw it, "We'd made a mess, and we had to fix it."

The question was, how? John Pepper lasted as CEO for only three and a half years in the mid-1990s because he had been unable to get the tired old consumer products company on the road to profitable growth. Jager's new-product and globalization strategies were aimed at fixing a fundamental problem at the company. So just backtracking from Jager's radical changes would not fix the ailing company. But doing nothing was also not an option.

The company had an "emergency room" full of problems, and Lafley had only a finite amount of time and personal energy. He had to decide where to apply his limited resources to gain the most leverage and produce the greatest benefit. So he started with people issues.

Judgment calls about people are the most critical ones that leaders have to make. This is because they have a huge impact on everything a company does. Strategy calls are important because they set the objectives and the agenda. And crises are important because they, by definition, threaten the well-being of the organization. If they weren't high-stakes with a potential for disaster, they wouldn't qualify as crises. But when it comes right down to it, it's the people who make things turn out well or not. A good team member can fix a call that is going wrong, and a bad one can mess up even the most brilliant decision.

The P&G board's decision to accept Jager's resignation was thus the critical first step toward fixing the company's problems. As the new leader, Lafley needed to pull the company out of its current crisis and devise a strategy that could turn the company around. But most important, he needed to build a strong team that could make the necessary judgments and take the effective actions to carry the company to success.

In many ways the process for making good people judgments is similar to that for making other types of good judgments. A leader has to recognize the need, frame the issue, and mobilize and align the parties who can provide the information and advice needed to make a good call. Then the leader must make the call at the appropriate moment, and follow through on the execution to make sure that the result turns out as well as possible.

People judgments are the most complex of the three domains for several reasons. First, a judgment about whether someone will be a good leader is a judgment call about how well they will do making other judgment calls. Will they be able to build a good team? Develop effective strategy? Deal with the inevitable crises? Fundamentally, a judgment about selecting a person should be based on how well he or she will operate in all cells of our judgment matrix.

The evaluations do not have to be made explicitly, and sometimes they are made intuitively, but to make a solid call about the likelihood of the person's success, a leader needs to consider them all. The judgment matrix plays two roles in making good people judgments. First, the leader making the judgment needs to follow its process; second, the matrix provides the framework for measuring the candidate. It is a template for examining the candidate's track record across the three domains—people, strategy, and crisis—as well as his or her depth of self-knowledge and capacity for knowledge creation at the social network, organizational level, and contextual level.

People calls also have other distinct challenges. Unlike strategies, the "objects" of people judgments are humans who make their own judgment calls and engage their own political circles even as the process unfolds. In a competitive world, no judgment call is ever made in a static situation. But in people calls, the dynamics are more complex, if not more fluid, than in other realms.

Leaders do, of course, get attached to ideas. They become enchanted with a visionary dream. They fight so hard to explore an intriguing possibility that they become too invested, emotionally and/or financially, to accept outcomes that fall short of their goals. But with people, the emotional stakes are much higher.

No matter how hard-nosed some leaders may appear, they all have emotions that affect their judgments. They have feelings about other people. They become attached to them, or maybe detest them, to degrees that hardly ever apply when they are considering strategic business plans. And it's these feelings that can keep them from making good, objective calls.

Wayne Downing, the late four-star general who ran the Special Operations Forces, told us that "most of my bad judgment calls were generally about people. There have been times when I knew I had to take people out of a position. I knew they weren't going to change, and they weren't going to do what had to be done. But it's traumatic when you do that. The higher up you go, the more traumatic it is for the organization to remove people, and you don't like to do that, but in the final analysis you have to."

Even Jack Welch, who is highly regarded for his track record in hiring and developing thousands of leaders during his tenure as CEO at GE, told us that at the end he was still batting only about 800. He estimated that as a first-time manager starting out, he only got about 50 percent of his people calls right, but even after twenty years, he thought he still got 20 percent wrong.

Of course, Welch set the bar for talent very high, so probably some of the hires that he considered failures would have been roaring successes in the eyes of others or in other organizations. But the point is that getting people judgment calls right is very difficult.

In our research for this book, we interviewed and polled hundreds of people about their good and bad judgment calls. An amazing number of them told us that many of their bad judgment calls occurred when they had overridden their gut instincts. You have to remember that these conversations were influenced by hindsight, when the results were in and the person was second-guessing him- or herself. But one interesting thing about people calls, we discovered, is that many leaders said the reason that they messed them up was often just the opposite. It was because they paid too much attention to emotions ("gut feelings"), and not enough to logic and intellect.

Joe Liemandt, CEO of Trilogy, an Austin, Texas–based enterprise software company he cofounded in 1989, frames the issue in terms of the compassionate Nobel Prize–winning missionary Mother Teresa and Mr. Spock, the stony half-human/half-space alien of *Star Trek* fame.

"You know, I don't know what the percentage is, but a huge percent of bad decisions around people I feel are made because they misalign the emotional and the logical. I know personally for me that that's what I struggle with. I come to a good logical answer (to a situation) but then I can't make myself make it because I don't want the emotional pain."

So, Liemandt explained, at Trilogy

> we have a framework we actually use internally around tough people decisions. These are the ones like whether you lay off your friend or whatever. We call it "Spock and Mother Teresa." What I mean is that when you're faced with a tough people decision, most people feel uncomfortable, so they sort of Mother Teresa it. They don't really give the good feedback to the person or they don't make the decision to move them out. They stall, they delay, you know, they're vague in their feedback, whatever it is. And then, because of a crisis or whatever happens, that they finally are forced to make a decision, they then become Spock and they basically become an asshole to the person. Then, they very abruptly deal with it.
>
> What we try to do around it is the exact opposite, which is, when you're faced with a tough decision you've got to be Spock upfront. Be super-logical, super-analytical, really ask yourself: "What is the right answer?" and don't worry about the downstream implications right now. Just come to the logical right answer.
>
> But, then once you make the decision, absolutely Mother Teresa how you deal with the person. Be super-good, make sure you don't delay six months before you tell someone you think they're bad and then cut them off and give them a lousy severance. It's tell them six months earlier that you're going to be moving them out of the organization and give them six months extra severance or help them find a new job. That framework all of a sudden makes making the right decision six times easier.

SELECTING THE TOP TEAM

In the six years that A. G. Lafley has been CEO, P&G has turned around. Its earnings and stock price have climbed more than 58 percent. It has consolidated its position in its core businesses, including diapers. And it has made several substantial acquisitions, including Clairol and Wella, in the hair care markets. Its 2005 $80 billion purchase of Gillette has given it a solid entry in men's care.

A. G. Lafley's success in the months and now years since his appointment in June 2000 is a reflection of his good judgment calls. Ironically, many of the steps he has taken, including the acquisition of Gillette, Jager had attempted. The difference was that Lafley was able to get them executed while Jager did not. One of the primary reasons is that Lafley did a better job selecting and leading people.

"I came in during the middle of the night in June of 2000 in sort of emergency circumstances," Lafley told us. "I actually was thinking on that long flight back from San Francisco, when I had four hours to think alone, that we had a pretty good team. Some were team members or individuals who were de-motivated for various reasons. But I honestly thought that the team had talent and a lot of experience and would come together. But in the first hundred days, all of a sudden guys that looked pretty good as colleagues didn't look like they were going to have the right mind-set to take on the tough calls and choices we would need to make, and to take their game to the next level on a collaborative team. And it was clear that we had other up-and-comers with more appetite for change and more courage to make tough calls." So, over the next two years, more than half of P&G's top thirty executives left the company or moved on to other assignments. "It wasn't that they were failing. It was that they were not going to take us to the next level. So we worked through that, and then we worked through the priorities, which ones we have to change first, second, third."

LAFLEY'S P&G STORYLINE

Lafley's storyline for the future success of P&G gave him the stage to make critical judgment calls. Here is how he told it to *CEO Magazine* in late 2005:

> Everything begins here with our purpose. It's very simple. We provide branded products that improve everyday lives. The values of the company are integrity, trust, ownership, leadership, passion for service and winning. Then we have principles such as "respect for the individual" and "innovation is our lifeblood." Every employee has one of these little pamphlets. It's on every

Web site and in almost every conference room everywhere in the world. We're quite public about all that and we're even, in a shorthand kind of way, pretty public about our strategy. We're not surprising our competition. They know broadly what we're trying to do.

Then we turn to strategy, which is choices. Our whole focus has been to grow and profit from the core—and that means core businesses, core capabilities, core technologies. Our second choice was to expand our portfolio in health, personal care and beauty care because that would serve more consumers' needs for longer lifetimes. Then the third one is to serve low-income consumers who can't always afford our products, especially in developing markets. I say this because I live it. But I guarantee you that if you dropped into any group, anywhere, in the company, they could explain all this.

Then (the other piece of this is) selecting, developing, training, teaching and coaching the leadership team. They are the leadership engine. We'll do at least $68 billion in sales post-Gillette. We're in 80 countries. We sell in 160. We have over 100,000 employees. It's going to go to 130,000 or 140,000. This company is run by 20 presidents of line businesses and 100 general managers and their functional leadership that supports them. So that's about 250 people. It's one team with one purpose and one dream and one set of strategic choices.[1]

Although Lafley refined his storyline as time went by and he gained experience, the essentials were in his mind from the beginning. So when he became CEO, he went business by business evaluating and judging what he needed to.

One of the biggest calls that Lafley made early on was to pick Deb Henretta to be in charge of the baby care business. With the storyline in his mind that the overall success of P&G would depend on the quality of its leadership team, he made a judgment for the baby care business that surprised a lot of people. He selected someone with no expertise in the area because he thought that she was a good leader and would be able to bring a needed new perspective to the business.

The steps he took as he worked his way through this judgment call are instructive. He didn't get everything right the first time. He had to circle back and cover some bases that he missed. The result was a success because he was constantly aware of the importance of getting each phase right and because he stuck to it until he got it right.

ANATOMY OF A PEOPLE CALL

The unique aspect of people judgments is that the full judgment matrix is the framework for making a key people judgment. Whether someone is a good leader or not is based on their track record of past judgments about people, strategy, and crisis; it is also a prediction about how well they will do on judgments in new and future settings. This is unlike strategy or crisis judgments, which only deal in their unique domain.

Leadership Judgment Process

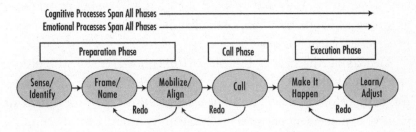

JUDGMENT PREPARATION PHASE

Step 1: Sense and Identify

The first thing Lafley had to do before making the judgment call was to sense and identify the problem that needed solving. The sensing part was easy. "Baby care is our biggest single category after laundry. It was struggling," Lafley told us.

> Kimberly-Clark's Huggies took leadership of U.S. baby diapers in the mid-'80s because we made a huge strategic mistake. We had a Pampers brand with about 65 percent market share. Then we introduced a new technology—shaped diapers—but instead of making the new shaped diapers on the flagship Pampers brand

for better fit and performance, we introduced them on a new brand. Luvs was a huge success."

Overnight, it went to like a thirty-plus market share. But we, of course, were cannibalizing unmercifully. So we took most of it out of Pampers. We reduced Pampers from a 65 percent to 70 percent to a one-fourth share. We have Luvs at a 30 percent share. And Huggies came right up the middle with an improved shaped diaper. Pampers ended up being third into the market with the new shared diaper technology. When the dust settled, they had the biggest brand. We had the biggest company (total), but we divided our forces. We weakened our position. In addition, they introduced the pull-up or pull-on diaper. We all had the technology at about the same time. We all had the patents, but they went to market, and we didn't. So we were in tough shape in baby care.

P&G's dominance in the baby care market was flagging. It had two successful brands of diapers, Pampers and Luvs, but neither was as strong as Kimberly-Clark's Huggies. The reality that there was a problem in baby care was obvious.

Identifying the exact problem was not, however, as straightforward. Lafley needed to "fix baby care," but there were many ways to go about doing that. He could have identified the problem as an issue of management performance. The unit currently wasn't running very well, but maybe the problem was that people weren't working hard enough or smart enough. If they were coached, or removed and replaced with better performers out of the same mold, maybe things would turn around.

Alternatively, Lafley could have focused on marketing. Since diaper sales weren't as strong as they once had been, maybe the problem was the marketers. Or he could have decided that the problem he needed to fix was distribution or research. But he didn't choose any of those.

Instead he identified the problem as having a business model and approach to the business that was off the mark. "I felt that we were technically competent in baby care," he says, "but that the machine guys and the plant guys and the engineers were running the show. And our problem was on the consumer and the brand equity side."

Step 2: Frame and Name

Once he had identified the need for a total transformation of the baby care unit, Lafley framed the issue as leadership. The problem wasn't that the unit wasn't well managed, and it wasn't that the people in the unit were poor players. The unit needed a new strategy, and the only way to get that new strategy was to get a new leader and a new top team in place. He framed his task specifically as finding a transformational leader. He needed someone from outside the division who would be able to look at the business with fresh eyes.

Baby care was technology and machinery-centric rather than customer-centric. The goal that he wanted to achieve was to transform the culture and the way the people in the baby care unit thought and conceptualized their jobs. "I wanted someone who had not spent a minute in baby care to go in. I wanted a good leader, and an outstanding consumerist and brand builder." The framing of the people judgment that Lafley had to make for baby care was to look for a leader who would, in turn, make good judgment calls. He needed someone who could build a good team, align people throughout the organization, develop a smart new strategy, and pull the unit out of its current crisis.

Lafley created the frame and specifications for the new leader as someone who would make good judgment calls, and then he started thinking about specific candidates who could successfully fill the role. The judgment matrix is how Lafley both intuitively and explicitly framed the leadership judgment. He wanted a leader who could make good people judgments so as to quickly assess who should be on or off the baby care top team; then he wanted a leader who could make the strategic judgments to turn the business around; finally, the leader had to be good a making crisis judgments as the business was in a crisis.

Step 3: Mobilize and Align

Once he had framed the call as finding a leader who could make a series of good judgment calls, Lafley began mobilizing others to help create a slate of candidates. He worked with Dick Antoine, former head of Human Resources; and with Mark Ketchum, former group president with responsibility for baby care, family care, and feminine care, both of whom agreed with his framing. They quickly came up with a slate of candidates, at the top of which was Deb Henretta.

Then they began to assess her, based on her ability to perform in the various boxes of the judgment matrix. The process involved both explicit reviews of Henretta's past performance and her HR assessments, and more general discussions with a network of people who knew her and had worked with her.

Here are the kinds of questions that leaders need to consider to answer in each cell of the matrix.

Deb's Judgment Matrix

Domains

	People pre-call-execution	Strategy pre-call-execution	Crisis pre-call-execution
Self Knowledge			
Social Network Knowledge			
Organizational Knowledge			
Contextual Knowledge			

(left axis label: Knowledge Creation)

Questions for Each of the Cells of the Matrix

1. **People/Self:** Does she have a solid sense of herself? Does she have a Teachable Point of View; ideas, values, and emotional energy to guide making good people judgments? Is she comfortable making tough decisions that affect the lives of others?
2. **People/Social Network:** Does she know how to draw on the resources of those around her to get the input she needs? Is she able to figure out who she needs to involve? Can she align and energize them to support the ultimate call on key people?
3. **People/Organizational:** Does she know how to design and implement organizational processes that support her in making good people judgments?
4. **People/Contextual:** Is she willing to tap relevant stakeholders for input? Does she know when to ask, and how to get meaningful input?
5. **Strategy/Self:** Does she see herself as a change agent? Does she look over the horizon? Can she conceptualize new opportunities and execute new strategies?
6. **Strategy/Social Network:** Will she get the people with the right expertise and right chemistry in the room? Will she have the discipline to exclude those with little to contribute? Can she frame the issues so that the best solution is reached?
7. **Strategy/Organizational:** Can she build the processes to get all levels of the organization aligned to execute the new strategy? Can she energize them to deliver on it?
8. **Strategy/Contextual:** Can she teach the rationale of the strategy to key stakeholders and get them aligned with her? Can she create recognizable benchmarks and deliver on them?
9. **Crisis/Self:** Will she assume personal responsibility for dealing with crises? Does she have a strong Teachable Point of View to guide her? Is she clear on her ultimate goal? Does she have strong values to shape what is acceptable and what is not? Does she have the self-assurance to make clear, firm decisions when necessary?

10. **Crisis/Social Network:** Does she have a high-trust team? Can she mobilize them quickly? Can she efficiently elicit a range of options and honest discussions of them? Can she manage conflict so that it is productive?

11. **Crisis/Organizational:** Can she focus the organization on essential actions? Can she impose the needed discipline without sapping morale?

12. **Crisis/Contextual:** Can she manage while in the spotlight? Can she manage external expectations? Can she build/maintain the trust of others that will buy her time to develop and implement effective solutions?

After going through all the cells of the matrix, Lafley concluded: "She was a laundry person, but I knew what she really was, which was a tough and decisive leader. She was great at understanding consumers and great at branding and great at building innovative programs. And that's what we needed."

At this stage, Lafley made a big misstep. Having been at P&G for over twenty years, rotating through jobs with increasing scope, Lafley knew who was in the candidate pool. He didn't do a big search, because with his own knowledge and the supporting information provided by his HR chief, Dick Antoine, and Mark Ketchum, he didn't need to. He knew Deb Henretta, and he had the information about her he needed to answer the questions about how she would perform on the matrix questions. He was confident that she could do the job.

Still, his failure to mobilize a search team cost him, and cost him dearly. He didn't need a lot of input from others in order to make a good choice. But by not consulting his top team members, he missed an opportunity to get them aligned behind her. While he didn't feel that he needed their advice, Henretta would need their support, or at least their acquiescence, to succeed in the job. Lafley jeopardized the outcome of his judgment call because he didn't pay sufficient attention to the politics involved or to the feelings of the other senior executives who had their own candidates.

As a result, on the day he announced that Henretta would be the new head of baby care, "there was almost a revolt," he says. "I announced Deb's appointment at the morning management meeting. It was before the announcement went out to the company. It was to go out in a day or two. By three o'clock the revolt was well under way. All of the vice chairs and group presidents were ticked off because they had their own candidates ready for promotion."

JUDGMENT CALL PHASE

The "call" phase of judgment-making is often as quick as the flipping of a switch. As Jeff Immelt describes his style, he does a lot of consulting with others, and then, "boom!" he makes the call. In truth, most judgment calls actually are made in the blink of an eye. At one moment a leader hasn't chosen a course of action and by the next, he or she is ready to move on to the execution phase.

Even though many calls do go this smoothly, leaders who have good judgment track records never assume that anything will happen so easily. Aware that the ultimate goal is to produce a successful outcome, they are always vigilant. They are constantly checking to make sure that conditions are as favorable as they can possibly make them to support the success of the judgment. If they need to take time and expand the decision-making process, they do.

In this case, that is exactly what Lafley did. When the revolt broke out, he stopped action and called the top team together. With everyone sitting around he invited each one to make their case against Henretta and/or for someone else. "I said, 'Okay, here's what we're going to do. I want you to take your list. I want you to make the best case you can for why your candidate or candidates are a better choice than Deb.' So we went around the table and I listened . . . sequentially, publicly in front of everybody else. Then I said, 'Okay, you know there were a couple of good cases. But let me tell you why I chose Deb.' "

Lafley didn't expect that he would change his mind as a result of the meeting, and he didn't change it. Nonetheless, he did open himself up to the possibility. He heard his colleagues out and responded to their concerns directly and respectfully.

Lafley knew that even if the powerful vice chairmen and business heads were not transformed into supporters of Henretta, they were no longer justified in any visible resistance to the call. The important thing here is that he did not try to slam-dunk his decision. He made time before moving on to set the stage for success.

EXECUTION PHASE

Step 1: Make It Happen

At the end of the day Lafley knew the powerful vice chairmen and business heads were not all transformed into supporters of Henretta. Her selection was a gutsy one. At the time, the baby care organization was very male. Its values were around technical degrees and the ability to build innovative machinery, and Henretta was not at all technically oriented. She was interested in consumers and marketing.

"They thought she was from outer space because she was talking about the consumer. She was talking about how to create an innovation program to attract customers. She said, 'I don't even understand how that machine works. You need to understand what the consumer wants, then make the machine work for them.' We were running an operation that had a machine as boss. We needed an operation where the consumer was boss." (Think back to chapter 1 when IBM's Lou Gerstner proclaimed that the company needed a customer in the CEO's chair. Lafley came to that same conclusion for his baby care unit.)

Lafley clearly understood that making the call was part of a longer process that required his active role in the execution phase. He knew that if he was not careful to maintain his support of Henretta during execution, there were plenty of political land mines that could make his call go bad. Lafley clearly understood that his role was to stay with Deb not only in the "make it happen" first step but to be an active partner in the "self-correction" process.

So, after backtracking with the top team to defuse their rebellion, Lafley stayed on the job. This included giving her the political backing to replace key members of her team, to make sure that everyone knew that he was in full support of her success. He also made himself available for mentoring and coaching Henretta.

"I had a pact with her that if she needed to change somebody out to let me know, and we would do it," he said. "I supported her every step of the way. In fact I pushed her to make all her decisions. I learned this in Asia: make as many of your people decisions as you can in the first one hundred days, because you have to get your team on the ground."

Step 2: Learn and Adjust

This is where many CEOs and other leaders end up with bad judgments: they do not stay the course on execution and their failure to do so costs them the ball game. Lafley clearly understood that he was the head leader/teacher at P&G and that he had to own the judgment through all three phases. This meant being available to Deb as a sounding board, as a coach, and as a political backer when the going got rough.

Henretta was handed a massive transformation challenge, which included dealing with resistance to change, putting together a new team, and coming up with a new strategy while dealing with the very real crisis of a business in a downward business spiral. This all had to be done in a much bigger arena than she had played before. Thus the scale, the complexity, and the political dynamics were at levels far beyond anything she had ever dealt with. Stretching a leader to achieve Olympic standards required Lafley to be an Olympic-level leadership coach to Henretta. This included giving her the political backing to fire and replace key members of her team, to make sure that everyone knew that he was in full support of her success.

The judgment matrix provides the template for what the leader needs to accomplish and therefore it is also the template for what coaching and help might be required by Lafley. He, in turn, helped Henretta base her people judgments on the matrix, and build a team that was going to be able to make good people, strategy, and crisis judgments and develop others.

Lafley declared his judgment call on Deb Henretta a victory only after the business turned around and there was irrefutable evidence of her success as a leader. As we reflect on this example, we can see how

Lafley used his storyline for building a leadership team that would take P&G to success and his TPOV, ideas, and values to make the judgment on Henretta.

As a result of her success in turning the business around, Lafley subsequently promoted Henretta to head of P&G's Southeast Asia business, a position that has considerably more career runway (i.e., potential) for her and will stretch her in new ways around people, strategy, and crisis. She handled it well and was then promoted to group president for all of Asia.

Later, in looking back on the early days of his tenure, Lafley would explain:

> We did four things:
> 1. We faced up to the reality of our situation.
> 2. We accepted change, and stopped trying to ignore or resist it.
> 3. We starting making choices, clear choices, tough choices.
> 4. We put together a strong, cohesive team to lead the business.

As we noted in laying out our framework about how leaders make good judgment calls, these four elements are all critical. We might not put them in that order. We would probably move the "strong cohesive team" up to the number one, but all of them are important.

TEAM FIRST/STRATEGY SECOND

We have taken the position that people judgment comes first. If there is not a team of trusted leaders, it is impossible to make good strategy judgments as the people politics will undermine what is good for the enterprise. This is what happened at Ford with Jac Nasser, in a company with a long history of politics and leadership changes.

Nasser was leading a massive strategic transformation of Ford and was handling a crisis, the Firestone tire troubles, when a small group of his top leaders pulled off a coup d'état. It is not possible to lead an organization through such turbulence without trust. In Nasser's case he was too trusting, or did not have the authority to make the people changes that were necessary. When the crisis hit, Nasser spent his time and attention focused on curing the company's ills while three members of his team used it as an opportunity to lobby Bill Ford to oust him so they ended up with all the power.

Carly Fiorina, former HP CEO, was fired not because of strategic judgment, but because she did not have the leadership teamwork with the board and with her own internal team. Her perfect storm hit, starting with missed earnings in August 2004 followed immediately with the firing of three senior leaders: Mike Winkler, head of customer solutions; Jim Milton, CSG senior vice president; and Kasper Rorsted, CSG senior vice president. This internal political turmoil, coupled with poor financial performance, dropped the stock price another 15 percent and gave the anti-Fiorina HP board members a window to go after her, which they did, getting her fired in early 2005. The lack of teamwork with the board exacerbated by the internal political turmoil without financial performance was the perfect storm.

Ray Gilmartin at Merck could not get the strategy right because he could not get a team of trusted leaders at the top. He simply grew too removed. Once there is a team that is reasonably cohesive, then the strategy judgment process can unfold with a reasonable chance of success.

When Jim McNerney spoke to us about his experience, he concluded that it is always people first, then strategy:

> It's all about understanding what organizations can and can't do. That's where the judgment comes in. It's not about strategy. Strategy's relatively easy to define. You can do a market assessment, you can do a competitive assessment, you can figure out a way you can differentiate yourself, and if you can do it, then you can make money and grow. That is . . . It's not easy, but I'm saying that is more commonly done well than the assessment that a leader has to make about execution—whether it can be done.
>
> So if an organization's standing in front of you with this

great strategy and says that to implement it we're going to do this using skills we've never managed before, selling to customers we've never seen before, yet it fits the strategy beautifully, judgment has to be applied. As to whether it can be done, how long it will take . . . And that is really derived from experience. I have a very different view of that than I did twenty-five years ago when I was a McKinsey consultant.

6

PEOPLE JUDGMENT:

CEO SUCCESSION

■ **Selecting a CEO Is the Most Critical People Judgment Call**
- All other calls flow from CEO judgment.
- Hiring from outside signals a failed process.

■ **Winning Organizations Build Leadership Pipelines**
- They prepare multiple candidates.
- They build leaders at all levels.

■ **A Good CEO Succession Process Is Transparent**
- The requirements for the job are clearly framed.
- The success of the organization is the ultimate consideration.

◆ ◆ ◆

> I think many correct decisions are messed up in
> execution . . . because you've bet on people that you
> thought could deliver and they couldn't.
>
> —Steve Bennett, CEO of Intuit

On February 10, 2005, the front page of the *Wall Street Journal*,
New York Times, and London *Times* all reported that the HP board

had fired Carly Fiorina as CEO. This came four and a half years after the board made a judgment call to go outside HP to find a CEO. Our premise is that whenever a company has to go outside for a CEO, they are exhibiting bad people judgment; the company has failed to build a leadership pipeline that produces the leadership talent to successfully guide the company in the future. HP ended up with a double failure. First, there were no internal candidates. Second, the outsider they hired was a bad judgment, as she failed at the CEO task and was fired in a very ugly board process.

The bad CEO judgment in hiring Carly Fiorina must fall on the shoulders of the same board that ended up firing her; they did not do a good job in the preparation phase of the judgment process. The sensing and identifying step was clear, but there was no adequate bench. Where the board fell short in its judgment process was the framing and naming of the CEO candidate. HP is a multibusiness company with many profit-and-loss (P&L) businesses and with both hardware and services to sell. The framing needed to take into account finding a leader with a track record of running a variety of business units that were true P&L businesses. Carly Fiorina was a product of the old AT&T monopoly that spun off Lucent, the old Western Electric switchgear and hardware producer for the captive AT&T phone companies, which were then spun off to become the RBOCs, the regional Bell operating companies such as Ameritech (now part of SBC, renamed AT&T), US West (now Qwest), Bell Atlantic and NYNEX (now Verizon), and Bell South. Carly was a sales and marketing person in Lucent, prior to becoming president of one of Lucent's Global Service Provider business units. She basically sold to a "good old boy" network of phone companies at a time when the ramp-up in the Internet and phone investment was going wild. She road the wave, and within months of going to HP the Lucent stock crashed along with the dot-com bust.

The point is that the board did not do a good job framing and naming the criteria for the CEO. They needed a leader who had extensive P&L business experience and who had led organizations through transformations. She also did not have any CEO board experience as she was heading up a unit of Lucent. The board mobilized and aligned themselves and the press and the HP staff into supporting a bad judgment. It is no wonder that, rather than the tough internal team building, execution, and driving of the business, Fiorina spent most of her time on external showboating and "selling." That is what she knew how to do. She lacked the requisite skill set to do anything else. Her track record showed that clearly coming out of sales and marketing in a very protected, near-monopolistic business at Lucent. She also had trouble building a team to augment or supplement her weak areas; instead, her team was in constant turmoil at HP, including the firing of three of her senior leaders months before she got fired. The implication was that they, not her, were why the company missed its earnings. HP had to go outside again when she left and hired Mark Hurd from NCR. Hurd has turned out to be a hands-on, in-the-trenches leader who has turned HP around and driven the stock price to almost double what it was when Fiorina left. The board made a good judgment the second time around.

A good CEO succession story occurred at PepsiCo. In mid-2006 PepsiCo announced that Indra Krishnamurthy Nooyi was the new CEO. She took over for Steve Reinemund. This was an internal candidate, a product of the Pepsi leadership pipeline. Pepsi has leadership talent because of a judgment made years earlier that succession planning—leadership development—was a CEO priority and commitment. Roger Enrico, former CEO prior to Reinemund, turbocharged the Pepsi process by conducting his own leadership development program for the top 240 leaders at Pepsi. He personally conducted a program with nine vice presidents at a time, which included a five-offsite, sixty-day project and a three-day follow-up. He had no outside faculty, no staff teaching, just himself, eight in the morning till eleven at night. This program was in part how Indra was both developed and discovered. To this day Pepsi executives can remember more than ten years ago the session at Roger's Montana Ranch, where the group went horseback riding and Indra could barely walk afterward but was a great sport and fully engaged that night singing around the campfire.

The Enrico leadership program was a part of the long preparation phase for CEO judgments. Steve Reinemund continued the program and Indra is now designing her own version. Contrast that with HP: no real knowledge of the outside candidate, no idea how she would lead or get along with the team at HP, and no knowledge by Fiorina of the HP businesses, culture, and strategic challenges.

THE #1 PEOPLE JUDGMENT

Who heads up an institution is by far the single most important people judgment. CEO succession in any type of organization—from political, to not for profit, to business or military—is the key determinant of organizational performance. This seemingly blindingly obvious premise must be examined in light of the empirical reality of success in the last decade. The track record in many companies has been abysmal. Given the importance of this judgment, the grade among blue chip companies is probably no more than a D, as many blue chip companies failed to have developed a successor CEO.

In the early 1990s IBM's board of directors fired John Akers and had to go outside to hire Lou Gerstner as CEO. Then AT&T's board pushed Bob Allen out and brought John Walters in from the outside. He only lasted a few months and he got fired. So they brought Michael Armstrong in from GM's Hughes unit. He ultimately failed and AT&T got bought by SBC, who has taken over the brand, but the company is basically gone. These bad CEO judgments had huge negative consequences for the companies and cost thousands of workers their jobs and careers. Both IBM and AT&T were touted by the academics as role models for management development and career planning right through the 1980s. The reality was that they were bureaucratic dinosaurs producing leaders for yesterday's economic reality; both were in monopolistic positions in their industries and kept coasting on the momentum of the past, much like GM and Ford. The boards and the predecessor CEOs exercised bad judgment.

At Merck the one internal candidate, Dick Markham, was let go at the eleventh hour, leaving no other internal CEO candidate to succeed Roy Vagelos. The board ended up hiring Ray Gilmartin from Becton Dickinson, a very small medical instruments company, best known for its medical needles. Gilmartin ended up being overwhelmed by big pharma. He was in an unfamiliar world where huge research and development (R&D) investments led to an occasional blockbuster, multibillion-dollar drug. Thus the role of R&D and drug testing and approval process, unknown in the world of Becton Dickinson, proved to be unmanageable by him. He ended up as a weak CEO who got ensnared in the Merck Vioxx drug recall and ensuing lawsuits. Ultimately he was pressured into resigning in May 2005 (the Merck stock had peaked at $90 and was in the low $30s when he resigned).

At 3M Jim McNerney was brought in from outside after losing the horse race at GE to Jeff Immelt. When McNerney left 3M to take over the Boeing CEO position, 3M was forced to go outside again. Even though one of McNerney's priorities was to rebuild the leadership pipeline at 3M, he was not there long enough to produce any CEO candidates. McNerney is now in his second outsider CEO position, 3M, then Boeing. Motorola pushed out the family CEO, Christopher Galvin, and brought in outsider Ed Zander as CEO who did not last, either. Another outsider, Greg Brown, took over for Zander.

Blue chip companies that one would have expected to have leadership pipelines developing CEOs came up empty: for example, Kodak, Nortel in Canada, and Honeywell in the United States.

The bottom line of these CEO outside hires is that they represent bad judgment in building a leadership pipeline for succession. Not to have a successor at the top of an institution is the ultimate in bad people judgment. The preparation phase includes a long-term commitment to developing a stream of talent, a leadership pipeline, designed to develop leaders at all levels and ensure a flow of leaders. There are multiple candidates and a succession pipeline that feeds opportunities at lower levels in the organization.

Bad CEO judgments happen because of broken leadership pipelines; that is, there are not any good candidates and the building of appropriate leadership bench strength has not occurred. There are a variety of underlying causes. In some cases it is family nepotism, such as putting Bill Ford in as CEO at Ford. After only a few years Ford has stepped out of the role and brought in an outsider, Alan Mulally, from Boeing as CEO in mid-2006. Other causes of broken leadership pipelines include lack of a disciplined succession planning process, board neglect, poor understanding of changing world and talent requirements (3M, IBM), and ego issues with the CEO not wanting to let go. Any combination of these problems contributes to bad CEO succession judgment. We consider having to go outside to be the ultimate in bad people judgment. However, when the board has to go outside, one certainly wants them to make a good judgment. It was good judgment for the 3M board to bring in McNerney given their situation, and it was good judgment for the Boeing board to woo him away.

There are two types of bad CEO succession judgment, the operational flaw and the systemic flaw.

OPERATIONAL FLAW

A good leadership pipeline but a bad CEO judgment: a good process is in place but the organization makes a mistake and self-corrects with a candidate from within the company. This was the case with Durk Jager at P&G. The board made a bad judgment in putting him in as CEO, and in eighteen months corrected it with a good CEO judgment, namely putting A. G. Lafley in as CEO. The P&G leadership pipeline had the right talent inside the company and was able to self-correct without going to the outside.

SYSTEMIC FLAW

A broken leadership pipeline: There is a failed process, there is no choice, no depth of leadership, and the board must go outside for CEO: HP, 3M, AT&T, Motorola, Merck, Boeing, and Home Depot are examples.

There are only a few companies with a track record of leadership pipelines producing good CEO judgments. ExxonMobil has a track record of always having leaders from within and a winning performance in the industry. At the close of 2006 they were the most valuable company on the planet with a market capitalization of $434 billion. Pepsi is another solid leadership pipeline. GE also has long had a leadership pipeline, which not only produces an abundance of candidates for the GE CEO position but also produces CEOs of other major companies.

LEADERSHIP PIPELINE

The long-term responsibility of the board and CEO is the creation of a leadership pipeline with the capacity to develop leaders at all levels. An increasingly narrow stream of those leaders move to the top. Done right, there are multiple great candidates to make the final CEO judgment call. Jack Welch had that luxury, but it came after twenty years of focus on the leadership pipeline.

BAD CEO JUDGMENTS DESTROY ORGANIZATIONS

To illustrate how critical the CEO judgment is, let's go back in time and examine a specific case that Noel was close to at the time. Roy Vagelos was a very successful CEO of Merck. He propelled the company to number one in the industry, and Merck was named *Fortune*'s most admired company for nine years in a row from the 1980s and early 1990s.[1] Roy was a very dedicated physician researcher who, as CEO of Merck, transformed it into the leader in the industry. He did care about development of a leadership pipeline and invested in it. However, his story reflects the centrality of having a robust leadership pipeline that provides options at the time of CEO succession. Roy's tragic flaw was having a "crown prince" CEO succession process, namely only one contender, Dick Markham. In 1993 Noel was set to do a leadership program with Vagelos and Markham, the heir apparent at Merck. The program was to launch on a Monday morning. The Friday afternoon before, Roy called Noel and told him that there would be no program, that Markham was let go for what the press ended up calling unexplained "personal reasons." Thus, Roy was stuck with no successor and had to go outside.

It is not enough for a CEO to drive short-term performance and then fail to have a good successor to drive long-term success; that is how we judge Roy Vagelos, a leader who was very successful at strategic judgment during his tenure as reflected in the outstanding business and stock performance of Merck. His judgment vis-à-vis his succession, the most important people judgment, was bad, there was no successor, and the one finally selected from outside, Ray Gilmartin, was a failure as measured by the performance of Merck. Its market cap went from $185 billion to $141 billion when he left (versus Pfizer at $209 billion).[2]

PREPARATION PHASE

As we examine the roots of the bad judgment, it clearly rests with a weak leadership pipeline at Merck, namely, overreliance on one candidate, Dick Markham, the "crown prince." When he was out of the running, there was no alternative.

Ironically, the launch of the leadership program that Vagelos and Markham were to cosponsor and lead was designed to help prepare Markham for the CEO role as well as to invest in developing more leadership depth in the top ranks of Merck. As laudable as this was, it turned out to be too little too late. The grooming of a CEO needs to take years and needs to create bench strength so that there is not just one candidate. To Vagelos's credit, he made a tough people judgment when Markham crossed an ethical line. However, Vagelos had a serious people judgment problem: there was no number two alternative CEO candidate inside Merck.

The Merck board and CEO framed the new issue as having to go outside to find leadership for the future. They offered the job to one of the board members who was an active CEO of another company at the time; that person turned it down. This set the stage for bringing in an outside to Merck and to big pharma, namely Ray Gilmartin.

The framing phase of the people judgment call looks highly questionable. What was the framing of the CEO role and specifications for success to offer the position to Gilmartin, who lacked the background to deal with the scale and scope of the world's largest pharmaceutical company at the time, with no experience in the complexities of pharma R&D and product development? R&D at Becton Dickinson consisted of 139.14 million dollars of expenditure on simple product extensions and improvements, not multibillion-dollar, highly complex drug research, with a Merck R&D budget of $1.2 billion at the time. The dynamics of the industries the two companies operated in had little commonality except that they both supplied the medical field.

MAKING THE JUDGMENT CALL

The board and CEO Roy Vagelos mobilized and aligned sufficient support to make the judgment call to hire Gilmartin. The die was cast due to the inadequate framing of the judgment. With Merck at the peak of the industry, it is inconceivable that a successor from within the pharma industry could not be found. The pool of talent included CEOs of other pharmaceutical companies, some of whom would have left to take the bigger and more prestigious CEO role at Merck (just as Jim McNerney left 3M for Boeing in 2005), as well as succession contenders in other big pharmaceutical companies, or leaders in much larger related medical suppliers such as GE Medical Systems, J&J, and Medtronic. The point is the judgment call set the stage for a rocky and ultimately failed execution phase.

EXECUTION PHASE

Gilmartin had trouble from the beginning. He went through several heads of human resources, he never had full control of the company, and he was unable to build a team of loyal and aligned team members. In big pharma, the key is new blockbuster drugs. His lack of experience and background training, having a Harvard MBA, not an MD or PhD, made it hard for him to gain credibility and provide leadership to the very powerful Merck R&D group headed up with a very strong-willed leadership group. Vagelos was an MD and a world-class researcher before becoming CEO, and he had the respect and capacity to lead R&D.

MAKING IT HAPPEN, LEARNING, AND ADJUSTING

This never happened at Merck. Gilmartin was over his head when it came to any judgments that needed to be made in R&D. The lack of technical background and the lack of a power base within Merck doomed him to failure in exercising leadership in this domain. The downfall of Merck was the mishandled Vioxx case; it led to pushing

Gilmartin out and finally promoting an insider to try to right the ship. Richard Clark was appointed in a controversial people judgment call. With all the turmoil, the board had to step in and play the part of the role of CEO, with Larry Bossidy on the board being named an active chairman, overseeing far more of the running of Merck than would normally happen with a CEO the board and Wall Street had total confidence in. It was almost as if the board made a judgment that Clark needed "training wheels" for a while. A bad people judgment was made a decade earlier when GM split the leadership between CEO Bob Stempel and retired CEO of P&G John Smale. This ended in failure as Stempel was fired.

The lesson from the Merck case is all too frequently replayed. The CEO puts all of his eggs in one basket with a "crown prince" succession process. In some cases the leader gets away with it, like ExxonMobil. In the late 1980s it was known that the CEO, Lawrence Rawls, would be turning then-named Exxon over to CEO Lee Raymond in a few years. He operated as chief operating officer, no other contenders, and then became CEO. Lee Raymond just repeated the process with now CEO Rex Tillerson. The risk is that something happens and then ExxonMobil is in the same situation that Roy Vagelos found himself in with Dick Markham.

AT&T's demise is clearly wrapped up in bad people judgment calls at the top, starting with Bob Allen, an old-time Bell leader who could not kick-start a transformation, then the bad judgment call of bringing in John Walters, former CEO of R. R. Donnelley and Sons printing company. He lasted a matter of months, and then John Armstrong came in from Hughes Electronics, a subsidiary of GM. Prior to that Armstrong was at IBM. AT&T needed a transformational leader. The board made a bad judgment call with Armstrong. He was at IBM in its heyday when they printed money and no one except at the top ever had real P&L experience. Hughes was a small entity under the GM portfolio. There is no way Armstrong had a chance to develop the capabilities to transform a behemoth like AT&T. Contrast that decision with the decision IBM made to go outside and get Louis Gerstner, who had the experience and skill set. The IBM judgment call turned out to be a great people judgment.

The lesson from the AT&T series of bad people judgment calls is in the preparation phase. They were slow to sense and identify the need for a new CEO. Their real problem was then in the framing and naming process. There was little or no capacity to frame the position requirements for a transformational leader and once that happened it was pretty clear that they would not find the right leader. They had no clue what "good" looked like.

The HP bad judgment call must be understood in the context of a board and senior leadership team who did not build a succession leadership pipeline, so that when Young was retiring they had adequate bench strength to fill the CEO role from within. That was the first bad judgment; they compounded the first bad judgment with a bad call on who to bring in from the outside. Very similar to the AT&T case, the specs were inadequate: poor framing, thus poor judgment call.

Because of varying board involvement, the CEO needs to orchestrate the dynamics of the board. These are not the calls of a CEO alone. CEOs need to manage a board in the execution if they're making the call. If not, the board dynamics and prep have a great deal to do with the selection.

Making Good CEO Succession Judgments

We will start with one that happened over twenty years ago but led to the world's largest and so far most successful organizational transformation. How did Reg Jones select Jack Welch in 1980 to be the GE CEO, who ended up being touted as the "Manager of the Century" by *Fortune* and *BusinessWeek*,[3] among other earned accolades?

When Noel was doing the research on his GE book, *Control Your Destiny or Someone Else Will*,[4] he interviewed Reg Jones on this very topic. In his Stamford, Connecticut, office, Jones proudly took out a piece of paper from his desk drawer and showed Noel a chart that had eight potential CEO candidates for his job. The chart was dated 1974, seven years prior to Jones's anticipated retirement. In addition to the typed names, Jones had handwritten a name, a young executive at the time running GE Plastics, Jack Welch. Jones said that he had his eye on

Welch even though he was not on the radar screen for CEO potential. That is why he was not on the formal typed list but was handwritten in by him. Welch in 1974 was a young manager. Running Plastics for GE, he was thirty-eight years old. One important point about the GE succession is that there is a very disciplined leadership development and succession process in place that has been there since the 1960s. Thus Jones had a process that helped in his framing of the judgment.

Jones carefully orchestrated a CEO succession process made famous by a three-way horse race: Al Way, John Burlingame, and Jack Welch. The final judgment was going to be made after the three were judged while each was running a big sector of GE. Jones wanted the candidates at corporate headquarters to watch them up close. The GE human resources team, headed by Ted LeVino, played a key role in the process as well. In the *mobilize and align* phase of the preparation, GE's CEO, HR staff, and the board used multiple methods to help shape the judgment. A great deal of time, debate, and disciplined analysis went into the process.

Ted LeVino's team carefully wrote up assessments and supported Jones's selection process. They were evaluated by the HR staff on a number of leadership characteristics. The process also included each candidate writing a letter to the CEO making a case for his candidacy and what he would do to lead the company.

One of the downsides of what Jones did was to have all three contenders for his job at GE politically attack one another. None of them was running a specific business; they were sector executives often in the same meetings and with time and staff to undermine one another. The political jockeying was very destructive and hurt the company during the preparation phase. Welch learned from this and did not replicate this part of the process.

On the positive side, Jones clearly framed and named the judgment call with the activities described above. The final phase of preparation was the mobilizing and aligning of his board, including his vice chairman at the time, who had their own candidates in mind. Walter Wriston was a key board member, and at the time CEO of Citibank; he provided Jones the political power at the board level to make Welch the choice, even though he was ten years younger than the other contenders, so that on April 1, 1981, Welch became CEO. It was a great judgment call because the outcome resulted in GE's twenty-year success under Welch's leadership. Without Jones's careful orchestration of the preparation phase, the judgment call would probably have been a different, more traditional candidate and the twenty years might have looked more like the death spiral Westinghouse went into during the same era.

THE WELCH JUDGMENT TO SELECT IMMELT AS CEO

Welch made a judgment call to select Jeff Immelt over Jim McNerney and Robert Nardelli as the CEO to replace him. The preparation phase began at least fifteen years prior to the judgment call. In 1985, when Noel was head of GE's leadership development, Crotonville, Welch involved him and a team of HR leaders to help frame a new GE leadership pipeline designed to help produce the new CEO. Welch told us at the time, "However I got to be CEO is irrelevant, we are a different organization, we will continue to change, we need to look into the future and figure out how to produce the CEO for tomorrow's world." He charged us to look at the whole leadership pipeline from "off-campus hire" to new manager, to senior leader in a function, to head of a multibillion-dollar business, thus, candidates for his job. He wanted us to help him articulate the "soft" people, leadership and cultural capabilities at each level, as well as the "hard" business capabilities (strategy, finance, and so on). Welch and then vice chairman Larry Bossidy worked with us over eighteen months to develop this framework. In 1987 the whitepaper that we produced framed the developmental challenges for a leader getting ready to be in the hunt for CEO.[5]

- Develop multifunctional integration skills required to manage a business measured on a profit-and-loss basis.
- Learn to effectively exercise power to make those decisions only the leader can make.
- Develop a vision for the business. Effectively articulate this vision and ensure it is adopted within the business.
- Develop projects and extrapolation skills in order to deal with

situations where he/she has not had firsthand experience. Learn to pose perceptive questions.

- Develop the capacity to conceive and manage change (as opposed to stewardship over the status quo).
- Develop an effective understanding of the dynamics of the industry in which his/her business participates.
- Develop sensitivity to "practical politics" and the forces that motivate people to behave as they do.
- Develop a balanced posture between the leadership of the business and integration/cooperation with other businesses in the company.
- Develop a capacity to effectively manage community relations.

In order to be a candidate for CEO the following criteria were established.

- Demonstrates mastery over the role of multifunctionally scoped, profit-and-loss-accountable general manager over a worldwide business.
- Demonstrates decisive business leadership and effectiveness in exercising power. Shows courage in making decisions and taking action.
- Demonstrates the ability to lead his/her team in the development of a meaningful vision for the business. Effectively communicates and gains understanding/acceptance of this vision across the business.
- Demonstrates excellent business judgment accruing to his/her intuitive processes and willingness to fully explore the inputs of many sources of information.
- Demonstrates the ability to catalyze total business turnaround situations in a timely and effective fashion. Has effectively managed organizational renewal or change.
- Demonstrates the capacity to handle ambiguity and paradox constructively.
- Demonstrates effective understanding of the dynamics of the industry in which his/her business participates and is able to uti-

lize this understanding to develop creative yet realistic strategies and tactics.

- Demonstrates the ability to effectively handle high-level political situations both inside and outside the company.
- Demonstrates the willingness to put company results ahead of the more parochial interests of his/her own business. Supports other company business and is successful in engendering this outlook with subordinates.
- Demonstrates the ability to effectively manage community relations.

Note that while this was going on, the normal succession-planning process at GE was occurring where as many as twenty potential CEO candidates were being carefully discussed and assessed. As Welch entered the 1990s, the preparation phase ramped up. A couple of things began to occur, the list started getting smaller, and Welch shared his judgment calls on who was no longer in the candidate pool with the board and with the individuals. For example, John Trani was at one time a potential. He was CEO of GE Medical Systems starting in 1986. By the early 1990s, it was clear to Welch and the board that he was not going to be a candidate. Welch gave Trani the feedback and worked with him to move out of GE. He left and became CEO of Stanley Works. Gary Wendt, the very successful head of GE Capital, was another one who was helped to leave.

The most interesting part of the preparation phase was how Welch managed the final horse race. He did the opposite of Jones, who had the three contenders working at headquarters. Welch said the politics were awful, they were in the same building and same meetings, and they were trying to kill one another. He felt that it really hurt the company.

In order to avoid those politics, he kept the candidates out of headquarters and made sure that they were very busy running their own businesses. They could compete; however, it was by outperforming one another in their own businesses. Nardelli had Power Systems, McNerney had Aircraft Engines, and Immelt had Medical Systems. Welch framed and named the judgment call for the board and worked closely with head of HR, Bill Conaty, to do all kinds of assessments of the leaders. A best practice was the way in which the board was engaged. Welch had a subcommittee of the board spend time in the field with each of the candidates without Welch present. The candidates had to host a dinner and day with the board committee. It was up to them to design the agenda, in order to give the board more unfiltered data on the candidates. The board then had to produce a written report assessing the candidates. This was in addition to the extensive data as part of the normal GE succession-planning process.

When he and the GE board made the final call, Welch set in motion a very unique execution phase in which the two who lost out to Immelt—McNerney and Nardelli—left almost overnight. It was done to avoid the political price Welch felt he had to pay when he got the job.

Simultaneous CEO Succession and Transformation

Not many companies have the long tradition of GE's deep leadership pipeline. Sometimes the leader has to simultaneously take the organization through massive change while developing and selecting a new CEO in record time. This was the case at Ameritech in the early 1990s when Bill Weiss, then CEO, had to make both a strategic set of judgments for the company and make a judgment as to his successor.

We worked with CEO Bill Weiss at Ameritech to help him structure his judgment process for selecting the next CEO. He sensed and identified the need for CEO succession three years before his retirement. On July 20, 1992, Weiss came to visit Noel and his business partner, Patti, in Ann Arbor, Michigan, at the recommendation of Jack Welch. Weiss laid out the challenge he had to both transform Ameritech and select the next CEO in the coming two years. Noel remembers telling him, "You simply need to select your successor now and retire, get out of the way so that the transformation can happen." He said, "I can't do that, I am not sure I have the right successor and we have to transform Ameritech starting now."

We agreed to help him with his succession process while driving a massive transformation. The first step was a three-day offsite at Pinehurst in October with his top team. At the end of the workshop, which focused on diagnosing Ameritech's strategic situations and options for the future, Noel told Weiss, "There is no one in that room who is a viable succession candidate for you." Bill Springer, an old confidant of Weiss and the vice chairman who was going to retire before Weiss, sat down with us and framed a judgment process for selecting the next CEO. It involved identifying younger talent in the organization who might have the potential to take over for Weiss in several years.

In a watershed event, the Breakers workshop in February 1993, the top thirty executives worked on a diagnosis of Ameritech and took a look at strategic options for the future. Weiss made a big step in the preparation phase for CEO succession. Weiss and Springer met each evening of the workshop in Weiss's suite at the Breakers with Noel and Patti to discuss what we observed of the key leaders in the workshop, who was leading, who had good ideas, who was being a team player, and so on. By the last evening it was clear to Springer and Weiss that there were four younger leaders—Dick Notebaert, Dick Brown, Barry Allen, and Gary Drook—who were the going to lead the Ameritech transformation effort and who were going to be looked at very closely as CEO candidates.

The last morning of the workshop, Weiss, who could be very imposing and formal, announced the cancellation of the normal Monday morning management meeting, something he had not done for ten years. He was replacing it with a meeting of the new transformation team leaders, Notebaert, Drook, Brown, and Allen. The room of thirty-five executives was surprised and everyone was trying to read the tea leaves: What does this mean for me? What does this mean for my career? What is Weiss up to?

Weiss then set in motion a transformation process for Ameritech. Each of the four had a team of thirty high-potential executives assigned to work on four strategic initiatives for the future: (1) the network; (2) customer segments; (3) regulatory strategy; and (4) human resource strategy. The 120 executives were carefully selected by the new "transformation team" and Weiss. The 120 kept their day jobs while working 30 percent on these strategic task forces. The team of four met with Weiss at least once a week for half a day to go over progress and to help each other. There were multiday workshops for the 120 to deal with the need for change, team building, and leadership development so that Weiss was seeing how the four could lead, how they could frame the future, how they could work with one another, and simultaneously how they could create the new Ameritech.

The first six months were intense and by the fall of that year, the company was reorganized based on the work of the 120. The power shifted to newly created customer segments, such as residential, small business, and big business. The state organizations—Illinois Bell, Michigan Bell, Ohio Bell, Indiana Bell, and Wisconsin Bell—were turned into regulatory organizations with little or no staff. The organization downsized from sixty-six thousand to forty-five thousand. A massive transformation was unleashed, led by Weiss and the four contenders for his job.

One critical event was the four transformation leaders confronting Bill Springer, vice chairman and close confidant of Weiss, with their skepticism about the whole process because Weiss and Springer had not gotten rid of a vice chairman and a president who were former contenders. The transformation leaders felt that if Weiss had courage, he would get them out of the way and send a message to the organization and to this team that they were the future. Springer agreed and so did Weiss. Weiss removed the two leaders and sent a very powerful message that they were playing for real and that the four better deliver or would be next out the door.

Weiss made it clear to the team, "If I catch any one of you undercutting another colleague, you are out of the game for my job. Only the best team player can be a candidate." No one was perfect; he took several of the players out behind the woodshed a couple of times on this issue. Noel remembers Weiss letting Dick Notebaert know that his behavior in a particular meeting looked more like scoring points against his colleagues than team play.

Weiss would also meet regularly with each of the contenders, one on one. He got input from others, including the team Noel was heading up to work with Ameritech. The board was regularly exposed to the players as well. The next year Weiss was ready to make the judgment call. He did and named Dick Notebaert CEO. Dick Brown stayed as vice chairman, and the other two moved outside Ameritech.

Weiss clearly sensed and identified the need for transformation and new leadership. He framed and named it as a simultaneous transformation and CEO succession process. Time was of the essence and he needed to do both quickly. The mobilizing and aligning were accomplished by creating the transformation process led by the four and engaging the 120 senior leaders. This preparation process set the stage for the team and Weiss to make judgment calls on the four domains, which they did. Then Weiss kept the team together to execute, go out, and hire heads of the new business units, build the businesses, revamp the network, change the regulatory strategy, and totally revamp human resources for the company. The same discipline and process used to prepare for the judgment calls was used for the execution of the strategy.

This compressed transformation gave Weiss all the data he needed to make the judgment call on who would best lead Ameritech, namely, Dick Notebaert, who became CEO two years after the Breakers meeting. Notebaert was viewed as a transformational leader, with clear strategic ideas for leading Ameritech. He embodied the values that Weiss and the board felt were essential: the unyielding integrity, the team focus, the commitment to developing leaders. Notebaert clearly had the wherewithal to energize both himself and thousands of others with the guts and courage to drive the transformation. He ultimately sold the business to SBC for $70 billion, after he started his tenure with the market capitalization at $20 billion.

CEO Succession Judgment Lessons

These examples illustrate the key elements of good people judgments. Jones, Welch, and Weiss each architected a judgment process that led to a successful CEO selection. Here are the lessons:

Lesson 1. Sensing and Identifying: Anticipating the Need for Key People Changes

The leader needs to ensure that the key people judgment is identified with plenty of time to lead a disciplined process. Jones was mobilized ten years early. Welch in 1985 was wrestling with the new leadership pipeline and succession fifteen years early. For Weiss, it was much later in the game; with only three years left he realized the world had changed and he did not have the right candidate pool. Timing is a key element of the judgment process.

LESSON 2. FRAMING AND NAMING: SPECIFYING THE LEADERSHIP REQUIREMENTS BY LOOKING INTO THE FUTURE, NOT IN THE REARVIEW MIRROR

Welch set the bar for all leaders. "Don't look at how I became CEO; it is irrelevant. The world has changed, GE has changed and will continue to. Look at what we need for tomorrow." The framing and naming of developing a leadership pipeline for the future is an unnatural act for the vast majority of companies who not only wait too long, but then do a poor job of framing the future. HP had no candidates internally two times in a row, resulting in the Fiorina misjudgment. In the Fiorina case the judgment was flawed because of the framing and naming work of the board. Had they framed the job requirements of transformation HP, it would have been clear that Fiorina lacked the requisite skill set. The hiring of Hurd with real hands-on leadership experience in technology bodes well for the second outside CEO judgment call made at HP. 3M went outside to hire Jim McNerney from GE and when he left in 2005 for Boeing, they did not have an internal candidate and had to go outside again. The root cause of the lack of CEO candidates is that lack of framing and naming succession judgments as critical to the success of the enterprise and that this gets put in motion with serious processes many years ahead of the need for the judgment.

LESSON 3. MOBILIZING AND ALIGNING THE SOCIAL NETWORK TO SUPPORT THE "RIGHT" CALL

Weiss used the 120 high-potential senior leaders engaged in revolutionizing the company as not only the testing ground for his four leaders but as a way to mobilize and align them around the new CEO. Dick Notebaert emerged as the leader key organizational leaders most supported and respected. Welch carefully engaged the board in the process by getting them mobilized and aligned through multiple meetings with the contenders and in-depth reviews and discussions. This phase requires repetitive, disciplined processes to ensure constructive conflict and dialogue. It was the step that A. G. Lafley short-circuited and then had to do a redo loop back and correct in the Deb Henretta judgment call.

LESSON 4. MAKING THE CALL: MAKING THE PROCESS TRANSPARENT AND JUDGED FAIR

Lafley basically failed at first. His top team felt the process was not transparent and fair. By setting up the meeting of the top team and telling them he was willing to give everyone a fair hearing, even though he was honest in saying that it meant changing his mind with a better approach, he was able to gain sufficient mobilization and alignment to move to execution. Welch orchestrated not only the board but the press, the leadership team, and all the stakeholders to understand his judgment call.

LESSON 5. EXECUTION: MAKING IT HAPPEN

Welch did something very powerful. He took care of the winner, letting Immelt know, and he also explained it to everyone why. He dealt with the losers. He rented a jet so no one would know he was traveling. The press was watching Welch at the end to try to figure out who would be the next CEO. He wanted to make sure that the two who did not get the job were told by him before hearing any rumors and were dealt with honestly and with respect. He flew to Albany, New York, to sit face-to-face with Bob Nardelli to tell him he was a great leader but that he and the board had decided on Immelt. It was a tough emotional meeting but part of the "making it happen" process. He then did the same with McNerney, flying to Cincinnati, where McNerney was running the Aircraft Engines business.

LESSON 6. LEARN AND ADJUST: PROVIDING CONTINUOUS SUPPORT TO HELP THE LEADER SUCCEED

Welch overlapped with Immelt in a coaching role for a year. In part he stayed longer because of the ongoing attempted acquisition of Honeywell, which in the end did not occur and extended by six months his overlap. The first six months were terrific for Immelt, because, as he told Noel, he had never been at the top of GE, leading across all of the businesses. He found Welch to be an invaluable coach. Weiss did the same for Dick Notebaert, coaching him with the board, with Washington, and how to fill the CEO role.

◆ ◆ ◆

1. The most important people judgment needs time, attention, discipline, and constructive conflict.
2. The judgment needs to be on a storyline for the future success of the organization—Merck had none, so had to run around to find a leader; versus Weiss, who came up with a new strategy judgment, and that judgment along with CEO succession go hand in hand; Immelt the leader to make new judgments for GE.
3. In the future we can watch as companies like Best Buy unfold. The CEO successor to Brad Anderson needs to be selected for tomorrow's world, not yesterday's or today's.

7

STRATEGY JUDGMENTS

▍ Strategy Judgments Constantly Evolve
- The big storyline provides the framework for many substories.
- Each strategic action sets the stage for the next call.

▍ Leaders Must Develop Their Own Strategies
- Calls cannot be delegated to bureaucratic "planners."
- They require constant review and updating.

▍ Strategic Thinking Is a Blend of Logic and Feel
- It requires leaders' intellect to frame questions and answers.
- It requires their emotional energy to mobilize others to execution.

◆ ◆ ◆

As I take over GE in 2001, and I see a GE that has these traits, that Jack fixed a lot. It is faster moving, it is more entrepreneurial, it is leaner, but it doesn't have the heart that it needs, it doesn't have the context I think it needs. And this is what I want to do in GE and the next twenty years. And that's how I want to end it. I want to end it with the fact that GE—Jack—took a big, respected company and made it a valuable company by doing a bunch of

> things, that was great, I believe in them. Now we're going
> to build on that and make it have a bigger impact on
> society, for ourselves and for our people.
>
> —Jeff Immelt, GE CEO, personal interview, October 2001

When Jack Welch handed over the reins as CEO of General Electric to Jeff Immelt in September 2001, Immelt knew that he would soon be making some changes. GE was at the time the most valuable and competitive enterprise in the world. During Welch's twenty-year run as CEO, GE had dramatically outperformed the economy, creating close to $400 billion of new market value for GE (when Welch took over the company was worth $13 billion and when he retired on September 7, 2001, it was worth over $400 billion). It had transformed itself from a company that steadily grew with the rate of U.S. gross domestic product (GDP) by being a solid producer of appliances and industrial equipment into a high-tech provider of industrial and financial services. In anticipation of his departure, Welch had put the company on a trajectory that almost assured several years of rising earnings, and he had cleaned house by getting rid of top executives who were in contention for the CEO spot and might not be supportive members of an Immelt-led team. GE was a smooth-running machine the day Jack Welch walked out the door.

Still, for all the success that GE was enjoying, Jeff Immelt knew that his job was to make big changes. If he just tinkered around the edges and focused on making GE's current business model run better, the company would not retain its preeminence for long. Jack Welch had been a brilliant leader, but he had succeeded by, as he put it, "relishing change." Immelt had risen through the ranks at GE and been mentored by Welch. He had won the top job in large measure because he was such a successful change agent. "Great leaders," Immelt told a group of Michigan MBA students, "drive change. I tell people within GE, we've got enough institutional momentum that if all we were going to do is stay the same, you sure don't need me. Leaders drive change. Leaders drive change. That's your job."[1]

In the weeks before he officially took office, Immelt was circumspect about the changes he would make. "I'm inheriting a company with no burning platform, no business sucking up cash, every business returning its cost of capital," he told the *New York Times*. "If you ask the question, 'Will the portfolio look different five years from now?' I'd say, 'Sure it will,'" he told another reporter. "Do I feel like I need to come out today and make a big announcement on the portfolio? I don't think I have that need. I don't really have underperforming businesses, and we don't need the cash. I think that gives us a chance to really look through the portfolio in an aggressive yet methodical way."[2]

When we interviewed Jeff Immelt a few weeks later, in October 2001, he still didn't have many specific plans for where and how he would lead GE in the future, but the world had changed dramatically, and Immelt was moving closer to embracing a Teachable Point of View that would develop into an overarching storyline and ultimately shape his strategic judgments for leading GE into the twenty-first century. A key element of that TPOV was that being a great company wasn't enough. GE needed to build on its heritage of giving back to society and the communities it operated in around the world, as well. It needed to become more focused on contributing to the greater good of the communities around the world that they operated in. He made a strategic judgment that global corporate citizenship would be more of a focus.

Immelt officially became the chairman and CEO of General Electric on September 7, 2001. Four days later, terrorists attacked the United States. In just a few hours, just about every aspect, every assumption, about the future direction of the world's economies and of geopolitical life was called into question. People's points of view about their own lives and their personal relationships were also cast in a serious new light. Jeff Immelt already knew that his job was to change GE, but the events of 9/11 made the need startlingly clear. "I get the job September seventh, September eleventh happens four days later, you know, and I watch, it's an unspeakable tragedy. I lost friends in that and it, it's extremely sad. But from a business standpoint, I saw planes with our engines flying into buildings we insured, covered by NBC, four days after I become chairman." September 11, he says, "helped me kind of say, '(Screw) it, I'm going to do it my way.'"

One of the themes that Immelt had been exploring before 9/11 was how to make GE perhaps not less corporate, but more human. "One of the things that just rolls around in my mind is we've got great people, but so much of their own self-worth and so much of their own personal worth is around the stock price. And if you get into a market that really is going to be dead for a couple of years, people need new psychic pleasure. They have got to love their work again. They have got to love the people they work with again. They have got to love the challenge of getting up in the morning again, versus saying, 'Hey, I have a beach home. I have $10 million in the bank.' The point I want to make is . . . Look, if the stock price doesn't go up, you're going to have new leaders, don't get me wrong, I know that, I know how important that is, but I think it's just encouraging people to remember why you went to work in the first place."

"The other thing that is stirring around in my mind," he told us in October 2001 as he considered how he wanted to move GE ahead, "is, in a time when employees are worried about their own safety, you can't have a (jerk) managing them. . . . You know, the fact that we still have some (SOBs) out there. We've got to get rid of them. I mean nobody's talked about it, but when your number-one concern when you're driving to work in the morning is, are you going to open up an envelope with anthrax in it, can you imagine combining that with working with (an SOB)?" This conversation occurred in Immelt's conference room the day that Tom Brokaw and some of the NBC staff received an envelope with anthrax inside.

"I think the first thing is this has got to be a place where people are put first, people are treated with respect. Start with people. You know, it's got to be people. Community may be part of it."

Those words coming out of the mouth of anybody but Jeff Immelt might sound like superficial platitudes. But the handpicked successor to Jack Welch as CEO of General Electric doesn't spend much time thinking or talking about things that aren't directly related to business and the success of GE. "Fundamentally it's my life," he told us. "This company is all I think about, it's who I am." Thinking about community and GE's role in the worldwide community was where he started developing his strategy for how he would lead GE to success in the coming years. It led him to a business model whose key elements include building infrastructure for developing countries, creating environmentally friendly products for both developed and developing countries, and investments in health care.

For a leader, developing strategy is a never-ending job of crafting the storyline for success. It is rarely an "aha" clear vision. It is an evolving story that starts off fuzzy, as Immelt's did when he stepped into his role. It gets continuously revised and becomes clearer as strategic judgments are made. Each big acquisition or divestiture, or judgment on a big R&D investment, changes the company's position and the possibilities for the future. These judgments are not only manifestations of the storyline, but also shapers of it going forward.

This big storyline provides the framework for many substories with the GE portfolio. For example: Immelt's judgment to acquire Amersham by GE Healthcare for close to $10 billion reflected Immelt's storyline of building a medical business around tomorrow's technology for personalized medicine. Thus he manifested his storyline by making an acquisition consistent with where he wanted the business to go. The judgment then sets up a process of reshaping the business in new and unforeseen ways; the Amersham judgment leads to authoring the next chapter of the future. The iterative process of making judgments to further the storyline, which then helps write and revise the future storyline, is how leaders like Immelt drive successful transformations.

Immelt makes it clear that making strategic judgments, along with picking people and handling crises, are his most important jobs. He must execute his strategy to win, but in a changing world he sees the formulation of strategy as critical. "There's more importance today on strategy, picking businesses, than ever before," he told a group of business students in 2004. "When you're chairman of GE, one of the things you really do is spend a lot of time thinking about businesses. Which businesses to pick, investing in health care, investing in entertainment. And we have very clear standards for what makes a great GE business. But the notion of strategy, in the environment we're in, good execution and good operations aren't enough to fix a business with a flawed strategy. So you need to spend time understanding what businesses you think are going to work, what business models seem to make sense. And strategy is more important than ever before."[3]

When we look back over the last three decades, the academics and consultants have not been all that helpful for CEOs like Jeff Immelt, A. G. Lafley, Jim McNerney, and the others in this book.

A REVIEW OF STRATEGY CONCEPTS

Many of the leaders with whom we've discussed strategy mentioned how unhelpful the overly simplistic, rationalistic models of strategy created by the business school professors and consultants are. These models offer by-the-cookbook linear recipes for making strategic judgments. They generally follow the same basic formula, which is:

Step 1: Look at your environmental threats and opportunities.
Step 2: Look at your internal strengths and weaknesses.
Step 3: Come up with products and services that will win, etc.

Within each step are all kinds of substeps and analytic models and approaches that can be applied. All commonsense, but not very helpful.

These models come out of the 1960s "scientific management" school of thought many developed or first applied at GE in the late 1960s along with a host of strategic planning tools. At GE there were almost two hundred people on the strategic planning staff when Welch took over as CEO in 1981. They were doing sophisticated computer modeling and had amassed a vast database called PIMS (Profit Impact of Market Strategy, which Sidney Schoeffler and colleagues developed at GE in the 1960s) that enthralled business school faculty and was taught to MBA students as the way to approach strategic decisions. The famous "cash cow," "dog," "stars," and "question marks" two-by-two matrix depicting market share and projected market growth was developed at GE with the help of the Boston Consulting Group (BCG). There was a second famous matrix developed at GE with McKinsey, a nine-cell one that plotted businesses on two other dimensions: market attractiveness and competitive strength. As business school professors in the 1970s and into the 1980s, we recall the strategy books, articles, and courses built around teaching these tools to MBAs, giving them the illusion of how to become great business strategists. At GE the actual results of all this supposed rigor was a huge bureaucracy of planning, which Welch knew was adding no strategic value to GE; quite the opposite, it was undermining good leadership. In fact, when he was running the Plastics business he would go along with the process by hiring McKinsey to produce impressive strategic planning books, often leather-bound, to show to the corporate staff and CEO. In fact these books were marginally irrelevant to what he was doing to grow his business. Welch's strategic judgments were made through highly interactive, informal, and rigorous dialogues with his team, customers, and suppliers. As he would say, "Real staff with real people."

When leaders of businesses came in to do a business review when Welch first became CEO in 1981, many had their strategy planner present the business strategy to the CEO and vice chairman, almost like an academic conference. Welch would often press the leader for answers and have the business leader turn to the strategy manager for the answer. He felt this was nuts—leaders need to own strategy, not staff bureaucrats. In vintage Welch fashion, he made a very clear judgment call. He fired all of the strategic planners in the first few years and made it clear that CEOs of businesses needed to make their own judgment calls on strategy. It is the leader's responsibility to use a combination of analytic tools, intuition, empirical data, and analysis to come up with the strategic judgment calls for his/her businesses.

Many academics also came around to "firing" the rationalistic school of strategy by grounding their critique in psychology and the human capacity for using these tools and the social dynamics of group and organizational decision making. Amitai Etzioni laid out the critique of the rationalistic approach in a *Harvard Business Review* article. Etzioni pointed out that

psychologists have shown—1. The human mind cannot hold the complexities . . . brains are too limited and can only focus on eight facts at a time. 2. Our ability to calculate probabilities, especially to combine two or more probabilities essential for most decision making, is low. 3. We learn slowly and make the same mistakes over and over. 4. We are all prone to let our emotions get in the way—especially fear-evoking anxiety.[4]

These factors can all add up to bad judgment as the outcome.

In addition to the limits of the individual leader being able to act in a totally rational fashion, the judgment process is even messier when we start to include the social context of making judgments.

One groundbreaking piece of work dealing with the social context was Irving Janis's "groupthink," in which he analyzed how smart people with dysfunctional political dynamics make bad judgments. His famous analysis of President Kennedy's Bay of Pigs fiasco versus the successful judgments made with the Cuban Missile Crisis show how good and bad social dynamics lead to good and bad strategy judgments. Janis argues that bad judgment occurs because of human problems: "1. Defensive avoidance (delaying decisions unduly), 2. Overreaction (making decisions impulsively in order to escape the anxious state), and 3. Hypervigilance (obsessively collecting more and more information instead of making a decision) . . . political facts are another complicating consideration . . . important decisions have political dimensions—individuals have conflicting goals . . . successful decision-making strategies must necessarily include a place for cooperation, coalition building and the whole panorama of differing personalities, perspectives, responsibilities and powers."[5]

Another dominant tradition in the academic world has been to view strategy as a "muddling through" process where events and political trade-offs have organizations stumbling into their future.[6] Thus we have two traditions in the literature that do not appear to reflect the empirical reality. Strategic judgment is far from a rationalistic process, as many of the normative frameworks taught to our MBAs and sold by consultants, nor is it a purely intuitive and political muddling process.

Good strategic judgment is a blend. It is built off the leader's capacity to intellectually frame the world of opportunity and the organization's potential as well as the leader's ability to mobilize and align key leaders to help make a smart judgment and get it executed. Like all good judgments, strategic judgments need to be a process: (1) preparation, (2) the call, and (3) execution.

Etzioni has come closest to our view of judgment, in what he calls a "mixed scanning model." He posits that mixed scanning involves two sets of judgments: (1) broad, fundamental choices about the organization's basic policy and direction (for Welch it was his strategic framing for GE's portfolio of businesses: number one or number two; fix, close, or sell). In our model, this framing represented Welch's Teachable Point of View, which then was crafted into a living storyline for the future, one that provided the context and platform for: (2) incremental strategic judgments that implement and particularize the storyline.[7]

Rationalism is a deeply optimistic approach that assumes we can learn all we need to know; mixed scanning is an adaptive strategy that acknowledges our inability to know more than part of what we would need to make a genuinely rational decision. Mixed scanning seeks to make the best possible use of partial knowledge rather than proceed blindly with no knowledge at all. The mixed scanning model applies in medicine, and it has many parallels to how our organizational leaders make good strategy judgments. Mixed scanning only works if there is an underlying Teachable Point of View. In medicine it means a clear set of *ideas* regarding physiology, diseases, and treatments; *values* (how to treat human life as captured in medicine's Hippocratic oath); and *emotional energy* (how to motivate the patient, other health providers, and family to rally around the patient). For serious illnesses good physicians develop a storyline for the patient, that is, a future scenario for how the patient will do in the future. It is upon that platform that the "mixed scanning model" is descriptive of how medical judgments get made.

This is the same for organizational leaders: (1) the Teachable Point of View is the conceptual foundation; (2) the storyline is the pathway to the future; and (3) good judgments are made on that platform and reflect Etzioni's "mixed scanning" model.

Mixed Scanning Model by Physicians

They know what they want to achieve and which parts of the organism to focus on . . . unlike rationalists they do not commit all their resources on the basis of preliminary diagnosis; they do not wait for every conceivable scrap of personal history and scientific data before initiating treatment. Doctors survey the general health of the patient and then zero in on his or her particular complaint. They initiate tentative treatment, and if it fails, they try something else.

1. Focused trial and error—adapting to partial knowledge . . . knowing where to start the search for an effective intervention and choking outcomes at intervals to adjust and modify the intervention . . . differs from outright trial and error, which assumes no knowledge at all . . . feeling one's way to an effective course of action despite the lack of essential chunks of data . . . and adaptive, not a rationalistic, strategy.

2. Tentativeness . . . a commitment to revise one's course as necessary . . . physicians telling patient to try medicine for x number of days and then check in . . . change directions on the basis of results . . . humility in the face of reality (Welch changing course as the facts change . . . stop or start and activity).

3. Procrastination . . . delay permits the collection of fresh evidence, the processing of additional data, and the presentation of new options . . . it can also give the problem a chance to recede untreated.

4. Decision staggering—form of delay. . . . Federal Reserve adjusting the rate a half a point at a time.

5. Fractionalizing . . . treats important judgments as a series of subdecisions . . . Staggering and fractionalizing allow the company to relate turning points in the decision process to turning points in the supply of information.

6. Hedging bets . . . diversified portfolio.

7. Maintaining strategic reserves—another form of hedging bets . . . reserves to cover unanticipated costs to respond to unforeseen opportunities.

8. Reversible decisions . . . avoiding overcommitment when only partial information is available.[8]

LEADERSHIP AND STRATEGY JUDGMENTS

In the remainder of the chapter we will discuss good and bad strategy judgments made by leaders. We will examine how leaders deal with the total process: preparation, the call, and execution. First, there is Michael Dell, whose lack of a timely judgment on a new Dell strategy threw the company into a crisis and led to the forced resignation of his CEO, Kevin Rollins. Then there is Brad Anderson's strategic judgment to move Best Buy from product-centric to customer-centric and how he engaged his expanded leadership team and his social network to support the judgment process. David Novak, CEO of Yum! Brands, made a monumental strategic judgment to leverage his multiple brands—KFC, Taco Bell, Pizza Hut, Long John Silver's, and A&W—with multibrand stores, including the unique hybrid restaurants with one-half Taco Bell and the other half KFC, or Pizza Hut and KFC, or any other combination. Jim McNerney at Boeing made a strategy judgment not to change the strategy he inherited at Boeing but to turbo-charge strategy execution. Jim Owens at Caterpillar did much the same as McNerney.

In the next chapter we will then delve deeply into the very complex and dynamic strategic shifts being led by Jeff Immelt at GE. What makes Immelt's strategy judgments fascinating is that GE spans the widest swath of businesses inside any one company on the planet, including retail financial services, commercial financial services, jet engines, medical equipment, power generation equipment, TV, movies, theme parks at Universal, lightbulbs, and refrigerators, to name just a part of the portfolio. Immelt crafted a new TPOV for GE, started writing his storyline and making strategy judgments over the last five years that have yet to result in breakout stock performance; it is a massive work in progress.

Leadership Judgment Process

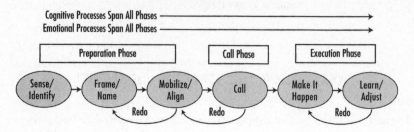

Dell Judgments: Slow to sense/identify need for change. Set up a strategic judgment.

Best Buy Judgments: Extensive engagement of dozens of leaders in preparation of customer-centric strategy.

Yum! Brands Judgments: Multibranding did not mobilize and align leaders at first.

Boeing Judgments: McNerney made strategic judgment to stay with existing strategy.

Caterpillar Judgments: Owens executed strategy judgment over many years.

Strategy Judgments at Dell

Bad strategic judgments result in stocks collapsing and CEOs being forced to resign. One notable case is Dell, which ended up in a crisis in early 2007, leading Michael Dell and the board to force the resignation of the CEO he had handpicked and supported for five years. He blamed Kevin Rollins for not making a timely judgment to change the Dell strategy in the face of renewed HP competitiveness. Strategic judgments were missed, resulting in Dell stock declining over 45 percent while HP's rose 90 percent. The leadership of both Rollins and Dell misread the customer and his competitors. In early 2007 Dell was still in a crisis. He personally jettisoned key leaders and brought in new talent, all key people judgments. Dell then started making strategic judgments aimed at turning the company around. The turnaround challenge he has created for himself is his own doing. (This is a very different story than that of founder Steve Jobs's coming back to Apple after seven years away, thus not having to own up to any bad judgments during that period. Jobs has been able to make strategic judgments that have completely and successfully transformed Apple.) Whether Dell is able to make good strategy judgments will also be his own doing; to fail would mark the beginning of the end for Dell as a company. He needs to exercise exceptionally good strategic judgment to successfully compete with companies such as HP, Lenovo, and Acer.

Good judgment starts with sensing and identifying the need for a judgment. Dell failed to see the competitive world unfolding. In the judgment process Michael Dell and Kevin Rollins failed to sense and identify the need for a new strategy. HP was on a rebound and caught Dell by surprise. Dell therefore missed the opportunity to frame and name a need for a strategic judgment to stay ahead of HP, which resulted in creating a crisis. In early 2007 Dell's judgments in the crisis were to go back to the basics and build a new team around him. By mid-2009 Dell's market capitalization was $24 billion while HP's was $89 billion; the market clearly registered its opinion of Dell's strategy. Michael Dell and his team will need to do more than cut costs and go back to the basics to strategically turn the company around and be truly competitive. The Dell Teachable Point of View building blocks need redoing and a new storyline developed for the future.

Best Buy Strategy Judgment: Customer Centricity

Best Buy has been tremendously successful as a mass-market retailer of consumer electronics. With more than eleven hundred retail locations, a fast-growing dot-com outlet, as well as services (the Geek Squad), Best Buy's 140,000-plus employees have a North America market share of more than 20 percent and revenues of over $45 billion. Best Buy's large-store, noncommissioned format, coupled with wide product assortments and strong process controls, has made it the leading U.S. consumer electronics specialty retailer and a strong performing stock on the New York Stock Exchange (NYSE).

After a great run, five-year best-performing stock, the world changed in early 2002 and Best Buy was challenged by new and encroaching competitors seeking to take advantage of the proliferation of digital devices and the convergence between electronics and entertainment. Formidable competitors such as Dell, Walmart, and Amazon all aimed to take market share in consumer electronics. Brad Anderson, a newly minted CEO in 2002, took a stock hit and had to make a huge strategic judgment in early 2003 to transform Best Buy from a product-centric, one-size-fits-all (each store basically the same with the same products, labor models, etc.) into a customer-centric retail company with deep consumer insight. He differentiated value propositions so that individual stores were tailored to their markets, which include services and installation and the ability to build sustained customer relationships. What makes this strategic judgment particularly interesting is the process Brad Anderson used to engage hundreds of Best Buy leaders in the process of preparing him to make the big shift from product-centric to customer-centric strategic judgment. It is a process that one of the authors, Noel, had the opportunity to help architect and be an insider/outsider working with Brad Anderson and his team of leaders.

PREPARATION PHASE

Best Buy began in 1966 with a single store in St. Paul, Minnesota, called Sound of Music. During the 1980s the company expanded into video, appliances, and other electronics, adopting the name Best Buy in 1983. Best Buy pioneered its superstore format with forty-five-thousand-square-foot stores in 1985 and featured noncommissioned salespeople. Much of its aggressive store expansion happened during the 1990s. The company continues to open sixty to seventy new store locations per year.

During the 1990s the company more than doubled in size and head count. It historically managed scale through uniformity of business process, competitive hiring practices, and a culture biased toward execution. Store performance has been measured on published scorecards, creating a culture of aggressive competitiveness.

In early 2002, Brad Anderson took over as CEO. The stock took a dive after a five-year positive run and he sensed and identified a need for a new strategy. In meetings with Larry Selden (coauthor with Geoff Colvin of *Angel Customers and Demon Customers: Discover Which Is Which and Turbo-charge Your Stock*), Noel, and Best Buy's senior team, Anderson framed and named a "shift to customer centricity" as the strategic judgment being contemplated.[9] By the autumn Anderson was working to mobilize and align the nearly two hundred officers in a meeting at an upstate resort in Minnesota. It was at this meeting that he told his team that this was not a trivial transformation; it would require a wrenching cultural change in which they looked at the customer-value proposition, which in turn made them change the store offerings and in turn meant they would have new leadership in the store and at the associate interface with their customers.

It took about six months of work, engaging over one hundred of Best Buy's senior leaders to discover the customer segments they would go after, figuring out the value propositions for these segments, and then developing plans for how to execute on those segments. The mobilize and align phase of the process was led by Brad Anderson and his senior team using an action-learning process, one in which teams of executives, six or seven per team, worked part-time, mostly putting in an additional 30 to 40 percent of time beyond their day jobs. They mined data, interviewed current and former customers, visited competitors and interviewed their customers, debated new value propositions, and benchmarked other companies including ones outside the industry, such as Royal Bank of Canada and GE. They also went out in the field to figure out what competitors were doing, what Best Buy was capable of doing, and then formulating recommendations for Anderson and the top team. The process was highly engaged, chaotic at times, but highly energized; all the participants knew that they were going to come up with judgments that would reinvent the company. This was a look over the horizon at what was emerging in the industry. While diving deeply into customer segments they had to reinvent for an anticipated new competitive landscape. When the teams were launched in January, the expectation was clearly set that implementation would take place four months later, with actual new physical store layouts and product and service offerings, coupled with a new store set of process and extensive staff development. It was to launch a handful of stores in one market. The other expectation created at the launch was that the leaders of the new segments would be selected from among the action-learning participants, which increased the pressure in an already intense, high-expectation setting.

Brad Anderson and his senior team did not make the actual judgment call to commit totally to a customer-centric strategy until midway through the spring of 2003. By May not only was Best Buy committed strategically; it was well into the execution process. Six segments were selected, including Best Buy for business, a high-income female segment, and a high-end male customer segment. Best Buy for business aimed at small-to mid-six-figure businesses as well as segments for younger up-and-comers. In order to execute, each segment got a leader and team assigned full-time to drive the segment into the targeted stores.

Anderson and the top team spent days with the action-learning teams, learning about the segments, visiting stores, and finally engaging in a workshop for several days, spending three to four hours per proposed segment to make the judgment call, yes or no, to move ahead.

EXECUTION

The customer-centric transformation required a massive strategic shift impacting Best Buy's employees in corporate functions, field support, and retail stores. Starting in 2005, elements of customer centricity were in all stores. Not all stores had physical changes, but all stores made "soft changes" including sales strategy focused on the needs of individual customers. By early 2007 most of Best Buy stores were operating in the new customer-centric model with focused segments and new product and service offerings tailored to the local markets. In preparation, there had been massive training of the store associates, introduction of new labor models, and implementation of totally new performance scorecards.

Today, the customer-centric stores track daily P&Ls, which include data at the customer level (segment profitability, value proposition performance, and so on), product/department level (category revenue, department profit, specialty labor productivity, and so on), and store level (traffic, average selling price, close rate, and so on). In order to develop the leadership capacity to execute on the strategy, the first wave of customer-centric stores taught all the associates new capabilities. A key element of the execution was that every morning these customer-centric stores conducted "chalk talks" with key store personnel to review the previous day's performance, share their learnings, and prepare for improved performance the next day. All of this was supported by multiple workshops with thousands of associates being taught business acumen, leadership, and customer-centricity training.

These changes represent a profound divergence from Best Buy's practices in the past. In an effort to create more nimbleness and innovation, Best Buy is "unleashing the power of its people" to think like business owners. This will require store leaders to create a culture of "owner operators," instead of asking employees to adhere strictly to centrally defined policies and procedures. This translates into associates in the store making judgments that are in support of the overall customer-centric storyline.

BEST BUY REDO LOOP

A new set of strategic judgments are being made at Best Buy in 2007; namely, how to be truly customer-centric in a consumer electronics world where 65 percent of the purchases are controlled by women, and fully 90 percent are significantly influenced by women.

This is in an industry where the workforces and the focus have been almost totally male dominated. Julie Gilbert, former senior executive at Best Buy, who headed up the high-end male segment when Best Buy launched customer centricity, whose track record included launching and developing this highly profitable segment, engaged the brainpower of thirteen thousand of Best Buy's employees in a "redo loop." She drove a "learn and adjust process" during the execution of the customer-centricity strategy, utilizing the insights of Best Buy female associates and customers. The redo loop is coming up with new ways of capturing the female purchasing power while simultaneously developing women leaders at Best Buy using an innovation-action-learning approach.

Gilbert launched a unique woman's network in 2004 called WOLF (Women's Leadership Forum). All thirteen thousand are on teams. In addition to workshops around the company for women to innovate and improve Best Buy, develop leadership skills, and give back to the community, Gilbert has launched a high-level strategic redo loop.

Winning with Women

A Key Company Strategy

What the market says:

- Women spent $68 billion on Consumer Electronics in 2005, which is more than ½ of all spending
- Women influence 89% of ALL spending in electronics
- Women are the key purchasers of services tied to electronics
- *USA Today* article "Study: Women like tech toys more than shoes" indicates that 3 out of 4 women said they would:

  - Choose a plasma TV over a diamond solitaire necklace
  - Choose a top-of-the-line cell phone over designer shoes
  - Choose an iPod over a little black dress

If we don't win with women, we lose more than half of EVERY market opportunity

COMMITMENT • NETWORK • GIVEBACK

There are over one hundred teams of women—with men helping—specifically dedicated to redoing the business model for Best Buy to embrace the female customer base.

Gilbert's personal judgment to start was framed and named through her personal journey as a leader. She describes it as follows:

> I was touring Best Buy stores as part of my high-end male customer segment job where female employees frequently hugged me. One day, about two and a half years ago, I asked one why she did it. She said, "You give us hope that we can one day become you." It made me want to help women more directly. That night I had a dream and woke up at two A.M. Growing up in South Dakota, I often heard the howls of wolves or coyotes howling in the distance during full moons. In my dream, I heard the same thing, but instead of wolves or coyotes, it was

WOLF Innovation – Teams Across the Country
Let the unique voices be heard
Unleash the passion to drive the business

Reinventing Best Buy as we know it—to serve women and create the future female focused businesses internationally

Some Areas of Innovation:
- New Selling Strategies
- New Products
- GeekSquad Service Offerings and Marketing
- Trend and Fashion Products
- New Store Design
- New Concept Design
- Relationship Selling
- Recruiting and Retention
- Marketing
- Multi-Channel purchasing experiences
- Store Environment
- New Services
- New Product-Tags In All Stores
- New Female Concept

Some Key WOLF Wins:

- **WOLF Trend and Fashion Accessories team**
  Partnered with key designers to launch new product collections in 100 BBY stores including BBY Mobile concept by Back to School.

- **WOLF lifestyle product signage team:**
  Changing ALL product tags in all BBY stores to be lifestyle oriented vs. "speeds and feeds" oriented. *Example:* instead of a washer saying: 4.385 cubic square feet, it will say "washes 3 laundry baskets in one load." Launching June 1 in all stores as new skus hit the shelves.

- **WOLF Job Share team:**
  The Iowa WOLF pack led the innovation to reduce turnover amongst our employees by creating a program to enable employees to share a role and maintain benefits—thereby reducing turnover of talent and increasing employee morale.

- **WOLF.com gift registry team:**
  The team revamped .com to ensure gifts purchased on .com can include a note to the receiver of the gift as to who it is from along with a note from the sender. Currently in phase 2 of implementation.

COMMITMENT • NETWORK • GIVEBACK

women's voices. Inspiration struck me and I realized that each of us feels alone, like a stray, but if we are loyal like wolves are loyal to each other, and we bond together with other males, we can reinvent the company and the industry. *And* we can build amazing leadership skills in the process.

Brad Anderson, CEO of Best Buy, sees the wisdom of what Gilbert is doing:

Women now influence 90 percent of consumer electronics purchases, from the type and look of the big-screen TV to the color
of the iPod speakers for the living room, Best Buy says. The
Consumer Electronics Association estimates their influence is
less, but still significant and growing. It says women influence
57 percent of purchases, or $80 billion of the $140 billion spent
on consumer electronics this year.[10]

"Sure, our stores used to have one primary customer in
mind . . . that was the young, techno-savvy male," says Best Buy
CEO Brad Anderson in an e-mail interview. "Today we know there
are more than just young men in our stores—men and women, all
ages, all ethnicities and uncountable backgrounds."

But, he concedes, "Women likely will notice and appreciate some
of the changes more."

The WOLF network is transforming all aspects of the business.
Best Buy owns Geek Squad, which is thousands of technicians who
can install and support the technology hardware that Best Buy sells.
The Geeks started out as a very catchy unique brand with an image of
white male "geeks," just as the name states. Gilbert is helping transform the Geeks to be an active change agent on the female journey.
As he states

The Geek Squad is a company within Best Buy that helps customers trouble-shoot their electronic problems. Recently we've
seen where the women geeks, we call DIVAS [Dynamic Intelligent Vivacious Agents with Solutions] have turned up more
business simply by being . . . well . . . women. They may be
called out to a home for a computer problem, and then the
homeowner feels so comfortable with them that they take them
to a second electronic snafu and so on. Sometimes they even
invite them to dinner. . . . DIVAS are fairly new, but because
they see things from a woman's perspective they are uncover-
ing issues the guys might miss. One of our Geek Agents—
Kat S.—was very passionate about educating parents on the
risks their kids face on the Internet. [Child predators can easily find kids based on information they share freely with the
emergence of sites like myspace.com and others.] She created

a brochure and training for parents so that they will be educated on this and ensure their children are safe. It's called the *Internet Lingo Guide for Parents, Keep Your Kids Safe.* This is illustrative of many new innovations coming out of the initiative. We frame this as a "redo" loop as it does not alter the fundamental strategic judgment to go from product-centric to customer-centric; it is a quantum "redo" in the execution phase as it has the potential to turbo-charge Best Buy's execution. One example that foreshadows what is possible is how the change in staffing ratios in some of the Best Buy stores has a big impact:

Best Buy has the numbers to show that the more women they have per store, the higher the sales. In stores where the staff is comprised of five men for every woman, the comparative store sales are up an average of five percent. When the ratio is 4 to 1, it's up seven percent and when it's 3 to 1 it's up ten percent.

This is just staffing ratios. What is ahead are the results of the hundred teams coming up with new product offerings, new services, new store formats, as well as new career and staffing models for the whole of Best Buy. This is no small "redo loop" that Anderson, Gilbert, and colleagues are driving.

One exciting example of how the WOLF effort is paying off is the work led by Geek Squad associate Moria Hardek in the community. The Geek Squad created a summer academy for three hundred girls to get them engaged in learning about technology. This summer academy represents not only a way for developing these young women, but a great way for WOLF to both give back to the community and groom future potential Geek Squad members. At the conclusion of the camp, Moria Hardek sent Julie Gilbert an e-mail showing why this was a good judgment. We (the Agents) are leaving Summer Academy trying desperately to remember what it's like to return to our "real lives" . . . but I know we will never know because our lives have been changed forever. We are utterly exhausted after having pushed ourselves to the limit physically, mentally, and emotionally for the past fifteen days, but I still find myself having a little spring left in my step as I think about the future of Summer Academy work.

Geek Squad Summer Academy: Mother McAuley

Building female leaders around technology

What is it:

4-day summer academy for 300 school girls to get them actively engaged in learning technology (building PC's, networking, etc.)

Our main objective:

Increase the number of women in the IT pipeline. Women do not automatically choose technology due, to a lack of "proper" exposure to technology at a young age, and also due to the stereotype that woman and technology do not belong together. We are out to destroy that myth. Hopefully we will create the next generation of Geek Squad Agents with a much larger number of them being women. This can only mean great things for our business...having our workforce reflect our customer base, which is 65% women.

Current Plan:

Scale this program nationwide to impact girls, including minority groups.

Why Mother McAuley:

Mother McAuley is the largest private girls' school in the United States and has been building female leaders for over 161 years.

Classes for the girls:

- PC Build and Operating Systems (building a computer)
- Networking (wireless and wired)
- Digital Imaging
- Programming and HTML (make your own webpage and beginner object-based programming)
- There were also "fun techie activities":
  - Jewelry Making
  - Geocaching (a scavenger hunt with GPS)
  - Dance Dance Revolution (video game)
  - Guitar Hero (video game)
  - Wii Olympics (video game)

We create environments to build female leaders in our communities

COMMITMENT • NETWORK • GIVEBACK

WOLF GOES GLOBAL

In early 2009, Julie Gilbert left Best Buy to launch Wolf as a global, multicompany effort. She continues to support the Best Buy Wolf organization from outside while mobilizing companies and women around the world to be part of "Wolf means business" which Gilbert says the goals are to:

- Drive business in the female space and diversify your company at the same time
- Make your company the place for women to work and shop.
- Create a decentralized innovation capability
- Build leaders through innovation, automatically

Yum! Brands Multibranding Judgment

David Novak, CEO of Yum! Brands, was struggling with how to get more unit volume. He said:

> For years McDonald's has been the envy of the industry for their high average U.S. unit volumes, at about $1.6 million, almost twice that of the average Yum! Brands restaurants in the U.S. One reason why McDonald's has such high volumes is they offer the consumer more choices. In fact they offer seven different types of food—everything from burgers, chicken, fish, shakes, and breakfast. McDonald's has something for everybody and this drives sales. Historically, each of our brands has focused on one food category. Pizza Hut has pizza in its name. KFC means Kentucky Fried Chicken. Taco Bell stands for Mexican style food. And every time we've tried to broaden our appeal by moving into new categories, it fails because our brands stand for just one thing. No one is looking for a KFC or Taco Bell hamburger. But at the same time, consumers do want more choice and convenience. And what we've proven is that consumers love the idea of getting variety with branded authority—accessing two brands in the same restaurant—multibranding . . . we started with combinations of KFC–Taco Bell and Taco Bell–Pizza Hut. We learned that we were able to

add $100,000 to $400,000 per unit in average sales, dramatically improving our already strong unit economics. . . . Because of the significant sales increases we are generating with multibranding, we are remodeling much of our existing U.S. asset base by adding a second brand.

Novak made the strategy judgment for multibranding and then hit a brick wall in the execution phase. The two brands in a box, two stores within one store, were not possible to execute due to the siloed nature of Yum! Brands. David Novak talked to us in an interview and took ownership for his problems in getting good execution on his strategic judgment to multibrand:

> One of our challenges in this is that we've got five brands that have stood alone for years. Culturally, there's great pride at each individual and you want that. When you talk about bringing two brands together, under one roof, well, that's breaking new ground in the industry. It's breaking a lot of cultural history and tradition.

These were historically stand-alone brands—KFC, Pizza Hut, and Taco Bell—with their own merchandising, their own operating mechanisms, marketing, and so on. In the new format they were expected to work together. Novak's judgment was dependent on flawless execution of teamwork in these new-format, dual-brand stores. The organization resisted and it did not work. The execution required a lot of learning and readjusting.

Novak took personal ownership of the problems in executing his strategic judgment. He told us that the expectation got bogged down because:

> People thought I loved it too much, and that I wasn't seeing the issues and the complexity that was associated with it. I didn't do a good enough job as a leader stepping back and saying, "Hey, look, I know that we've got a lot of challenges here." I was ready to charge the hill without taking full account of the cultural pride of each individual brand. I would have been more effective if I said, "Hey, I realize that culturally we're proud of each brand and there's lot of complexity with this new

approach. Let's take the time to really think this through so we can satisfy our customers who want branded choice and convenience under one roof."

I got a lot of feedback from our people that they didn't think I was looking at the executional issues. They thought that I was just pushing towards the vision. People knew I was so passionate about it, they felt like I wasn't really open to even hearing it.

So what I heard from my team was, these were the issues. And I realized that a lot of the issues fell right in my lap. So I would say that I didn't change my strategic direction, but I was still behind multibranding. We're making more progress because I listened to people who had the productive conflict with me to get me to understand that I was seen as the guy who had his head in the sand on some of the issues that needed to be addressed.

Boeing Strategic Judgment: Execute Flawlessly

Jim McNerney came into a troubled company and told his team: "My goal is not to replace or reinvent Boeing's vision and strategy. It is to reinvigorate the Boeing culture, spur growth and provide the tools for every individual in the company to make a greater contribution." He quickly developed his Teachable Point of View and storyline presented in chapter 2, which supported his big strategy judgment, namely, stay the course.

It's all about understanding what organizations can and can't do. That's where the judgment comes in. It's not about strategy. Strategy's relatively easy to define. You can do a market assessment, you can do a competitive assessment, you can figure out a way you can differentiate yourself, and if you can do it, then you can make money and grow. That is . . . It's not easy, but I'm saying, that is more commonly done well than the assessment a leader has to make about execution—whether it can be done.

McNerney was on the Boeing board of directors for several years prior to becoming CEO. He was CEO at 3M while Harry Stonesipher was CEO at Boeing and thus was involved in approving the Boeing strategy. When Stonesipher was dismissed and McNerney accepted the CEO position, he quickly articulated his Teachable Point of View for

Boeing and started to craft his future storyline, which led him to conclude that no fundamental change in strategic direction was his big judgment. He told us that his job was to make sure the organization could execute. He told us that this was a different stance than he would have taken early in his career as a consultant.

> So if an organization's standing in front of you with this great strategy and says that to implement it we're going to do this using skills we've never managed before, selling to customers we've never seen before, yet it fits the strategy beautifully, judgment has to be applied. As to whether it can be done, how long it will take . . . And that is really derived from experience. I have a very different view of that than I did twenty-five years ago, when I was a McKinsey consultant.

Caterpillar Strategy

Jim Owens has had a very successful run as CEO of Caterpillar. Since he has been CEO he has added more than 50 percent new market capitalization to the company. He has made strategic judgments to continue to drive globalization and position Caterpillar against its traditional cyclicality. Owens made a strategic judgment to break free from the automotive industry model of stuffing dealers with inventories and products, which creates a lot of the ups and downs in the industry. Owens told the *Wall Street Journal*:

> We want to keep some dealer inventory out there so they can see it and buy it and try it, but we want to get away from having them carry significant amounts of inventory. If you look back . . . dealer inventory swings have in every case aggravated the business cycle of Caterpillar. We work overtime to build inventory in the up cycles and then in down cycles help them get it moved by price discounting or other bad practices . . . this is a huge cultural change.[11]

Another strategic judgment made by Owens, which is related to his overall "stay the course" with the basic TPOV and storyline for

Caterpillar, is regarding his focus on the bottom line and execution. Owens stated:

> What we're really about in this near term is just a relentless focus on execution. We're focused on introducing a Caterpillar production system that is universal across all of our manufacturing operations worldwide. We've had a propensity to do things at least slightly differently all over the world. We've . . . created our own recipe book. Whether our top-line sales are $45 billion or $60 billion is going to be a lot less important than pulling off that operational excellence. The Holy Grail is not top line sales growth; it's bottom-line profit growth.[12]

For Caterpillar, 2009 was a very rough year, requiring layoffs of 22,000 and retrenchment due to the global recession. In spite of this very tough year, one has to judge Jim Owens' tenure as CEO an extraordinary success. His stock has consistently outperformed the S&P in good times and in the 2009 recession. He has made strategic judgments that have repositioned Caterpillar for the next decade. The current economic crisis will be weathered. In June of 2009 Jim Owens said: "It is a tribute to Caterpillar's strategic 'trough' planning and financial strength that we are maintaining the dividend rate in the face of the worst economic crisis since the Great Depression. Just as we have in previous downturns, Caterpillar is positioning itself to emerge from this recession as a stronger company."

◆ ◆ ◆

Strategy judgments alter where the organization is heading. They require the leadership to have a clear TPOV and storyline and then have the courage to make the calls and see that they follow through on the execution.

In the next chapter we will drill down in depth with Jeff Immelt's strategic judgments at GE.

8

STRATEGY JUDGMENTS AT GE

■ **Immelt: "My Job Is to Lead GE in . . . a New World."**
- He foresees a global environment of slower growth, more regulation.
- He envisions a route to success through emerging markets.

■ **Greatest Opportunities Are in Two Broad Areas**
- Developing economies will make big infrastructure investments.
- The biggest needs in developed areas will be medical and environmental.

■ **GE's Competitive Strength Will Be Its Technological Expertise**
- It will develop new technologies to serve new markets.
- It will find new uses for existing technologies.

◆ ◆ ◆

IMMELT'S GROWTH JUDGMENTS FOR GE

The number one question is the organic growth rate, how much cash you generate to drive growth. Our goal is two to three times the global GDP. A company of GE's

size requires developing a $12 billion company every
year. GE has to create a company the size of Nike every
year to be able to have that kind of growth, and that's
the challenge.[1]

From its earliest days, General Electric has had a tradition of using
groundbreaking research and professional management as a means
for enhancing performance. The brilliant inventor Thomas Edison
started the company with his patenting of the incandescent lightbulb
in 1878. GE's first CEO, Charles Coffin, set the fundamental building blocks of an integrated yet diverse company in 1893.

The company was integrated by common management discipline
and practices, centralized financial and human resource controls,
and the creation of the nation's first industrial R&D center. It was
a diversified electrical company making lightbulbs, streetcars, tur-
bines, and related products that fed off a common R&D base. Coffin
also created a set of standard management practices. By the 1920s,
GE was conducting management retreats every summer in the "Thousand Islands" in upstate New York, with the leadership duo of Gerard
Swope and Owen Young, president and CEO. This was the precursor
to the current-day leadership development center at GE's Crotonville.
The Crotonville center, now officially named the John F. Welch Leadership Center, was created in 1956.

The GE DNA has always sought to add value across a diverse
portfolio through technology transfer, financial and managerial disciplines, development of managerial and leadership talent, and common processes and systems. As Jeff Immelt has made judgment calls
about how to reshape GE, the building blocks of this DNA of integrated diversity has informed his thinking and actions. Immelt articulated this DNA in the company's annual report for 2005:

> There are many companies that have been created through
> acquisitions that are frequently compared to GE, called con-
> glomerates. However, our business model is designed to achieve
> superior performance through the synergies of a large, multi-
> business company structure. The following strategic impera-
> tives provide the foundation for creating shareowner value:

1. Sustain a strong portfolio of leadership businesses that fit together to grow consistently through the cycles
2. Drive common initiatives across the company that accelerate growth, satisfy customers and expand margins, and
3. Develop people to grow a common culture that is adaptive, ethical, and drives execution.[2]

This model is very different from that of a holding company or a portfolio of investments such as Warren Buffett's. Buffett does not engage in any form of "integrated diversity." So his strategy judgments are about which assets to buy or sell rather than about how to operate them. This holding company model is very different from the GE multibusiness operating company model.

At GE, strategy judgments are made in a much more hands-on context than in a holding company. But there are many paradoxes in the GE model. The heads of GE's businesses have a great deal of local autonomy; yet there is also a lot of central control. For example, businesses at GE are of themselves *Fortune* 100 in size. (Infrastructure with sales of $46 billion ranks ahead of United Technologies, which is number 42 on the *Fortune* 100 list, and GE Industrial is bigger than all of Honeywell.) Jeff Immelt works closely with the CEOs of the businesses on their strategy, their budgets, their succession planning, and involvement in corporate initiatives such as lean Six Sigma quality program, growth platforms, leadership development, and technology transfer.

Immelt's calendar reflects these tasks. He is personally teaching at Crotonville every few weeks. He visits the Global Research Center as many as four or five times a year. He gathers the heads of the business together with key corporate staff four times a year for multiday sharing workshops at Crotonville. Immelt also goes out to each business unit to do succession planning reviews, twenty days' worth of reviews. He also holds all-day strategy reviews with each business, and operating plan reviews. Not one of those activities exists in a pure holding company. Judgment at GE is much more of a team sport, even though paradoxically the CEO makes the final call on the big items. During the preparation phase there is a great deal of mobilizing and aligning of key stakeholders for any given strategy judgment. This occurs in the various GE face-to-face forums for the heads of the business.

GE is also not like a new entrepreneurial company that starts with a clean sheet of paper. It has a legacy of 130 businesses, organizations, processes, and practices involving over 320,000 global employees. Thus, Jeff Immelt's strategic judgments are, to some extent, limited and constrained by the past. But the success the company has enjoyed in the past also opens opportunities to him. GE's size and wealth allow him to take risks and make bets that would be impossible for weaker companies.

Storyline

As he indicated in our early interviews, Immelt began crafting his storyline for where he would take GE by thinking about the in-house GE community. He wanted to make GE a better and more energizing place to work. But he quickly expanded his horizons to look at the global community.

To be effective a leader's narrative storyline has to answer three questions: Where are we now? Where are we going? How will we get there?

In the early months of his tenure, Immelt began answering the "Where are we now?" question by describing the environment that he believed GE would encounter in the coming years. "I have taken over for a pretty famous guy, Jack, but to be honest with you, I have never thought of my job as replacing Jack," he told a group of students. "It is a 120-year-old company. He happened to run it for a while, but it is a company that has staying power. My job is to lead GE in a new set of circumstances and a new world. Post 9/11, it is a different world. Even Jack would have had to change his style if he had stayed in the company in this environment. The job of the leader is to do the job of leadership in the time you are in."[3]

In his first annual report letter in early 2002, Immelt described the world where GE had to operate. It was, he said, a world marked by slower growth and more volatility: "Jack left us a financially strong GE, as well as a culture that loves change. This is important because the world we knew in the late 1990s—a world of global growth, political stability and corporate trust—has changed. The U.S. economy began to slow in late 2000 and entered a recession in 2001. The world followed, with Europe and Japan in decline."[4]

By September 2004 he had expanded on the storyline and made it more concrete. Here's how he described the challenges that GE needed to overcome:

> I look at it pretty optimistically. But it's just going to mean that there's not going to be a rising tide to lift all ships universally. There are going to be businesses that win and businesses that lose. There are going to be countries that win. There are going to be countries that lose. And so the need to be competitive has never been greater . . . which you're going to see in the next five, ten, fifteen years."[5]

In addition to the economic challenges of slow growth and volatility, Immelt saw important social changes that would affect how GE needed to do business. To attract and motivate good people, Immelt believed that GE needed to become more humane. But he also believed that better corporate behavior would be demanded by society and government.

It's going to be "a world with more regulation, more laws, more cynicism about companies. And so that dictates that just being great isn't enough anymore. The companies and people have to be both great and good to be successful in the future."[6]

This reading of the state of the world informed the other elements of Immelt's storyline about the direction he needed to lead GE and the kinds of behaviors he needed to encourage and develop to get there.

Based on this storyline and the underlying foundational points of his Teachable Point of View, Immelt would make judgments about what businesses GE should be in and how it would conduct those businesses.

Those judgments included his own pay. From the start, Immelt made sure that his pay package was moderate compared to other CEOs and that all his incentives are tied to GE performance. It is an example of contextual knowledge, reading the signals in the environment and responding to them appropriately, making the right judgment calls.

Given the assessment of the state of the world, Immelt's next job was to figure out how GE could operate most successfully in that world. What products or services would be most in demand? And how could GE be the best at winning customers and delivering those goods and services? This is the "Where are we going?" part of the storyline.

The answer that Immelt arrived at was that the best way for GE to generate organic growth was to use its strong research and technology base to develop new markets. Some of the markets offering huge opportunities would be developing countries that needed to build infrastructure for power, water, energy, and transportation. In the more advanced economies, the best opportunities would be in as yet unserved, or underserved, markets. And these were most likely to be found in health care, in energy saving and production, and in environmentally friendly products. This assessment of where GE needed to go to succeed in the coming decades informed Immelt's strategic judgments. These included buying Amersham, a leading company in the diagnostic imaging agents and life sciences markets, and increasing investment in wind-generation and advanced technology for the oil and gas industry.

The third element of Immelt's storyline describes how GE will go about succeeding in these markets. His answer is, in part, about using the company's strong technology and management systems for sharing knowledge to develop winning products. It is also about corporate citizenship. It is about not only what the company will deliver to customers but also about how it will behave in the global community.

Corporations, in Immelt's view, would have to be more socially and environmentally aware. To be successful over time, they would need to make a greater contribution to the societies in which they operate. This would be mean greater efforts to support environmentally sustainable development and to attend to human capital issues such as housing, education, health care, and jobs.

Because he saw that global warming and the need for sustainable energy were serious concerns, he made the judgment to embrace the change and to come up with a GE response to them. In 2005 GE launched its Ecomagination initiative, which it described as "both a business strategy to drive growth at GE and a promise to contribute positively to the environment in the process."[7] It is a multidisciplinary campaign to apply GE technology to drive energy efficiency and improve environmental performance. He has always been clear that "green is green" for GE; he says that we are going to solve tough problems, yes, but Ecomagination has been a commerical enterprise from the start.

Immelt's storyline for the future of GE includes new elements of global citizenship. Continuing Welch's legacy of integrity, Immelt keeps reinforcing a commitment that GE must perform with the highest levels of integrity and compliance everywhere in the world. It must contribute and invest in the long-term well-being of the communities in which GE operates. It must build local capability, draw upon local resources to create jobs, and work with governments to implement solutions.

Finally, Immelt has provided much greater transparency to the investor community than in the past. He proactively set standards for other companies in the post–Enron, Tyco, Sarbanes-Oxley world. He is continuously pushing the boundaries of how transparent GE can become without giving away too much information to its competitors.

A leader's Teachable Point of View and his or her storyline are always interwoven. It is easy to think of leaders' storylines as a "fleshing out" or an animation of their Teachable Points of View, but in reality the action goes both ways. Sometimes leaders have TPOVs that they develop into storylines, and sometimes they have stories from which they draw foundational TPOVs. Most often a leader develops the story and the TPOV together. Sometimes the bullet points of the TPOV generate the narrative, but equally often a leader's listening to the story produces the TPOV. Jeff Immelt's TPOV for GE reflects his storyline.

Immelt Judgment Calls on Strategy

Based on his TPOV and storyline, Immelt has made a host of strategic judgments: some to get rid of businesses and others to add to existing businesses through acquisition. This is coupled with a massive emphasis on technology and R&D to build new businesses for the future. Immelt frames his judgments in terms of:

> There are five traits that I think are consistent across GE businesses that I look for. I like businesses that are technically

Immelt's Teachable Point of View

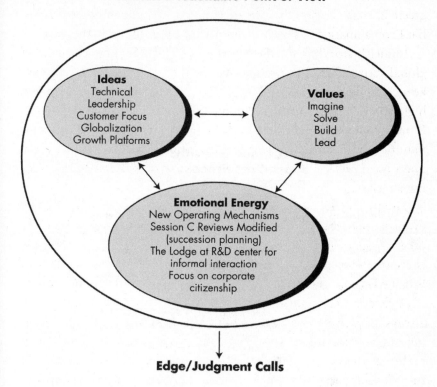

Ideas
Technical
Leadership
Customer Focus
Globalization
Growth Platforms

Values
Imagine
Solve
Build
Lead

Emotional Energy
New Operating Mechanisms
Session C Reviews Modified
(succession planning)
The Lodge at R&D center for
informal interaction
Focus on corporate
citizenship

Edge/Judgment Calls

based, global. I don't like selling through distribution, so I want to own customer interface. I like businesses that have multiple revenue streams, so you have product, you have service, you can do financing, and that are capital-efficient. I don't like businesses that utilize a lot of cash. I like businesses that generate a lot of cash because we've got a lot of ideas on how to grow businesses.

I have a real rule . . . we sold any business that we think somebody can run better than we can. So we sold our motors business. We sold our insurance business. We sold our global exchange business. We've sold our backroom sourcing business in India. Any business that I feel like somebody can run better than we can, we sell.[8]

Immelt has created a growth process for GE. These are a set of interdependent processes owned and driven by the CEO. They are

Growth Process at GE

Customers
Use process excellence to satisfy customers and drive growth.

Growth Traits

Lean Six Sigma
Net-Promoter Score

Growth Leaders
Inspire and develop people who know how to help customers and GE grow.

Innovation
Generate new ideas, and develop capabilities to make them a reality.

Imagination Breakthroughs

CECOR Framework

Execute for Growth: A Six-Part Process
General Electric's leaders use this diagram internally to explain how specific initiatives fit into a larger organic growth process.

Emerging Markets

Globalization
Create opportunities everywhere, and expand in developing global markets.

Great Technology
Have the best products, content, and services.

Commercial Excellence
Develop world-class sales and marketing talent, and demonstrate the value of "one GE."

One GE: Enterprise Selling and Brand

New Product Introduction

Ecomagination

judgment-shaping and enabling processes. It is part of his strategy judgment platform. The six-part process as shown in the diagram "Growth Process at GE" is used by Immelt and other GE leaders to teach leaders throughout GE about how growth is generated at GE.

Immelt took several years to evolve his six-part process:

> I knew if I could define a process and set the right metrics, this company could go 100 miles an hour in the right direction. It took time, though, to understand growth as a process. If I had worked out that wheel-shaped diagram in 2001, I would have started with it. . . . But in reality, you get these things by wallowing in them a while . . . Jack was a great teacher in this regard. I would see him wallow in something like Six Sigma, where easily the first two years were tough. . . . He'd get different businesses sharing ideas, and everything always crystallized in the end. He was a good initiative driver.[9]

GE's Growth Tools[10]

These are the tools GE uses to drive top-line growth.

- **Acquisition Intergration Framework:** outlines a detailed process for ensuring that acquired entitles are effectively assimilated into GE
- **At the Customer, for the Customer:** brings GE's internal best practices, management tools, and training programs to customers facing their own managerial challenges
- **CECOR Marketing Framework:** connects innovation and other growth efforts with market opportunities and customer needs by asking questions to *calibrate, explore, create, organize,* and *realize* strategic growth
- **Customer Dreaming Sessions:** assemble a group of the most influential and creative people in an industry to envision its future and provoke the kind of interchange that can inspire new plans
- **Growth Traits and Assessments:** outline and enforce the expectation that GE's next generation of leaders will display five strengths: external focus, clear thinking, imagination, inclusiveness, and domain expertise
- **Imagination Breakthroughs:** focus top management's attention and resources on promising ideas for new revenue streams percolating up from anywhere in the organization
- **Innovation Fundamentals:** equip managers with four exercises to engage people in innovation, and prepare them to transform new ideas into action
- **Innovation Labs and Tool Kit:** support business strategy, product development, and other cross-functional project teams with a variety of resources and materials relevant to innovation efforts
- **Lean Showcases:** demonstrate the power of "lean" thinking by allowing people to see how cycle times were reduced in a core customer-facing business process
- **Lean Six Sigma:** puts the Six Sigma methods and tools in the service of a critical goal—reducing cycle times in the processes that chiefly drive customer satisfaction
- **Net-Promoter Score:** holds all GE businesses to a new standard: They must track and improve the percentage of customers who would recommend GE. The scores are seen as leading Indicators of growth performance; business teams apply lean Six Sigma and other tools to analyze scores and identify and implement improvements

In addition to the six-part process, Immelt has a set of tools that are used to drive the six processes. These tools are levers and drivers for making the process work, such as "customer dreaming sessions" to drive innovation. These are one-to-two-day sessions held at Crotonville with the CEOs and key leaders from a business.

Ram Charan describes Immelt's dream sessions:

> He invites people from one customer industry at a time, usually CEOs and one or two associates for a one-or two-day session in which the conversation and presentations are geared toward what each of the participants visualizes over a long period of time—up to ten years. They discuss the external trends, the root causes of those trends, how they might converge, in what fashion and what the picture might be as viewed from as many different angles as possible, including the customer's customers, suppliers, regulators, special interest groups and trends in technology.[11]

Immelt's job as a leader is to create the platform for GE leaders to make good strategic judgments. He is the social architect of a set of processes to enable that and he is also the head teacher in getting these processes into the DNA of GE.

The Big R&D Judgment at GE

Growth through innovation is Immelt's number one priority. He does it with innovation projects, and with a massive investment in R&D. He made a strategic judgment to drive the execution of innovation through the use of his personal time and his commitment to new innovations. He describes some of his activities to drive innovation.

> We really, totally kind of focus on how do you get new ideas into the marketplace. In GE, we have a process now called imagination breakthroughs that are a hundred projects that have the opportunity of being $100 million in revenue in the next five years. And I am the program manager. I'm the person that makes sure that they're funded; I help pick who the

program managers are; I make sure that the risk and the time
horizon can be taken at my level; and really trying to find ways
to make size, to make this girth of GE a platform for innovation and not something that's going to choke off real creativity
in the future.[12]

Judgment Execution Phase at GE

MAKE-IT-HAPPEN STEPS:

Immelt's big judgment bet on technology depends on solid execution, so he has put in place a number of core execution supports.
These include increased capital expenditures for R&D, upgrading the
facilities, and opening new satellite R&D facilities around the world
in places as far-flung as Germany, China, and India. The most important of all is the way he is forging human linkages between Global
R&D and the leaders of the businesses.

Innovation requires people to interact, to be creative together, to
brainstorm, and to be able to make their own judgments about what
will and will not work. When Noel interviewed him in the fall of
2001, Immelt already knew that he was going to expand GE's focus
and expenditures on R&D. In the same way that Welch expanded
Crotonville and increased the focus on leadership at GE, Immelt
would make GE's R&D center the centerpiece of meaningful learning
and interaction that would shape the future of the company.

Attendance at Crotonville and leadership development are required
for business leaders at GE. All businesses send leaders to programs
that are mandated by corporate GE. GE's business leaders all teach
at Crotonville and the heads of the businesses attend Immelt's four-
times-a-year Corporate Executive Council. At these two-day meetings at Crotonville, they meet leaders going through programs and
also get action learning teams from Crotonville to report out to them.
It is a large part of what makes Crotonville an integral part of the
GE DNA.

Immelt made a judgment that all business leaders need to be in
the technology game as well. Along the same lines, Immelt made the

judgment to require all business leaders and their teams to go to the Global R&D center four times a year and "hang out," to interact and work with the technology groups there. To make sure that this could happen, Immelt actually built a mini-Crotonville. He built a lodge, a residential facility to house business leaders and their teams in an informal learning environment, right on the campus of Global R&D. The goal is to support informal sustained interaction with the technology colleagues.

Immelt also makes sure to pull all the other GE execution levers. Leaders have technology elements to their strategic plans. Succession planning discussions and judgments are tied into technology and innovation, and budgets must reflect a commitment to technology. One of the hallmarks of GE is this systematic alignment around key initiatives.

One of the most significant judgment execution levers is the GE value system. The judgment to grow organically through technology led to a dramatic change in the GE values. The values that Welch emphasized included speed, simplicity, self-confidence, boundary-lessness, and the four E's, which in Welch's words are: "Energy to cope with the frenetic pace of change. Energize the ability to excite, to galvanize the organization and inspire it to action. Edge the self-confidence to make tough calls with yesses and noes and very few maybes, and Execute, the ancient GE tradition of always delivering, never disappointing."[13]

Immelt has changed the values to be: imagine, solve, build, and lead. These four values are the ones that he feels will support the right behaviors throughout GE to execute on his growth strategic judgment. It means that all of the hiring and promotions screens at GE ask how well people have done and can be expected to do with regard to these values. Do they have imagination? Can they innovate, and have they done so in the past? Can they solve problems? Have they taken innovative ideas and turned them into solutions for customers? Can they take innovation that solves a customer need and build it into a viable business? And, finally, can they develop and lead others to grow through innovation?

Immelt operationalizes his development of growth leaders as follows. He states:

Our leaders are now trained and evaluated against five capabilities. They must:

- Create an external focus that defines success in market terms
- Be clear thinkers who can simplify strategy into specifications, make decisions, and communicate priorities
- Have imagination and courage to take risks on people and ideas
- Energize teams through inclusiveness and connection with people
- Develop expertise in a function or domain, using depth as a source of confidence to drive change.[14]

GE spends about $3.5 billion in R&D. Corporate Global Research and Development spends about $500 million of that, focusing on high-end technology, really deep, advanced thinking. The individual GE businesses, which also have their own R&D groups, spend the other $3 billion. The business and corporate R&D efforts work collaboratively to divide up the work based on expertise and need.

Learn and Adjust in the Execution Phase

A key player in Immelt's execution of his R&D strategy is GE Global's head of R&D, Mark Little. It is Little's leadership and the processes he puts together that will greatly influence how key leaders and technologists interact, and ultimately determine how well they are able to create innovations that get commercialized. The success of Immelt's technology-based strategy depends on this collaboration.

Mark Little describes his responsibility:

> I'm the Head of GE Research and Development. I watch out for all the technologists in the company. It's kind of interesting—GE has about twenty-seven thousand technologists working across our broad businesses. A few short years ago, we had almost no technologists in India or China. Today, 15 percent of our total technologists are in India and China, and we're rapidly going toward 25 percent. Why do I bring that up? Globalization is real, it's happening very fast, and we want to tap into the best global brains we can. We're finding great talented people in these places, and they're helping us change our business.

But there's another very real thing. We want to be close to the markets that are emerging in India and China. Over even the near term, I think, they are going to be huge, important marketplaces for us, and we really need to understand how to play there. And having people on the ground thinking about markets is very important for us.

We have things we call "In China, For China," and "In India, For India," which are technology plays about developing products for these local markets. So we're doing this across the entire business.

Little explained to us the processes he was setting up to make sure the technological advances at GE are understood by the people in the businesses and that the unmet customer needs are communicated to the technologists so that they can target their efforts to produce solutions.

The way it's been done here over time has been a little bit more unstructured than I'd like it to be. So, for instance, you hear Jeff talking about the growth playbook process for GE. We don't really have such a process here at the Global Research Center, and we're creating that. So we put together a growth team to work on: How do you generate ideas from the ground up; how do you get them in externally; how do you feed them; and then, how do you pick from them? So we're putting together a process that's in sync with GE's growth playbook process. It's called Session T. As the businesses build up their growth playbooks, they start thinking about what they need for technology. So we've got a well-defined process to do this where the marketing people, the engineering leadership and our scientists get together in what's called a Session T. And the way that works is, you spend a couple days, typically . . . first; saying what the market needs. Big picture, idea phase, brainstorming. Then you say, what can we do to develop some technology for that. And they'll bring forward some ideas to do that. And the output of a Session T is a set of what we might do. The follow-on to Session T is sort out what we can do.

To support this process Little's leadership role is to energize and engage his R&D technologists in a more productive way. He describes it, saying:

I wanted to get much more engagement from the folks here. There are tremendously smart, well-connected people here, and I really wanted to tap into their brain power and make it a more open process with a lot more debate, rather than having a bunch of smart people pitch their wares out and then having other smart people go into a room and decide what we're going to do. We're going to make it a much more open, interactive process.

Little wants all of his technology leaders to be able to conceptualize opportunities from the "outside in," meaning that they will be looking at customer needs and then try to couple them with emerging technology. The chart "GE: Big Market Opportunities" frames some of the opportunities for the GE portfolio of businesses.

This chart is key to how Little teaches his leaders to think not about what we are doing today but where the world is going so that technology and the R&D work execute on Immelt technology strategy.

In order to make the connection with the businesses work better,

GE: Big Marketing Opportunities

Big market opportunities for our future

	FROM	TO
Healthcare	See and treat	Predict, diagnose, treat, monitor & inform
Energy, Oil & Gas, Water	Scarcity threatening	Abundant & cleaner sources
Aviation & Rail	Steady progress	Breakthroughs in efficiency, emissions & noise
Security	Limited & intrusive	Fast, simple & safe
Appliances, Lighting, Industrial, Sensing	Commodities	Step-change in efficiency, cost & performance
NBCU	Living room & movie theater	Any time, any place
Financial Services	Developed markets	Funding the world's growth

> . . . all require innovation

 imagination at work

Little is setting out to orchestrate a new set of processes. He gave us an example from the Rail Business, which manufactures railroad engines.

> You'll start off with people who represent the businesses feeding ideas for trends that they see to Rail, for which they know they're going to need more efficient engines. They know they're going to have a lot of pressure on emissions coming out of our transportation engines. So they'll start to talk to the people in the laboratory groups about the need for low-cost, efficient, low-emissions transportation technology. . . .
>
> Then you ask the scientists to think about what can you do about that, and they start bubbling up ideas. Then you have the technical people vet those ideas. We have a process that gives people some money to play through the ideas and see whether they can be made to work or not. And if they can, then they'll bring it forward to another level of decision making, and it all will come together in the thought process.

Immelt's drive to increase the interaction with the businesses has had a positive emotional impact on both the R&D team and the business leaders, Little says. "People here are unbelievably self-confident and optimistic about what they can do. And the business guys love to come here for that reason, 'cause it's so refreshing." The scientists are teachers and learners with the business leaders. Because of the regular visits, the interactions are informal and include receptions and meals as well as opportunities to brainstorm; they are more productive than meetings where the businesspeople and the technologists just push one another on short-term deliverables.

GE Health Care and R&D

The acquisition of Amersham was a key element of GE's strategy to become a leader in personal medicine. But despite the enormous size of the acquisition, it was not the whole strategy. In fact, the acquisition came after GE technologists had already begun looking at ways to expand beyond GE's traditional diagnostic imaging business. The acquisition of Amersham furthered and redirected a strategic thrust that was aimed at taking GE more into bioscience. It gave GE a platform from which it could leap into the business. Little describes the course of events:

> We've got a world-leading diagnostic imaging business. It became pretty clear that there was a lot happening on the biosciences side that would be a very nice companion to that. So they started up a research program here to try to open up some doors for us. And it wasn't clear exactly what the doors were going to lead us to. But we started up a research center; started hiring some great people in. And then, as we started to think about that whole space, the [Amersham] acquisition came into play. We bought [Amersham], and now we're building off that. We've got tremendously great programs going on. We're going to change the face of medicine. There's just no doubt about it.

The health care execution included moving scientists from the UK Amersham home base to the upstate New York labs so that they could work with Little and his team of scientists.

THE HEALTHYMAGINATION JUDGMENT

Jeff Immelt made a big strategic judgment which he announced to the world on June 9, 2009. He announced that GE will spend $3 billion over the next six years on health care innovation that will help deliver better care to more people at lower cost. In addition, Immelt said, "The company will commit $2 billion of financing and $1 billion in related GE technology and content to drive health care information technology and health in rural and underserved areas. These investments are the foundation of GE's healthymagination initiative, which is built on the global commitments of reducing costs, improving quality, and expanding access for millions of people."

Under healthymagination, by 2015 GE will:

- **Invest $3 billion in research and development to launch at least one hundred innovations that lower cost, increase access, and improve quality by 15 percent.** GE will also apply its expertise in services and its suite of performance improvement tools for

impact in these areas. These actions will strengthen GE Healthcare's business model.

- **Work with partners to focus innovations on four critical
  needs to start:** accelerating health care information technology; target high-tech products to more affordable price points;
  broaden access to the underserved; and support consumer-
  driven health.
- **Expand its employee health efforts** by creating new wellness and
  healthy worksite programs while keeping cost increases below
  the rate of inflation.
- **Increase the "value gap"** between its health spend and GE
  Healthcare's earnings to drive new value for GE shareholders.
- **Engage and report on its progress.** GE will engage experts and
  leaders on policy and programs and create a GE Health Advisory Board, which will include former U.S. senators Bill Frist
  and Tom Daschle and other global health care leaders.

Healthymagination will draw on capabilities from across GE,
including GE Healthcare, GE Capital, GE Water, NBC Universal, the
GE Global Research Center as well as the GE Foundation, the philanthropic arm of GE.

"Health care is an important industry that is challenged by rising
costs, inequality of access, and persistent quality issues," Immelt said.
"Health care needs new solutions. We must innovate with smarter
processes and technologies that help doctors and hospitals deliver
better health care to more people at a lower cost.

"Healthymagination is our business strategy that seeks to help
people live healthier lives, support customer success, and help GE
grow," he went on. "We will invest in innovations that measurably
improve cost, access and quality. That means lower-cost technology
for more customers, products matched to specific local needs and
process expertise to help customers win."

NANOTECHNOLOGY APPLICATIONS

One exciting part of the execution of the Global R&D strategy is
looking for new applications for nanotechnology.

Big Swings: Nanotechnology

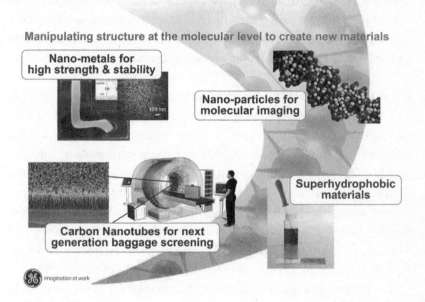

Manipulating structure at the molecular level to create new materials

Nano-metals for high strength & stability

Nano-particles for molecular imaging

Superhydrophobic materials

Carbon Nanotubes for next generation baggage screening

You know, people spend billions on nanotechnology, most of it semiconductor that we're not interested in at all. We care a lot about applications. For example, there's a lot of nanotechnology that feeds into the biosciences sides, because you want to find very, very small particles that can attach onto things and absorb quickly, and nanoparticles do that. You get material properties that are phenomenal out of nanoscience stuff. We're doing some fascinating things in lighting with nanotechnology. So it's just a basic material science that's very interesting and powerful and spreads across all our businesses.

The chart "Big Swings: Nanotechnology" is one that Little uses to show GE leaders about the potential applications of nanotechnology. The scientists in the lab are busy experimenting with these applications and are collaborating with the scientists in a number of the businesses to find new uses for them. This is one of the ways that Little supports Immelt's strategic judgment on technology by providing the channels to "make it happen."

In addition to nanotechnology, GE R&D is working on biotechnology. This is where physics meets biology to explore a new paradigm for early health detection. This will range from molecular and digital pathology for in vitro diagnosis, to targeted magnetic resonance contrast agents that make images far more accurate and clear and binders for disease-specific contrast agents.

CROSS BUSINESS TECHNOLOGY APPLICATIONS

One of the most promising aspects of the strategic execution of Immelt's technology judgment is what is occurring at the Global Research Center (GRC) with cross-business applications. When we visited the GRC we saw examples of this, such as the use of medical imaging technology—CAT scan and MRI—being developed for oil pipeline and refinery scanning systems that might have prevented catastrophes like the BP oil pipeline leak in Alaska in 2006, or the BP refinery explosion in Texas that killed fifteen workers. The chart "Core Technologies: Imaging" shows some of these cross-business applications of technology.

For example, X-ray and imagining technology are being used to do preventive maintenance assessment with oil and gas pipelines; other imaging technologies are being applied to security and aviation. The GE advantage is multitechnologies across a multibusiness portfolio. If GE can execute their technology strategic judgment, they have an unmatched portfolio on size, breadth of technology, and breadth of businesses.

◆ ◆ ◆

Jeff Immelt has made some very bold, bet-the-company strategy judgments. Initially, they have not paid off in terms of stock performance. In early 2007 the *Financial Times* summed up his challenges:

> Despite having long commanded a place in the pantheon of the world's most admired companies, the US industrial group enters the year having to prove its worth to the capital markets. GE shares have underperformed the S&P 500 index in the past six years . . . the challenge facing the company is disarmingly simple to make a convincing case that its strategy to drive profit growth across its sprawling portfolio warrants a high stock market valuation . . . the stakes are such that if 2007 does not prove a

Core Technologies: Imaging

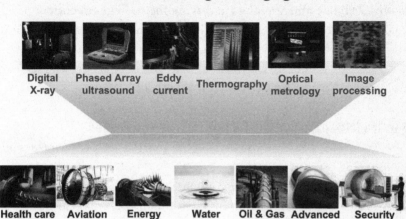

breakout year, there is a risk that capital markets may turn one of the following ones into GE's break-up years.[15]

As the quote indicates, Immelt is on the line in 2007 for his GE strategy judgments. He has spent five years repositioning GE for future growth; now he needs to demonstrate that his strategic judgments will yield the promised results. His is a work in progress. He has dropped businesses from the portfolio, a never-ending process, and is adding new ones through acquisitions and organic growth to create the GE future engines of growth. Five years into the transformation, his judgments were showing clear evidence of being rewarded in the stock market. Jeff Immelt states:

> To be a reliable growth company requires the ability to conceptualize the future. We are investing to capitalize on the major growth trends of this era that will grow at multiples of the global GDP growth rate. We are using our breadth, financial strength, and intellectual capital to create a competitive advantage.[16]

Below is a summary of how Immelt explains his strategy judgments to the world, both internally to GE and externally, including

Wall Street, the press, and key stakeholders. He is relentless in sharing his storyline and relentless in driving the strategy execution.

SUMMARY OF IMMELT'S STRATEGY JUDGEMENT FOR GE

The Transformation of the GE Portfolio of Businesses

- Focus on a faster-growing, higher-margin set of businesses is paying off.
- Since 2002, completed approximately $80 billion worth of acquisitions of faster growth. High margin business and close to $40 billion of dispositions of slower-growth, lower-margin businesses.
- Delivering consistent double-digit earnings growth of 10 percent 2001–06.
- Two straight years of organic revenue growth of two to three times GDP.
- Two straight years of expanding margin rates and increasing returns.
- Global revenue almost doubling from $40 billion in 2000 to $75 billion in 2006.
- Higher-margin service revenue doubling from $16 billion in 2000 to $30 billion in 2006.
- Net income almost doubling since 2000.

The Transformation of the Portfolio and the Investment in Technology Position GE to Capitalize and Key Growth Drivers

- Changing demographics
- Digital connections
- Liquidity
- Global infrastructure growth
- Emerging markets
- Ecomagination—clean energy

THE 2008–2009 ECONOMIC RECESSION HITS GE

All the predictions made for 2007 going forward went out the window with the recession. Jeff Immelt wrote a very candid and strong leadership letter in the 2008 annual report which came out in the first half of 2009. Here is some of what he said to shareholders:

> Despite our efforts, the GE stock got hammered. Companies with a presence in financial services, like GE, are simply out of favor. I can tell you that no one is more disappointed than I am with the performance of our stock in this tough environment. I assure you that we will work hard to restore your trust, and we will continue to work hard to build GE for the long term. . . . Let's face it: our Company's reputation was tarnished because we weren't the "safe and reliable" growth company that is our aspiration. I accept responsibility for this. But, I think this environment presents an opportunity of a lifetime. We get a chance to reset the core of GE and focus on what we do best. We can reset expectations for our performance. And we can participate in the changes required in the broader economy.
>
> The current crisis offers the challenge of our lifetime. I've told our leaders at GE that if they are frightened by this concept, they shouldn't be here. But if they're energized, and desire to play a part in transforming the Company for the future, then this is going to be a thrilling time to be a part of GE.

Jeff Immelt's leadership judgments will be tested as the global economy emerges from the recession. In the meantime he has made some tough crisis calls to stay consistent with his long term strategy and has not changed his team, thus trusting his people's judgments.

9

CRISIS JUDGMENTS

■ **Winning Leaders Take Personal Responsibility for Handling Crises**
- Ability to frame the nature of the crisis correctly is an essential skill.
- A factual, scientific response to a political uproar can be disastrous.

■ **A Common Mistake in a Crisis Is Losing Sight of Your Ultimate Mission**
- Responses that ease the tension don't always move toward the goal.
- The chaos of a crisis can offer unexpected opportunities.

■ **Bad Judgments on People or Strategy Can Lead to Crises**
- When faced with a crisis, a smart, loyal team is critical.

◆ ◆ ◆

On the day I was announced as the new CEO, P&G's stock fell another $4. After 15 days on the job, P&G's stock fell another $3.85; an early personal confidence builder.

The biggest crisis at P&G in 2000 was not the loss of $85 billion in market capitalization. The far bigger crisis was the crisis in confidence . . . particularly leadership confidence. P&G business leaders retreated to their bunkers. Leaders were lying low. Heads were down.

In too many businesses, best-in-class competitors were on the attack. P&G business units around the world were blaming headquarters for their problems. Headquarters was blaming line business units. Employees were calling for heads to roll. They were very vocal about their lack of confidence in leadership.

Analysts and investors were angry. How could this reliable company have screwed up so badly? Retirees were madder than hatters. They rely on P&G's stock for a comfortable and secure retirement. Their nest eggs had lost more than half their value.

We'd made a mess, and we had to fix it.[1]

A. G. Lafley
January 13, 2005

When A. G. Lafley was suddenly tapped as CEO of Procter & Gamble in June 2000, the company was in a crisis. Its stock was in a free fall. His predecessor, Durk Jager, had been ousted for failing to revive P&G's flagging businesses and missing a number of earnings targets. The company's operations were in chaos, and morale was in the dumps. Lafley's assignment was to deal with the crisis and, at the same time, immediately begin to solve the underlying problems that had led to the crisis. He successfully led a transformation of P&G that drove the market capitalization from $74 billion when he took over in 2000, to over $200 billion in early 2007.

Describing his crisis response plan in 2005, he said:

We did four things:

1. WE FACED UP TO THE REALITY of our situation. We started seeing things as they are, not as we wanted them to be.
2. WE ACCEPTED CHANGE. We stopped trying to ignore or resist it. We embraced change, we committed to lead change.

3. WE STARTED MAKING CHOICES. Clear choices, tough choices; what P&G would do and not do. Choice making is the essence of strategy.
4. WE PUT TOGETHER A STRONG, COHESIVE TEAM to lead the business. We put the right players in the right seats on the same bus headed in the same direction. We shared a compelling vision of what we wanted to achieve, and we worked as a team on strategies and action plans.[2]

Good judgments made during times of crisis follow the same process as judgments made under less stressed circumstances. There is a preparation phase, a call phase, and an execution phase. The preparation phase, however, needs to be done before the crisis occurs. The most effective leaders prepare for crisis even before knowing what kind of crisis will occur. It is perhaps even more true in crisis situations than with judgments about people and strategy that the likelihood of making successful calls is vastly increased if they are made in the context of a preexisiting Teachable Point of View and on the platform of the storyline for the future.

Leaders generally make bad crisis judgments either because they lack a clear TPOV and storyline, or because they have made bad people judgments. For leaders to handle crises effectively, they must have an aligned team. Otherwise, the crisis situation will splinter the team just when smart, coherent action is needed most. Bad people judgments or bad strategy judgments can precipitate a crisis, but once one happens, teamwork and focus make all the difference between survival and disaster.

THE TRIAGE NURSE AND CRISIS

"Is it ever morally right to make judgments about the worthiness or unworthiness of persons who lay claim to our services?" asks a triage nurse in an article on ethical issues in emergency rooms.[3] The answer by another triage nurse was, "Absolutely! Every patient we see has the potential to create an ethical dilemma in terms of priority of treatment and allocation of resources. Essentially, the proverbial 'red flag' is raised every time we triage a patient."[4]

One way to help understand what judgment calls are really about is to observe a busy inner-city triage nurse. As patients come through the door, the triage nurse makes judgment calls regarding who gets medical care and in what order. The judgment call is about the seriousness and urgency of the medical condition.

Noel remembers being in the Harlem Hospital studying how the emergency room operated. The triage nurse was making very quick judgment calls: this child with a fever and his parents were told to sit and wait, for over an hour, while the nurse mobilized a team to deal with a cardiac arrest on what appeared to be an eighty-year-old man. Then the nurse made a really fast, and what I thought would be difficult, judgment call. A pregnant teenage girl came in with a gunshot wound. But the nurse didn't hesitate. She pulled the team off the cardiac arrest case and put the resources into the pregnant girl. The girl and her baby survived but the cardiac arrest victim died. The nurse made a judgment call about how to use her limited resources and applied them to the pregnant teenager.

A leader's Teachable Point of View operates in a crisis decision framework much as it does for people and strategy judgments. The main difference is that the time frame is compressed, and there is often intense pressure, even chaos. This is clearly the case in a busy emergency room where the triage nurse's TPOV must be the bedrock of medical judgments.

The first two judgment calls, the boy with the fever and the cardiac patient, were fairly easy; they required using the nurse's medical experience (*ideas*) to come up with an initial diagnosis to guide the judgment call. The nurse's medical experience was necessary but not sufficient to make the tougher judgment call based on her *values*. The decision to stop treating a patient who had a good chance of dying without immediate care to save another patient was based on her value system, which said that it was more important to save the life of a young pregnant girl and baby than an older man with the heart attack. The nurse did not falter. Whether we agree or not, she had a clear Teachable Point of View on how to make the judgment calls.

Finally, the nurse had to generate *emotional energy* in herself and in the other people on the staff to execute on the judgment quickly and effectively.

How does a triage nurse develop the ability to make good judgment calls? Formal training is clearly part of the formula. But experience plays a huge role. An aspiring triage nurse starts by working as an apprentice with others who have more experience. Eventually, after a time of mentoring, the nurses are put into real situations where they must make their own judgment calls. A triage nurse might start out in a small emergency room and then keep building capability until he or she can take on a big, complex, fast-moving, and chaotic inner-city emergency room. To be a good triage nurse requires continuous improvement and learning. Experience without this preparation is a ticket to disaster.

While personal preparation is a key contributor to making good judgment calls, so is institutional preparation. Kathy Gallo, RN, PhD, MBA, currently the chief learning officer at North Shore–Long Island Jewish Health System, is a former director of an emergency department (ED) in a level 1 trauma center. She talked to us about how experience and preparation improve the quality of her tough judgment calls.

> With systematic planning, preparedness, training, cycles of improvement through debriefing, and experience, crises can be handled as routine events. You can't plan for everything so you plan for anything.
>
> While the arrival of a helicopter with a trauma patient and several ambulances with other trauma patients from the same accident scene showing up simultaneously on the doorstep of an ED may look like a crisis to the casual observer, it is not a crisis for prepared staff and facility—it's just another day at work. During this scenario the staff's roles are clearly delineated and protocols are executed before the patients even arrive. This team moves into action as soon as there is notification from the scene by EMS that patients are on their way. Once the patients are stabilized and transferred to their next point of care in the hospital, the trauma room is cleaned up and prepared for the next patient's or patients' arrival. The trauma room is always "ready to go."

Working in an area where emergencies are your business, you learn quickly that preparation is your best friend. In running the ED I was always thinking what would come through the door next, do we have a bed available, etc. I always had my ear to the ground—when will the next helicopter land—are we good to go? What decisions do I have to make now in order to handle the next critically ill or injured patient? This environment trains you to always be sensing, "What's next?" so there are no surprises and the patient and family receive the best care possible.

An even broader and more profound example of how preparation improves crisis judgment is her experience as the vice president for emergency services at North Shore–LIJ. Gallo told us this story. Through meetings that she had with a senior FBI agent in 1999 she was advised that the potential for a terrorist attack in New York City was great and that hospitals needed to prepare themselves for mass casualties. With the approval and support of her CEO, she led a team to prepare the health system for such an event. New emergency management plans were developed and deployed, and incident command systems were developed at each site as well as for the overall organization. All employees were rigorously educated regarding the new threat and why a new emergency response system was essential. Specialized training was also included regarding role delineation for all key personnel:

An empowered workplace is optimal for day-to-day operations, but once a crisis is on your doorstep, command and control is the order of the day and everyone moves into their roles.

Tabletop drills became the norm, and debriefing afterward provided learning opportunities for improvement of the emergency response. We also held a regional conference prior to 9/11: "Health Care Implications of Weapons of Mass Destruction" for all hospitals and EMS agencies in the tristate area. The speakers were senior FBI personnel as well as federal government personnel. We also met with the Office of Emergency Management for NYC, Nassau County, and Suffolk County to share our plans so we could be integrated with theirs.

During the overall preparation effort, I have to say it was a hard sell. A terrorist attack? Why do we need to put so much

time and effort into something so farfetched? I heard this over
and over again. But I guess it goes back to sensing 9/11 was the
"what's next."

Gallo and her team built a crisis capability into North Shore–LIJ
so that when 9/11 occurred, she told us they were more prepared than
they would have been if they ignored the warnings by the FBI.

> We pulled the trigger on our new emergency management
> plan—the one that we trained and drilled on. We sent our ambu-
> lances, EMTs, paramedics, and supplies into NYC, facilitated
> the movement of our patients to create room for any mass casu-
> alties, shifted resources within the health system to where they
> would be needed, and kept our critical care transport operation
> running to simultaneously provide care to any cardiac, neonatal,
> or pediatric emergency patients that needed to be transported to
> our hospitals. Our normal day-to-day business was kept intact.

The medical examples above follow the model we describe for all
institutional leaders who have to make judgment calls. There is a pre-
judgment call phase, the making of the judgment call phase, and the
execution of the judgment call. As with other leaders, we judge the
success of the medical judgment calls by the results of the execution.
In the case of the pregnant girl with the gunshot wound, the triage
nurse saved the lives of the teenager and her baby but lost the life of
the eighty-year-old cardiac patient. Was that a good or bad judgment
call? In the framework of that triage nurse, it was a good judgment
call. It accomplished her primary intended outcome, with scarce
resources. She was able to make the call so seamlessly because it was
clearly based on a set of values that she already had embedded in her
mind. She did not have to work them out on the spot.

For a triage nurse, the prephase in the emergency room happens
very quickly. It includes an assessment of the patient's condition,
often done informally without any tests: looking at the patient, reading major medical indicators. This sets up the judgment call decision,
to treat or not to treat. This is followed by execution, which requires
having the right team administering the right treatment.

All leaders have the same responsibility in making judgments:

They must read the situation to properly frame a judgment call, make the call, and then make sure that it is executed well.

TRIAGE NURSES VERSUS INSTITUTIONAL LEADERS

Triage nurses, firemen, and soldiers on the battlefield are all people who make lots of judgment calls in crisis conditions. There is limited time, limited data, often life-threatening consequences. In these situations, judgment calls must be made in real time. An institutional leader, a head of a corporation, university, hospital, or other organization does face the occasional crises, such as when an unwelcome acquirer comes along, a top management scandal, or a natural disaster. But most leadership judgment calls occur in calmer circumstances than those faced daily by first responders.

Nonetheless, the institutional leader can learn much from our professional "crisis" judgment call leaders: triage nurses, firemen, and soldiers. The calls that leaders make are not less complex than those made on the battlefield or in an emergency room. They are possibly more complex, and are equally important. The difference is that the leader enjoys the luxury of having more time to make them. And it is important to remember that if he or she makes good judgments in the two other critical areas we have described, People and Strategy, then the likelihood that crises will arise is reduced. But no matter what kinds of judgments a leader makes, eventually crises will come up. And, when they do, the leader with a good, clear strategy and a smart functioning team will inevitably be able to handle them better than a leader who doesn't.

Lessons from the Military: Trained to Perform in Continuous Crisis Environment

Wayne Downing, the late four-star general who headed the Special Operations Forces, told us that he was always on the lookout for unexpected opportunities in the midst of crisis.

> Crisis affects timing. An unexpected event can create chaos which, by definition, cannot be controlled. Yet so many of us in

a chaotic situation try to gain control. I have always felt that the way to handle this is to try to get some distance from the chaos. Zone out a bit and try to pick up what is going on, because what chaos does offer you is opportunities, sometimes opportunities you are never going to have during normal periods of time. If there is a crisis, the chaotic situation oftentimes offers you not only disadvantages, which is what we tend to focus on, but also tremendous advantages to do things that you couldn't do in any other way.

Downing led the Special Forces Operation during the 1989 raid to capture Manuel Noriega, Panama's military dictator. After weeks of careful planning with all the forces in position, and some already on the move, the situation changed and Downing faced a crisis judgment. He described it to us:

> We're in a crisis, a major crisis. Our surveillance has lost Noriega and we must get him at the beginning of the operation. We cannot allow him to escape to a foreign haven. And the clock is ticking. Rangers and paratroopers from the 82nd Airborne Divisions are already in the sky flying down to parachute into Panama from the United States. . . . Noriega has slipped away. So what is it we're going to do? One option was to execute the original plan . . . not the right thing to do . . . it would not have produced results. So what we did was stop our two major efforts to get Noriega and pull them back to a central location . . . what we ended up doing was reacting to where key personalities associated with Noriega were located. . . . We systematically went to their homes and captured them and brought them to a central location, and we collapsed his infrastructure so that ten days later we captured him. . . . Had we followed the original plan we would have given him a chance to elude us and get to Cuba.

Downing was able to make his good judgment based on a clear Teachable Point of View for how his organization was to operate, both in normal and crisis times. He had to change the Noriega storyline from "quickly extract him" to a "ten-day collapse the infrastructure" storyline. His crisis judgment worked.

Leadership Judgment Process

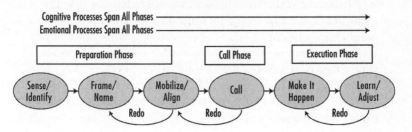

Note the judgment process flow does not change; Downing was able to sense and identify in time to then frame and name the crisis as a new situation. After that, he was able to mobilize and align the troops in a matter of less than an hour. Downing described the task of getting everyone on the same page quickly.

> We had to tell our forces that the tactics for executing the mission have changed. . . . Rather then execute preplanned raids on distant targets, we marshaled the Delta Force and their lift helos in a central location to react rapidly to intel on Noriega.
>
> We used their ground-force elements to start a series of raids on the homes of Noriega's friends—an entirely new mission. We established the SEALs on the Atlantic side of the isthmus to run down all of Noriega's haunts and friends and even airlifted their assault boats by Chinook helos across the Panama Canal. We changed the tactical plan we had been working on for over a year and a half because it was no longer appropriate to the situation. The goal was still to get Noriega and topple the government; we just had to do it differently. And we made these changes very quickly. There was no time for debate and long deliberations. My operations officer and old friend Colonel Dick Malvesti and I sat down and developed an entirely new plan appropriate to the new situation in about fifteen minutes. You have to be this flexible in combat because the enemy always has a vote. You develop your plans with the best information available but you must accept that things are going to change, sometimes radically, and you must be able to rapidly respond and make a clear and often immediate decision to respond appropriately.

For Downing's judgment to be a good one, he had to ensure that the third phase, execution, was successful. He led the ten-day execution of finding and capturing all of Noriega's cronies, learning and adjusting as they went along.

Downing described a very simple and powerful framework used in the U.S. military to guide leadership judgment in crises. It is also useful in less stressed times, but it is critical in crises. The memory aid is METT-T or Mission, Enemy, Terrain, Troops available, and Time. Downing states:

> Any military leader can METT-T. It goes like this:
>
> MISSION: What is my unit supposed to do? I cannot forget this in the fog and friction of the battlefield. It's easy to get caught up in activity that solves the immediate crisis and forget your purpose in being there in the first place.
>
> ENEMY: What are we up against? Although I have studied the enemy in great detail, they have done something unexpected. What are their likely actions? How many of them? Reinforcements?
>
> TERRAIN: This means the total environment, the ground, the air, the ocean, and the weather. How will this environment assist us or make us vulnerable?
>
> TROOPS AVAILABLE: This is more than soldiers; it is all the material resources we have available to us or can reasonably get our hands on. We can expect mortars, artillery, airstrikes, and maybe even other ground maneuver units who can strike the enemy on the flanks. We may not have to solve this situation alone, there may be others who can assist.
>
> TIME: This is key. How much time do I have to make this decision? I always want more information but waiting can also mean disaster. A 75 percent plan executed now is always better than a 99 percent plan executed an hour late.

Karl Weick wrote a powerful frame-breaking chapter titled "A Stress Analysis of Future Battlefields"[5] that has been extremely useful to us as we work with leaders in business and other sectors. It helps differentiate why crisis judgments are qualitatively different from people or strategy judgments. Although a battlefield is clearly different from other organizational contexts, the lessons to be learned

are relevant. Weick describes the modern battlefield as one that creates crisis and stress. (Note that this chapter was written over twenty
years ago and was quite predictive of the Iraq battlefield environment.) Many of these characteristics have clear analogs in today's
business environment.

1. The battle is longer, there are few replacements, and there is a
   greater feeling it could go on forever.
2. Objective danger is higher because the battlefield is larger
   (worldwide).
3. Will be impossible to run away from battle, because unclear in
   which direction safety lies, or whether persons will be able to
   avoid extended exposure while trying to locate safety.
4. Quantity of airborne metal will be greater, as well as destruc-
   tiveness.
5. More complicated equipment—tougher to repair, more break-
   downs.
6. To cope with increased pressure, officers may distance themselves more from battlefield—this means their judgments will
   be less sensitive to local conditions—and small units will be
   ordered to do more things that will be wrong.
7. Units smaller, more dispersed, connected by communication
   devices that are vulnerable to jamming—this will make it difficult for soldiers to get social support and an accurate view of
   what is happening.
8. Fighting will be continuous, which means people will be exposed
   at all times and therefore must constantly be vigilant.

Over the years we have used this list to help business leaders think
about their environments. Global competition creates many parallel
pressures. "Few replacements" equates to talent shortages. "Objective
danger higher" equates to global worldwide competition. "Officers
may distance themselves from the battlefield" equates with headquarters and units in a different part of the globe; and "fighting will
be continuous" matches up with the 24/7 pace of global business.

Weick developed a prescription for enhancing leadership capacity to make good judgments in such a battlefield. These include:

1. **Institutionalize overlearning:** overlearn core behavior necessary for winning so that under extreme stress behavior does not break down.
2. **Overlearn routines for improvisation:** Develop algorithm for dealing with novel solutions in high stress situations—new solutions found—swift episodes of trial and error, breaks rigid mental sets, imposes an orderly procedure when people feel a strong need for structure, creates complex strategies that match enemies' complex strategies, transforms difficult tasks of analysis into easier tasks, breaks tension by inducing laughter at some of the absurd solutions. Gain flexibility and confidence.
3. Practice under more realistic conditions.
4. **Simplify tasks**—under conditions of stress people sacrifice quality for speed—therefore design tasks to minimize quality loss under stress.
5. **Develop resistance resources:** people can improve their ability to reduce the more disruptive effects of stress by commitment to the overall mission; by enhanced perception of controlling their own fate (ultimately feel they can push the panic button) and are challenged with the belief that change is an incentive to grow rather than a threat to security.
6. **Develop skills of autosuggestion:** meditation, self-suggestion, imagery, have a vision of success.
7. Appraise individual differences on the team; know strengths and weaknesses of team members.
8. Identify substitutes for attention; learn how to build leadership functions into nonhierarchical structures with peers providing each other with new abilities, knowledge, experience, training, and direction.[6]

General Downing and Karl Weick ground us in the realities of crisis judgment at the extreme, in a life-and-death battlefield situation.

Other organizations rarely face crises that are so stark. However, they do face crises that are big—unexpected events that threaten the survival of the organization. With the battlefield context as a backdrop, we will build our framework for how leaders in all kinds of organizations can make better crisis judgments.

CRISIS JUDGMENTS, COMPRESSED TIME, AND ROOT CAUSES

The reason crisis is one of our three categories of key leader judgments is that all leaders have to deal with them. We have personally been in leadership positions dealing with crises and we have talked with scores of leaders about crisis leadership. The fundamental process of judgment is the same as with people and strategy. Have a solid TPOV, and make sure the judgments you make are consistent with the TPOV, or at the very least, do not hinder execution of the storyline for where you want to ultimately end up.

What Is a Leadership Crisis?

At a societal level we have lived through many crises. Warren was a young man when Japan attacked Pearl Harbor and he was a first lieutenant in World War II. Since then, there have been the Berlin crisis; the *Sputnik* crisis; the Cuban Missile crisis; both Kennedy assassinations; the assassination of Martin Luther King Jr.; the Vietnam War crisis; the Nixon impeachment crisis; the 1970s oil crisis; the Tiananmen Square crisis; the attempted coup of Gorbachev; the assassination of Gandhi, the prime minister of India; the 9/11 terrorist attacks; and the Iraq War crisis. Across these crises, we have been witnesses to good and bad leadership judgment.

In our work with business organizations, we have been eyewitnesses to or personally involved in many crises. These have ranged from the bankruptcy in 1977 of the Appalachian Regional Hospital System in Hazard, Kentucky, when Noel was running one of their clinics; to the explosion in 1984 of a Union Carbide chemical plant in Bhopal, India, when Noel was working with them on a leadership program; to the GE time card scandal when the government froze $6 billion of GE defense contracts because of false billing of time.

We have also been on the scene when it was discovered that a GE manager had bribed an Israeli general and when a rogue Kidder Peabody scammed the company. This last one ultimately cost the CEO of Kidder his job because the scandal happened on his watch. Noel was at Nomura Securities in 1999 when the CEO, Setsuya Tabuchi, was abruptly fired in the midst of a bribery scandal involving the mob in Tokyo.

The *Exxon Valdez* oil spill crisis occurred while Noel was running a leadership program at Exxon for then chief operating officer Lee Raymond. His boss, CEO Lawrence Rawl, made a series of bad crisis judgments that cost the company billions of dollars and inflicted major damage on its reputation. And at Shell, there were the Brent Spar and the Shell Nigeria crises that occurred while Noel was working with Cor Herkstroter, the chairman, and the top team.

Other crises we were personally involved with include Ford CEO Jac Nasser dealing with an explosion in the Rouge Plant and his handling of the Firestone tire crisis, and most recently some of our own organizational crises. We like to think that we don't cause crises, but we have certainly been onstage, or in the front row, often enough to have learned a lot about how they unfold and how leaders made good and bad judgment calls.

Painful Judgment Lesson: Bad People Judgments Can Create Crises

Downing told us, "Weak leaders let you down when you need them the most."

Some crises just jump up out of nowhere and bite you, but in many cases, a crisis is the result of one or several previous bad judgment calls. The bad judgment calls that are most likely to produce crises are ones made about people. As we were completing this book, Noel faced a very painful and difficult crisis because of a poor people judgment.

Noel heads up a small center at the University of Michigan, the Global Business Partnership (GBP). A trusted colleague and program director was responsible for running one of the GBP's most important programs that accounted for 60 percent of the annual revenue. The program was a partnership with five major organizations. Each CEO was to send a team of six executives for a six-month process. The purpose was to work on a strategic project for the CEO and organization while also developing leadership skills in the participants.

The six-month program was to include three workshops: a one-week launch at the beginning, a three-day workshop in the middle, and a three-day final workshop. Each team would spend 25–30 percent of their work time during the six months on the CEO's project.

The program was to be launched on a Monday morning in early 2007 with all five CEOs and their teams. At 3:09 on the Friday before the launch, Noel received a letter from his colleague. In the letter, the colleague confessed to having created an elaborate scheme to hide the fact that there were not five teams coming, but only one. The others, which had participated in the past, had dropped out for this year. They had told the program director months before that they weren't coming but he hid this information until the eleventh hour. It was bad enough to get this news at the last minute and have to inform the one remaining CEO, who then chose not to come.

The program was canceled and the GBP was thrown into a financial and image crisis. It was even more shocking to uncover the elaborate labyrinth of lies the colleague had built. He had made up a list of fictitious names, then assigned them hotel rooms, created seating charts, and had Noel sign books for them with notes that said, "Dear so-and-so, with best wishes, Noel." He also produced phony plans for projects purporting them to be from the CEOs, and then had the prework material mailed out to the organizations that weren't coming and calling them and blaming a clerical error for the mailing. The colleague's four-page letter that outlined the scam started with:

Personal and Confidential

Dear Noel,
I am not well. And I have done a terrible thing and—weakly—have allowed myself to be swallowed up by it. In the process, I've violated the very ethical standards that I have lived by for almost a half-century.

In short, the program is in shambles—a myth of my imagination supported by a series of lies—and I have not had the personal courage to own up to it. At this late hour, I must confess—and apologize profusely to you, my friend of thirty years, for my failures and, worse, my dishonesty as to what was really happening. I betrayed your trust and have been a lousy employee, an even worse friend. . . .

As a result of the former colleague's actions, people's jobs were jeopardized. Without this anticipated revenue, the budget was shot. The GBP brand and image were severely damaged. The organization was pitched into a crisis, not to mention the self-destruction of a colleague's career. But there was one benefit. Noel had some incredible leadership discussions with the leaders he had to call and tell the story to.

As Noel made the phone calls, each of the CEOs—every one of them—had a similar story to tell. They all talked about how they had put their trust in a key leader who turned out to be untrustworthy. At some point, every one of them had missed all the warning signs and created an organizational crisis.

There was the vice president who was the best salesperson for six months until he came forward and, much like Noel's colleague, confessed that he was making up his sales figures. He said he had a cocaine addiction and asked for forgiveness, help, and another chance. The CEO gave it to him, only to have to fire him after another six months of lies, cocaine, and organizational damage. Another CEO talked about an alcoholic head of a major division who created a crisis. Another told of a brother-in-law whom he invested in and who ended up bankrupting the company through lies and deception.

Blind Spots on People
This got us reflecting on how good leaders, with solid track records of sound judgments, can sometimes make such bad people judgments. Noel would like to consider himself a person who makes good judgments on people most of the time, but he is clearly susceptible to "blind spots" on people. We do know some leaders who do not have

a "blind spot," but that is because they are always bad on people judgments. These are the ones with sycophants hanging around, and who close their eyes to incompetence or disloyalty among members of their inner circle.

We have spent a lot of our professional lives helping leaders make sure they do 360 evaluations of their staff and are not caught without valid data on the leaders around them. Yet we cannot find a CEO who doesn't have at least one painful story of a bad people judgment leading to a crisis. They had a "people blind spot." Some of the more powerful examples include:

- Merck board of directors: They hired Ray Gilmartin to be CEO even though he was over his head as a leader. He didn't have the necessary experience. He mishandled the Vioxx crisis and ultimately lost his job.
- Carly Fiorina: She, too, lacked experience leading a large, diverse organization. She could not/did not put a team together, the company faltered, and she was fired by the board.
- Jack Welch: As CEO of GE, Jack Welch had the best track record in the world for selecting and developing leaders. Yet he too was occasionally blinded to human weaknesses. One outstanding example was the CEO of Kidder Peabody when the Joe Jett trading scandal occurred on his watch, creating a crisis and resulting in the CEO losing his job.
- Bob Knowling: A veteran telecommunications industry excecutive and developer of the New York City Leadership Academy, Knowling says that when he joined one company as CEO, he was forewarned about founders and that there were very few examples of founders playing key roles on the executive team. In his case, there were three founders, and each occupied a seat at the senior table. Knowling had the power and support of his board to deal with his founders if they didn't measure up, but he tried in vain to make it work, despite a dysfunctional relationship between two of the founders. When the company had its first stumble under Knowling's leadership, the dysfunctional founder played a key role in orchestrating Knowling's resignation. Bob learned a

valuable lesson in not taking action when all the data was there
for him to do so.

- Jac Nasser: As CEO of Ford Motor, Nasser overlooked the signals that many members of his top team were not loyal and not
really on his side. When the Firestone tire crisis came along,
they undermined his efforts. It took a couple of years for him
to finally be ousted by Bill Ford, but a number of very disloyal
executives were major collaborators in his downfall. Nasser
failed to clean house when he should have.

Good leaders have blind spots about people because of a complex
set of cognitive and emotional processes. Sometimes leaders will have
a sense of loyalty to those who did something helpful to them earlier
in their career. Sometimes subordinates are very talented at the "kiss
upward and kick downward" game. They abuse their subordinates
and undermine colleagues, but they present a picture of perfection to
the boss. This is why 360-degree evaluations are so important. Leaders also succumb to the halo effect, when the leaders generalize their
own talents and abilities to others around them.

Blind spots lead some of us to have defensive routines that systematically block out accurate data on a person and/or set up psychological barriers that keep others from sharing honest feedback on the
person. All of these forces add up to serious bad people judgments,
which can create organizational crises. Noel was blinded by thirty
years of friendship.

Learning from Bad Crisis Judgments

Shell Story

Noel was consulting with the Committee of Managing Directors
(CMD) at Shell in the summer of 1995 when he received a call from
Cor Herkstroter, the chairman of Royal Dutch Shell. Herkstroter
wanted to discuss a breaking news story. The front pages of the *Financial Times, New York Times*, and many European papers had unfa-
vorable stories about Shell. The company was planning to sink an old

oil platform in the North Sea and environmentalists from Greenpeace were protesting. British prime minister John Major was supporting Shell, but the environmentalists were up in arms. In Germany, there were organized boycotts of Shell at the retail level. The governmental support from the prime minister backfired when pictures of Greenpeace boats being sprayed by fire hoses appeared on the front pages of papers around the world.

We worked on framing the dimensions of the problem Shell faced. Noel recommended that Herkstroter call the CMD together even though they were on vacation. But the Shell team viewed the problem as a local issue that, with Major's support, was well under control. Also, their engineering mind-set had led them to conclude that the sinking was the safest action to take. Since they thought they had the science on their side, they believed that was enough. They lacked the broader geopolitical and public image framing to see how Greenpeace could exploit the situation and drive a wedge between the positions of the Germans and other Europeans and that of the UK. This is a story of how good people make bad crisis judgments.

When Herkstroter and his well-meaning top team failed to properly frame and name the judgment, they set the stage for a bad judgment. For them it was a clear analytic judgment that was required. They had an old oil platform and they wanted to dispose of it in a way that was minimally damaging to the environment. They framed and named the judgment as an engineering problem. Then they mobilized and aligned with the UK government and their own managers.

But as they began to execute that judgment, all hell broke loose; Greenpeace saw that they had a great opportunity to gain political and PR ground. They depicted Shell as a big, environmentally insensitive oil company polluting the environment. Once the Greenpeace campaign was launched, Shell's leaders stumbled again by not learning and adjusting. Herkstroter and his team stayed the course until finally the negative publicity stopped them, but the damage to Shell's image was done by then.

Had there been a process for getting and realistically weighing feedback, the story might have ended differently. The judgment should have been reframed as not just an engineering problem but as a political and public relations judgment. This could have led to engaging those concerned with the environment in a process to jointly agree on the best way to dispose of the platform. The CMD did not have a Teachable Point of View and storyline for the company that dealt with the emerging political and social context for big oil on the world stage. Thus, the conditions remained in place for a second big crisis judgment at Shell just a few months later. This once again put Shell in a negative light on front pages around the world.

This time, Noel and colleagues were facilitating a workshop with the CMD in the Amstel Hotel in Amsterdam. After ending the workshop at 10 P.M., we were debriefing in our hotel room at 11 P.M. when we got a knock on the door. John Jennings, one of the four CMD members, said that there were protesters organizing in both London and the Shell headquarters in The Hague because of the arrest in Nigeria of Ken Saro-Wiwa, a community organizer who was helping the Ogoni tribe push for more rights. As an antigovernment protester in Nigeria, Saro-Wiwa was a hero for many Nigerians.

The government was going to try him for treason. Sympathetic protesters were mobilizing in the UK and the Netherlands because they wanted Shell, whose oil fields were the major income producer for Nigeria, to intervene on behalf of Saro-Wiwa. The arrest was becoming an international cause. The protests had led the Shell security team to instruct the CMD to get out of the hotel to a safer place. At eleven at night they did just that.

This turned out to be another bad crisis judgment in the making. The CMD framed and named the issue as political. They decided that Shell should stay clear and let Nigeria resolve its internal politics. When protests occurred, the media, as in the Brent Spar crisis, portrayed Shell as insensitive, insular, and arrogant. We were with the CMD, and we can attest they were far from arrogant and insular. They were not, however, prepared to make appropriate judgments in this crisis. They made the decision as a corporation to frame the issue as political, and since it was a political issue, Shell should not get involved. As a result, they missed an opportunity to alter the course of

Nigerian history. As it turned out, Ken Saro-Wiwa was hanged, and he became the martyr in a story that had Shell playing the villain.

◆ ◆ ◆

Good crisis judgments are made when leaders have a solid Teachable Point of View and a storyline that sets up the platform.

The good that came out of these two Shell publicity disasters was that Herkstroter and the CMD came up with a new TPOV that included a community and citizenship agenda. This TPOV would provide them a different storyline for the future and new context for dealing with crises. This storyline took several months of active engagement of teams of leaders at Shell. It was widely taught throughout the company and continues to provide context for judgments around the world in communities in which Shell operates.

When a crisis hits, it is too late for a leader to develop a TPOV and storyline. Without a TPOV and storyline for how Shell would deal with political and public relations issues, it was almost impossible to make proactive judgments in the two cases.

Shell isn't the only big oil company to mess up big crisis judgments. The whole industry has a track record of making bad judgment calls in crises. Noel was running a leadership development program for up-and-coming executives at Exxon in March 1989 when the *Exxon Valdez,* a huge oil tanker, strayed from its course and went aground in Alaska. At the time of the accident, which spilled eleven million gallons of oil in an environmentally sensitive area, the captain was drunk and asleep. The spill made front-page news all over the world and resulted in massive long-term damage to the environment. It killed over half a million birds, forty-five hundred sea otters, and fourteen killer whales and damaged the salmon, herring, clams, and mussels in the region.

Lawrence Rawls, the then CEO of Exxon, definitely did not take ownership of the problem, opting instead for just the opposite, a bunker mentality. He did not go to the scene until two weeks after the spill. And when he did appear, he seemed insensitive to the environmental damage. On one television appearance he even said he was unfamiliar with the latest Exxon cleanup plans because as CEO, he was not responsible to read such reports. He blamed the media for making too big of a deal of the spill.

For months pictures of dead birds and fish, dying seals and plant life were shown over and over again in the press. There was never an apology. Instead, the Exxon legal staff and outside counsel prepared to defend the company against the inevitable lawsuits. An initial judgment against the company totaled more than $5.3 billion, the largest punitive damages ever assessed for corporate irresponsibility. After legal challenges and appeals Exxon got the punitive damages down to $2.5 billion in 2006, which equaled $4.5 billion with interest; Exxon is still appealing the case in 2007.

The public relations damage has still not been erased. As Professor Ron Smith at Buffalo State College says in summarizing his teaching case on the Valdez incident, Exxon management

1. showed little leadership,
2. failed to show concern,
3. failed to involve the media,
4. failed to respond to activists.[7]

As in the Shell case, this bad judgment occurred because the leaders did not have a TPOV and storyline that enabled them to deal with crises of this nature.

History repeats itself. As Barbara Tuchman points out in *The March of Folly,* people continue to make bad judgments despite many opportunities to learn from past mistakes.[8]

Lessons Learned from Other Crisis Judgments

The case that is held up as the exemplar of great crisis leadership is the Tylenol poisonings in 1982. Seven people were killed when someone laced Tylenol capsules with potassium cyanide and the bottles were distributed to store shelves. The tampering happened after the medicine had left J&J's control, but the company and its leader, James Burke, stepped in quickly to take ownership of the problem. They quickly pulled all of the product off the shelves and offered refunds for anyone who wanted to return bottles already purchased. Because of their quick, responsive action, they were able to save the brand and return it to its top-selling status.

Another leader who gets less attention for a well-handled crisis is Jac Nasser. When Ford Explorer SUVs with Firestone tires started rolling over in 2001, Nasser as CEO of Ford stepped out front and took responsibility for solving the problem. It wasn't clear why the accidents were happening, or whether Ford or Firestone was at fault. But Nasser took on the job of dealing with it. And he did it well, even though he did not have a united team around him and even though his intense focus on the crisis opened the door for others to undermine him and ultimately get him ousted. Had he been less urgently attentive to the Explorer crisis, he probably would have had the time to protect himself better from the threats within his senior management team.

Nasser set up a war room at Ford that he personally led, day in and day out. He took control and followed his TPOV, which had the customer as value number one even though it cost the company $2.1 billion after taxes.

For Noel, who was working with Nasser at the time, it was an opportunity to pull together all of his crises experiences and develop a TPOV to share with Nasser:

Personal and Confidential

May 30, 2001

Dear Jac,
I want to share some thoughts with you regarding your leadership during this very trying time at Ford. First, when I shook hands with you at the Ritz-Carlton several years ago, I said I was signing up for the long haul with you. I meant it then. I mean it even more today. I will do whatever possible to support you during this tough leg of the journey to build the "world's leading consumer company producing automotive products and services." I am here because I believe in you and your leadership. Second, I want to share some perspectives and thoughts on leading in a crisis.

Personal Benchmarks

You and I have both been involved in crises over our careers. I did a review of the ones I was personally involved with over the years. I took a look at them and have pulled out some of the lessons.

First, before I share the benchmarks, I want to remind you that I did live through the worst period of time with Welch at GE in the mid-1980s, when he was vilified in the press as "Neutron Jack," as "hollowing manufacturing in America," as the person who was setting the wrong model of management in contrast to IBM, Digital, HP, etc. It is why I started the *Control Your Destiny* book with "Jack Welch is the greatest CEO GE has ever had" and "Jack Welch is an asshole"—I wanted people to reflect on the role of a true leader, one who can lead when they are not winning the popularity contest.

Second, here are some of my experiences:

Union Carbide

The Bhopal explosion occurred when I was working with some of their management team—it ultimately destroyed the company. They did not mobilize externally and internally quickly enough.

Lesson
The critical need for speed and alignment—external and internal.

Exxon

Valdez—I was working with Lee Raymond, then COO who reported to Rawls, CEO, on a leadership program when the accident occurred. Neither Rawls nor Raymond went to Alaska, nor did they speak to their troops. They lost the PR battle and lost the respect of their people. The leaders underneath them were ashamed of their leaders and the company.

Lesson

Low profile and bunker mentality, leadership a problem externally, and even more so internally as you end up losing the trust and morale of your own people.

Royal/Dutch Shell

Brent Spar—the oil rig that Shell was going to dump in the North Sea that the Greens attacked Shell on. Shell countered with scientific data that they were doing the right thing. The CMD (top team) was totally out of their element, fighting the Greens as if they were in an academic debate while the Greens took it to the streets of Germany, played the German Shell head against the UK and left the prime minister in the UK holding the bag when Shell did a 180 due to losing the PR battle when the Greens sent a boat out to the North Sea, which got filmed on global TV as being defended with fire hoses, etc.

Lesson

The CMD had no clue. They fought a political and PR battle with engineering data and lost face totally.

Nigeria—the Nigerian dictatorship imprisoned and ended up hanging a dissident who had led rallies against Shell and their environmental practices in Nigeria. Public opinion pushed Shell to take a stance, they pleaded neutrality. Patti and I were in the Amstel Hotel the night the protesters started in the UK and Holland, and we had to evacuate at midnight. The CMD the next day was in disarray, having just come off the Brent Spar incident. They never got their storyline right and it ended up with both the *New York Times* running a front-page article with the dissident hanging from a Shell sign, which was run again in *Fortune*.

Lesson

Two crises in a row when they did not have their act together did tremendous damage to the brand. The good news is that it led to their corporate citizenship agenda, which they are actively living today.

GE

Time card scandal—in 1985 GE was nailed for engineers in the aerospace unit in Philadelphia falsifying their timecards—GE acquiesced of billing the government for millions of dollars—government all over GE, the press called GE a bunch of crooks, and the company was taken to task by all the major business and national press.

WELCH ACTIONS:

1. Personal audit of the problem to determine exactly what was going on
2. Plan of action FAST—the system was wrong, we at GE were wrong, we must fix this with the government. He took on national leadership role in the defense industry to clean up the problem (basically at the company level, managers juggled projects, if they overran one they took time from another, often with local government oversight person agreeing, they did it by having engineers sign off their time to the wrong project—well-intentioned engineers and managers wanting to make their projects succeed—yet highly illegal)
3. Clear storyline—the system was wrong—we participated—we have to clean it up and the government has every right to be angry—well-meaning people got caught up in this and unfortunately they will lose their jobs and GE has lost its integrity image—we all must realize that integrity is our most important asset—everyone needs to look in the mirror—I want all my leaders telling their people the real deal and using this to teach our values.

4. Welch led a national effort in the industry to clean this stuff up—CEO meetings, headed up the aerospace group on this nationally.

Lessons

GE and Welch come up looking very good—he spent time leading both externally and internally, made sure that his people heard the story over and over again, the top team, groups at Crotonville, etc. Saw it as his role to teach and dialogue so that people in GE and outside knew and believed the story.

Kidder Peabody

The first crisis came after buying Kidder, a group of traders were taken out in handcuffs on national TV. Welch and Bossidy were angry and embarrassed by having bought a firm that had fraudulent practices. Welch jumped in and made sure things were cleaned up. He put in Cathcart, a board member from the Midwest, a respected business leader, to clean the place up and get the respect of the SEC and others.

The second crisis was Joe Jett, the rogue trader, who got GE in trouble again and ended up getting Kidder fired. Dennis Dammerman was sent in to clean it up. Welch personally led a team of auditors down to Wall Street on Friday night after getting word of the problem and spent the weekend digging into the facts. *Fortune* did a cover story that year declaring the end of Jack Welch as CEO.

Lessons

Quickly face reality, bring your own independent team of auditors in to find out the truth for yourself, then get your own loyal people in to clean the mess up and work the external stakeholders personally—SEC, press, etc. Simultaneously communicate to your own troops over and over again.

Compressor Problem in the Refrigerator

GE put a bad compressor into millions of refrigerators which had to be recalled. Welch led the efforts and got the other business heads to come up with the money to meet the losses. Welch and his team learned the importance of having people in the room with real expertise when technical decisions were made. The leaders making the decision did not really understand compressors when they decided to put the technology derived from air conditioners into the refrigerator.

Lessons
Face reality, quickly clean up the mess, learn from it, and teach the troops.

Other crises for Welch include the Israeli general who was bribed by the GE sales manager—both went to jail. Also a scandal over the diamonds business where GE was accused of price fixing—Welch personally led the effort to clear GE's name. Finally, Welch has been involved in the Hudson River PCB issue since the late 1970s, it is still not resolved as the government is trying to get GE to pay hundreds of millions to dredge the Hudson and GE fighting it because they believe that it is not the right solution.

Things to Consider at Ford

Storyline
Simple and clear storyline that is understood by everyone and can be repeated and repeated. Starts with the top team, then they need to teach it to others.

EXAMPLE
Ford is going through a transformation to be the world's best consumer company producing automotive products and services. We have the right strategy, values, and tools for doing

so. We are going to have to fix things along the way. We are proud of our decision to put the customer as our number one value, which is why we are doing the recall. We feel it is dead wrong for Firestone to lash out in desperation and try to confuse the customer by failing to admit the tire problem and blame the problems on Ford. We will do everything possible to help our customers be safe and be treated in a way to engender trust. This storyline:

Must be repeated over and over and over.
Needs to be updated and give people understanding.

Personal Leadership

1. Face reality, keep getting the facts for self and all stakeholders.
2. Values guide action, keep reminding the organization that it is values driven.
3. Communicate but also teach others.
   External stakeholders: board, dealers, suppliers, partners, business community, business schools, government groups, journalists—need political plan for each.
   Internal stakeholders: need visible leader, Churchill and Roosevelt used broadcasts, fireside chats, etc., to build confidence and hope, the leader must be more visible than ever through all channels, through town hall meetings, plant visits, LDC teaching, Internet, and FCN.
4. Emotional energy for long period of time, take care of yourself, get positive energizers in the organization to feed your energy (selective town hall meetings, plant visits, LDC, etc., skip levels with Black Belts, etc., pick groups that will also energize you).
5. Top team: make sure that they are not pulling you in different directions such as "don't talk to the troops" vs. "talk to the troops," etc.—watch the bunker mentality— seek out other views—the new comers to Ford.

6. Street fighter when needed: take the high ground with
   Firestone but make sure that there are some tough street
   fighters for the down-in-the-trenches battles, always do
   things over to determine the outcome.[9]

Bottom Line

- Your emotional energy is key
- Your storyline is simple, clear, taught at all levels
- It is about people being aligned—internal more important than
  external
- It's about *edge*

Sincerely yours,
Noel

Nasser executed the crisis judgment process with precision. He
personally drove the process. He did a great job of framing and naming the crisis around doing what was right for the customer and for
the transformation of Ford to a customer-centric company. Still,
while he did a wonderful job handling the Explorer-Firestone crisis,
even without an aligned team, it cost him dearly. The lesson here is
that without sufficient preparation, a good strategy, and a good team,
a leader may be able to handle a crisis well, but the price and ultimate
costs may be very high.

BLIND SPOTS ON PEOPLE ARE KILLERS

As Downing told us, flawed people consistently fail you when you
need them the most, when you and the organization are in a period
of crisis and high stress. Nasser needed an aligned team during the
Firestone crisis. There has been a lot of revisionist history regarding
the Nasser era but the facts are that he was well into a transformation
that we feel would have positioned Ford to be in much better shape in
2007—certainly better than a year with a $13 billion loss, specula-

tion of bankruptcy, and rumors of the Ford Family coalition about to come apart due to the tens of billions of lost market capitalization.

Nasser's Teachable Point of View was very clear and he had developed a storyline that he was executing consistently. He wanted to create the world's premier automotive company that transformed from a domestic focused, "big three" car company with international operations to a "global organization with a single strategic focus on consumers and shareholder value . . . the new DNA has a couple of key components: a global mind-set, as I've said, an intuitive knowledge of Ford's customers, a relentless focus on growth, and the strong belief that leaders are teachers."[10]

Nasser made bold strategic moves, including the acquisitions of Volvo and Land Rover, to broaden the portfolio. He moved to create global technology and common systems while simultaneously customizing elements of the cars to the local markets. He centralized and decentralized around a clear Teachable Point of View, in his words: "All major decisions about brand positioning and technology will be made by a central group. Execution, however, will be local, with enough flexibility to ensure that local differences are accounted for." This was done in all areas including human resource practices around the world so as to be both global and local.[11]

He personally led an effort called "business leadership initiative," BLI, in which his top two thousand leaders personally ran three-day workshops for seventy thousand employees worldwide. Topping the agenda were shareholder value, customer focus, ways to drive new efficiencies into the fabric of the company, as well as executing change projects that yielded over $2 billion in cost savings for Ford. He was well into a multiyear transformation that included reinventing every element of the company, from product development, to manufacturing efficiencies, to the introduction of Six Sigma quality, to succession planning processes that accounted for leaders' performance and leadership behaviors, to massive investment in development of leaders at all levels. Having lived through the Jack Welch–led GE transformation as head of leadership development at Crotonville, Noel who was working with Nasser during this time, can attest to Nasser's relentless application of the lessons derived from GE and others.

The blind spot will get you; bad people judgments leave you totally vulnerable in a crisis. Nasser executed the crisis judgment process with precision. He personally drove the process, did a great job of framing and naming the crisis around doing what was right for the customer, and for the transformation of Ford to a customer-centric company. He failed in the mobilizing and aligning process due to bad people judgment. He did not have a loyal and aligned team. They ultimately took advantage of the crisis to form a small coalition that went to Bill Ford and pressured him to push Nasser out.

The blind spot existed in the context of a leader who had a long and storied career of good people judgments, who systematically assessed both performance and leadership behaviors, who used 360-degree feedback on leaders to overcome his biases. Why good leaders have blind spots is obviously due to a complex set of self-knowledge and social-network knowledge issues. The Nasser example is a painful lesson for all leaders: if the people judgments are not sound, it is very hard to have good crisis judgments.

10

CRISIS AS A LEADERSHIP

DEVELOPMENT OPPORTUNITY

■ **Leaders Who Make Good Judgments Are Prepared in Advance for Crises**
- They have built aligned and trusted teams.
- They have clear Teachable Points of View and storylines.

■ **When a Crisis Arrives, Winning Leaders Respond Immediately**
- They engage the appropriate people with the needed knowledge.
- They mobilize their team of aligned leaders for quick execution.

■ **Crises Provide Leadership Development Opportunities**
- Leaders role-model behaviors necessary for success.
- An explicit teaching process keeps everyone focused on critical issues.

◆ ◆ ◆

The most important task of an organization's leader is to
anticipate crisis . . . perhaps not avert it, but to anticipate it.

—Peter Drucker, *Managing the Nonprofit Organization:*
Principles and Practices[1]

Why are some leaders better equipped to deal with crises than others? Even when hit with totally unpredictable events, why do some leaders do a better job of responding? Why are some of them even able to turn organizational crises into leadership development opportunities?

The answer is because they anticipate crises. They aren't psychics. They can't see into the future and predict seemingly random events that are going to strike two days or two years hence. But they clearly understand that some crises *are* going to come down the pike, and they prepare themselves and their organizations to respond effectively and efficiently when they do. These leaders know that in order to survive crises, and perhaps even come out ahead because of them, they must have three things:

1. An aligned and highly trusted team;
2. A Teachable Point of View and storyline for the organization's future success;
3. A commitment to developing other leaders throughout the crisis.

David Novak, CEO of Yum! Brands, and Ricardo Salinas, founder and chairman of Grupo Salinas, are two leaders who have successfully navigated their organizations through several crisis situations. Both Novak and Salinas do three things simultaneously. They

1. Effectively, in real time, deal with their crises.
2. Mobilize, align, and engage the right social network of leaders in their organizations by tapping their brains and their emotional energy to handle the crises.
3. Focus explicitly on developing the leaders engaged in the process, taking the time to teach and coach in real time.

Leaders who succeed in crises are able to do so because they work on developing their own capabilities and on building them into the fabric of their organizations. The conventional wisdom regarding crisis management and communication, basically, nets out to be good public relations advice. It includes such things as (1) preparation of crisis contingency plans, (2) analysis of the crisis and public perceptions, (3) identification of the relevant audiences, (4) repairing a tarnished image, (5) suggestions for effective ways to repair the organization's image.

All of these are reasonable actions, but they do not address how to fundamentally help the leader deal with the crisis judgment process in a way that furthers the organization's storyline, builds for the future, and also develops a broader social network of leaders better able to handle future crisis judgments.

David Novak has successfully made a number of crisis judgments, including responding to the avian flu in China, which was affecting the perception of the safety of the KFC food supply chain, and the *E. coli* outbreak first believed to be associated with green onions at Taco Bell that resulted in sixty-three confirmed illnesses. Both of these crises were serious threats to Yum!'s businesses. In the Taco Bell case, it appeared that the unit's green onions were the source of *E. coli* causing illnesses in consumers. The source of the problem was never completely confirmed, but Taco Bell immediately ordered the removal of all green onions from its fifty-eight hundred outlets nationwide as a precaution after samples initially tested positive for *E. coli*. Subsequent testing ruled out green onions as the source. The CDC later determined that lettuce may have been the more likely source. Taco Bell replaced all its lettuce across the Northeast, and switched its regional produce supplier as an added precaution.

Novak has repeatedly exercised good crisis judgment for the organization while simultaneously developing his leadership team's capacity to handle future crises. In his business, most crises are likely to be around the safety of the food supply chain. He has a very clear Teachable Point of View for Yum!, and it is played out in his storyline for where the company is headed; this is the context for his crisis judgments.

Sometimes crisis comes at the worst possible time. After only five months on the job as Circuit City CEO, Phil Schoonover faced an earnings crisis with the collapse of pricing for flat panel TVs in the holiday season of 2006. Schoonover had seemingly resurrected a dying company by strengthening sales of plasma and LCD TVs and building a service department that earned fat margins for delivery and installation. In the span of several weeks, Walmart and Costco brought down the price of a 42-inch plasma flat screen TV from a 2005 price point of about $2,200 to $999 in one year.

The revenue plans for Circuit City's holiday season were based on old assumptions about price and profitability, as were its full-year projected profits. The holiday season is the major contributor to Circuit City's full-year profits. Because they were in the midst of a turnaround situation, they were much more vulnerable to price cuts than their much bigger and stronger key competitor, Best Buy.

The result was that Schoonover's team had to call a "time-out" and do a radical "redo" loop around the execution of the longer-term strategy for Circuit City. They had to radically reduce expenses while accelerating growth. This was done in an engaging process where eleven teams in sixty days worked on special "crisis" projects three days a week, plus managed their day jobs during the busiest season of the year and came up with ways of keeping Circuit City delivering on its Teachable Point of View and storyline. While working on the crisis, they also were coached and taught by Schoonover and the top team to be more effective leaders.

By mid-2007 the Circuit City crisis was still a work in progress, as reported by the hometown press:

> Circuit City Stores Inc. continues to have nagging health problems as it nears its 60th birthday.
>
> But the Henrico County–based consumer electronics retailer seems to be taking steps that could put it on the road to better shape.
>
> Sales have grown only slightly in recent years. Profit margins have shrunk. Earnings are unstable. In less than a year, its stock price has been sliced in half.
>
> Circuit City has opened a net of 38 U.S. stores since 2002 and is debating the sale of its Canadian operation. Rival Best Buy Co. Inc. has added nearly 350 stores during the same period, has a strong foothold in Canada and is expanding into China.
>
> After posting a net loss for the fiscal year, things got worse for Circuit City when the chain said last month that it expects a bigger operating loss—as much as $80 million to $90 million—than it had forecast for its fiscal first quarter, which ends May 31. The company said sales fell "substantially below-plan" in April.
>
> Philip J. Schoonover, Circuit City's chairman, president and

chief executive, knows he has his work cut out to get a grip on costs, boost sales and increase profitability.

"We're at the beginning of act two of a three-act play," Schoonover said last week. "Despite the choppiness in our near-term performance, we are staying true to our long-term strategy."[2]

YUM! BRANDS

David Novak is a veteran at crisis management. He is a seasoned leader who knows that crisis judgment starts with good people judgment. He painfully learned this lesson is his early days as CEO at Yum! Brands. As the company, then called Tricon Global Restaurants, was being spun off from PepsiCo, he compromised on a key people judgment, the CFO, and almost created a crisis for the company.

Novak has a clear Teachable Point of View and storyline for the company. However, when he was just taking over, he felt pressured to have a successful launch. He made a compromise that he later regretted. He told us:

> One of the worst leadership decisions I've made was hiring a CFO who supposedly brought expertise to the table that we thought we may be lacking. He was president of a competitive company and had a good pedigree. But my gut told me that this guy really wouldn't be a good cultural fit. He lacked the leadership style that I've found motivating in others. He was smart and PepsiCo thought he had the right technical skills for our new public company. It was in the very early stages of our company and I agreed to compromise on my decision. We had very little time to take our company public and with that time pressure, we didn't do enough homework on our own how to explore how he'd fit in with our other teams. I should have trusted my gut reaction and taken the time before making the call.
>
> PepsiCo hadn't given us a lot of time to staff with the right people. I was pressured on time. And we were looking for an experience that we didn't necessarily have. And those two things really drove, I think, a very poor decision.

The result was he got the CFO to resign in order to avert a crisis during a critical time for the organization.

AVIAN FLU CRISIS IN CHINA

This experience bolstered Novak's determination to have a very clear approach to crisis judgment. First and foremost he says it is critical at Yum! "to have process and discipline around what really matters and keeps you out of crises." But even with effective crisis prevention, and all the discipline on the planet, some crises can't be prevented. In 2005, for example, KFC in China had to cope with the avian flu scare. Many Chinese were afraid to buy and eat chicken, and partly as a result fourth-quarter profit dropped 20 percent. However, within months KFC sales rebounded largely because of how Yum! and KFC handled the crisis.

Preparation Phase

SENSE AND IDENTIFY

Novak and his team sensed and identified the need to make a crisis judgment regarding the sale of chicken at Yum!, most important in KFC stores in China, very quickly. As the World Health Organization (WHO) and the media chronicled the avian flu epidemic in Asia, the judgment was how to support the brand and keep selling chicken in the face of the flu scare.

FRAMING AND NAMING

The key was the framing and naming of the judgment. For Novak and his team the framing was that "people need education and understanding" regarding the safety of chicken at KFC. Sam Su, the president of Yum! Brands International Greater China, faced the reality of avian flu in his territory and then started educating the public on the myths and realities associated with the disease. He explained that chicken meat served at KFC outlets was safe because bird flu could not be spread via thoroughly cooked chicken or egg products. He also explained that authoritative organizations, including WHO, had shown that high temperature is one of the most effective ways to kill avian flu virus and that all KFC chicken is processed above the required temperature. This teaching was aimed at mobilizing and aligning both internal and external stakeholders so that the judgment call to keep selling chicken and defend the brand could succeed.

MOBILIZE AND ALIGN

The Yum! corporate team provided materials to all the store managers and staff worldwide so that they could answer questions and concerns of customers.

The Call Phase

The judgment call that was made by Novak, Sam Su, and team was to keep selling chicken in China and around the world by making sure that customers knew and understood they were safe. The way to do this was to keep teaching the community about avian flu and the food chain.

The Execution Phase

There were many actions taken to drive the execution of this crisis judgment. These included a preemptive campaign of putting small stickers on the lid of every KFC bucket, assuring customers that the chicken was rigorously inspected and thoroughly cooked, quality assured.

Novak and his team learned and adjusted as they went along and ultimately proved that they had exercised good crisis judgment, as the brand is doing fine and KFC is selling record amounts of chicken in China.

ANOTHER CHINA CRISIS: RED DYE

In addition to the avian flu crisis Yum! got hit with another crisis in China when a red dye used there was linked to cancer. Profit again plunged 30 percent until they worked out a solution. "A food safety issue can happen in any country," Novak told us. "We have to use education to insulate ourselves."

In talking about the food dye crisis Novak made his role as CEO clear.

> I trusted Sam Su (the local CEO). We gave him coaching, we
> gave him ideas but we knew he knew the Chinese government,

he knew the Chinese media, he knew the Chinese consumer better than us, and he handled it extremely well . . . my job was to let him know that we are 100% confident behind him. . . . I sent a letter to the Chinese team and said we'll come back, this is a short-term thing, I appreciate all the hard effort. . . . I felt that my big job as a leader was to understand what was going on there, provide whatever coaching I could . . . and provide support.

Novak reflected on another lesson: Even though not one customer was hurt, he made it clear that the red dye crisis never should have occurred. It should not have been in their supply chain. He told us, "No one ever got sick or would ever get sick by what was in the supply chain. But it shouldn't have been in there. It wasn't an approved ingredient."

TACO BELL GOOD CRISIS JUDGMENTS

As Novak predicted, the food supply chain created another crisis, this one the E. coli outbreak in the United States linked to Taco Bell. Once Novak identified the need for crisis judgment, he followed his well-developed approach. Based on the strong Teachable Point of View and a storyline that builds customer mania and growth, the team framed and named the judgment around how to support customers' safety and therefore the brand. The judgment to stop using any green onions in all 5,800 stores was how this judgment was executed, along with constant communication with the staff and the public.

The crisis judgment success led Novak to write in his 2006 annual report letter:

I'm particularly proud of the Taco Bell team for weathering a produce supply incident impacting our restaurants in the Northeast during December. Brands can go either forward or back on how they deal with a crisis, and our customers told us we did a very good job. As we move ahead, Taco Bell will be leading the industry by requiring our suppliers to test produce at the farm level, in addition to testing already being done by the produce processors. This additional precaution will enhance our stringent food safety standards for all our brands and give our customers added assurance that our produce is as safe as possible."[3]

Novak's Teachable Point of View on Crisis Judgments

David Novak personally teaches his leaders how to deal with judgments in times of crisis. He has a very clear Teachable Point of View on crisis leadership: First, "what you don't do is try to solve a crisis by jumping to the wrong solution too early. Seeing the total landscape and trying to instill the need to do that is important." This sets the stage for proper framing and naming, which takes some cool, cognitive thinking, not emotional knee jerking.

Second, it is important that the mobilizing and aligning be done by the right people. Rawls at Exxon missed this totally when he distanced himself from the *Valdez* crisis. Novak told us:

> You have to look to your senior leadership to get those crises. . . . When you're in a crisis, you don't hand off the problem to the rookie, because rookies haven't gone through it before. You show the rookie how to go through it when they have to go through it. You don't delegate crisis management. You're in there, you're helping people figure this out. When you do delegate, you delegate to people that know a heck of a lot more about it than you.

No matter what they do, Novak and his team will undoubtedly face more crises in the food supply chain. And there will probably be other crises caused by external catastrophes or by internal errors. What Novak is doing is developing other leaders who can drive his Teachable Point of View and in turn develop others who can make good crisis judgments. His last piece of advice to us on this matter was this important insight:

The worst thing that can happen in a crisis is to have some jerk sitting there saying, "We should have done this, we should have done that." You don't have time at that point to say, "We should have done this or should have done that." At that point you've got to help. It comes down to people. If you have people that you trust and believe in, you can handle crisis judgments. If you do not, you work with them, you coach them so they'll solve the problems and handle the crises. If you don't, you better get some different people.

PHIL SCHOONOVER AND THE CIRCUIT CITY CRISIS

Philip J. Schoonover took over as CEO of Circuit City in March 2006. Schoonover had been a key leader at Best Buy. He helped Best Buy's turnaround in the mid-1980s, led the building of its service business, and helped lead the transformation from product-centric to customer-centric, so he was a veteran in large-scale retail transformation. Still, he was taking over a company that had a number of serious problems. While the company had once been number one in its industry, it was then left to flounder and was underinvested both in terms of stores and human capital. The first thing Schoonover did was get a team in place and develop a Teachable Point of View and storyline for the future.

The transformation hit a serious road bump. After the stock shot up to $40, reflecting positive expectations for Schoonover's transformation plans, the wheels came off. The competitive environment changed, and Schoonover was dealing with a stock price that in the first half of 2007 was down to $16. Less than one year into the turnaround, Schoonover was faced with an even tougher environment than imagined.

This raises an important, albeit somewhat obvious, point about crisis judgments. While making the right ones at critical junctures can literally save a company so that it may live another day, successful crisis judgments do not guarantee the future success of an organization. The Circuit City/Schoonover case is a prime example of how a

CEO can make and execute one excellent crisis judgment and execute it to great precision, only to face other, even greater problems in the months ahead.

In the fall of 2006, Schoonover had been Circuit City CEO for about eight months. In baseball terms, that put him at about the bottom of the first inning. That is too little time to measure the success of a leader of a complex company like Circuit City.

There have been some painful lessons along the way. One leadership judgment that Schoonover made in March 2007 was to both shrink and grow simultaneously. He had to do layoffs in one part of the business while simultaneously adding head count to the Firedog services organization and other growth platforms. The judgment to make the cuts was good; the PR was not good. The press slammed him for cost cutting, something Schoonover knew was the right thing to do. From his point of view it was a necessary turnaround tactic, not unlike what Jack Welch did in the mid-1980s when he laid off more than one hundred thousand workers, garnering the "Neutron Jack" moniker that he detested (Noel was head of GE's Leadership Development at the time).

Even though the move set off a firestorm in the media, Schoonover is clear that he would make the same decision today, although he would frame it differently. Cost-cutting is seldom praised in the press, but it is often a necessary and critical step in executing a successful big-company turnaround.

What he learned was the importance of shaping and controlling the overall storyline that is part of a rebuilding for the future, a painful but necessary step in his journey. As controversial as that decision might have been, it shouldn't detract from Schoonover's handling of the flat-panel pricing crisis. His successful navigation of this crisis is a textbook example of how not only to weather a storm, but also how to build a leadership capability for the future.

When prices collapsed in flat-panel TVs, Circuit City's earnings, which depended largely on the 2006 holiday season, were headed for disaster, as were the plans for 2007 and 2008. Rather than attempt to respond as the "lone ranger" crisis leader, Schoonover created a crisis judgment platform for eleven teams of leaders at Circuit City. He led it; and it enabled his team to make the short-term crisis judgments needed so as to be able to drive the longer-term Teachable Point of View and storyline for Circuit City.

Circuit City Being Prepared for Crisis

The most important preparation for a crisis is the fundamental work on developing a Teachable Point of View and storyline for the organization, as these provide the context for crisis judgments. Schoonover led an effort in the first half of 2006 involving hundreds of top leaders at Circuit City to develop a long-term strategic plan and a TPOV and storyline. The top leaders then had to engage thousands in leader/teacher workshops to drive the new Teachable Point of View throughout Circuit City.

In August and September 2006, the top two thousand leaders taught several daylong workshops to thousands of employees throughout the stores, including the forty-five thousand part-time associates. These workshops were designed to teach everyone the storyline for the future of Circuit City. The chart "The Circuit City Teachable Point of View" is what Schoonover and the top team developed. It lays out the basics of the Circuit City Teachable Point of View. It reflects Schoonover's belief that what is good for associates is also what helps customers. Both groups need to be treated like they matter, be supportive, be inspired and excited, and have things made easier. Schoonover and his team together crafted that into a storyline for the future. They described what the stores and Web experience would look like, how the new Firedog services would be different and better than the competition, what the associates would be doing with customers, and how Circuit City would perform competitively.

One powerful exercise for helping the team get the narrative developed was to have Schoonover and each of the top team write a narrative, a story, taking place two years in the future, that they would each like to see it on the cover of *BusinessWeek*. These stories had to include a vision for where the company was going to be in two years in terms of sales, profits, organization, performance versus competi-

The Circuit City Teachable Point of View

Strategic Architecture

ENGAGE
Excite and Inspire Me · Treat Me Like I Matter
RESPECT

It's All
About
Helping
You

SIMPLIFY
Make it Easy for Me · Guide and Support Me
TEACH

MAINTAIN THE HIGHEST INTEGRITY

 This is a big shift for the company and will require significant investment

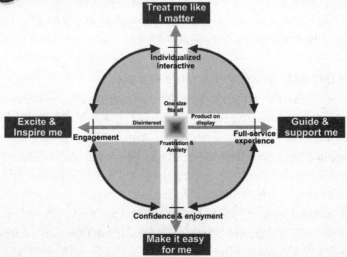

Treat me like
I matter

Individualized
interactive

One size
fits all

Excite &
Inspire me   Disinterest   Product on
                                    display
Engagement   Full-service
                                    experience   Guide &
                                                        support me

Frustration &
Anxiety

Confidence & enjoyment

Make it easy
for me

tors, as well as a blueprint on how Circuit City would transform itself from 2006 to 2008. The stories had to capture the leadership, the culture, and the challenges along the way, and they had to be living narrative stories, not PowerPoint presentations.

After an hour of writing, each team member read his or her story to the group and the group then listed the themes that were in each story. Generally, there were about ten critical elements, including the people who were running what part of the company, problems encountered along the way, expected performance and stock price, what stores looked like, how the company faired versus the competition, and so on.

The process ended with the team reviewing where they were aligned and not aligned. In situations where they were not aligned, they talked about what they would do to get there. This process of aligning leaders around a common Teachable Point of View and getting everyone to take a role in making it happen was cascaded throughout the company, as was the development of a future storyline for every associate in every part of the organization.

For example, the head of an individual Circuit City store had to personalize the Circuit City Teachable Point of View for that store and had to be able to have a future storyline for his or her associates. Noel facilitated this process and can attest to the total lack of focus on the potential for a price collapse driven by an aggressive competitive action on the part of Walmart, Costco, or others. They did not anticipate the severity of the problems created by what they later called the "perfect storm."

The Circuit City Crisis: Too Little Too Late

As heroic as the efforts were, the end game saw the demise of Circuit City. A year later, on September 22, 2008, CEO Phil Schoonover resigned under pressure from Mark Wattles, Circuit City investor and board member. By early 2009 Circuit City went into bankruptcy and its assets were sold during the first half of 2009. Circuit City was one more retailer that saw its demise in the 2008–2009 recession; others included Sharper Image, CompUSA, Foot Locker, and Wilson's Leather.

One very innovative attempt to save Circuit City was a new concept store. These were smaller, more efficient stores with new value propositions called "New City." The Acceleration Initiative New Concept team developed the new physical architecture and the new format in the stores as well as the all important human resource strategy, which included a completely new way of hiring, developing, and training the staff. The store associates all do the interviewing, selecting, and developing. The first of these stores was launched in the summer of 2007 and was dramatically outperforming other stores. The plan was to add hundreds of New City stores during 2008 and 2009.

These stores were successful in terms of sales and the return on investment, but were not able to prevent the mother ship from sinking as the base business of six hundred stores could not be turned around fast enough.

The leadership team under Schoonover had clearly framed and named the judgments needed and had made judgment calls needed to transform the company. Where the leadership judgment process failed was in the execution phase. Both the speed of the change and the scale of change required to save Circuit City were not there. It is probable that no leader could have saved Circuit City from the perfect storm—relentless competition from Walmart, Best Buy, and Amazon coupled with a massive recession. The Circuit City demise was set in motion over a decade earlier when it failed to keep up with competitors such as Best Buy in building new stores in new locations with new formats and labor models. The irony is that much of Best Buy's successful customer centricity transformation was led by Phil Schoonover while he was a key member of the Best Buy leadership team. When he left Best Buy and went to Circuit City to become their CEO, the expectations for him leading a successful Circuit City transformation were extraordinarily high, but his leadership judgments turned out to be too little and too late.

RICARDO SALINAS FRAMES THE ECONOMIC CRISIS AS AN OPPORTUNITY

In contrast to Circuit City, the Mexican entrepreneur, founder, and chairman of Grupo Salinas, Ricardo Salinas, has turned the 2009 global recession, which is particularly severe, into an opportunity. Salinas tells his leaders that now is the time to transform the organization and beat the competition. In 2008, as the recession was unfolding, Salinas, who spends a great deal of his time personally teaching and coaching his leaders, told a group of close to two thousand store managers, regional staff and headquarter staff that a crisis is a great opportunity. He has over one thousand retail stores selling consumer electronics, appliances, furniture, motorcycles, and cars, as well as a bank granting credit for customers to buy products. His customer base is the bottom of the economic pyramid in Mexico. These are customers who need credit and can't obtain it through traditional banks. He has a very loyal customer base.

The Bear in the Woods Story

Salinas told the story over and over again in 2008 to his leadership teams, thousands of them in workshops, about the two friends who were hiking in the woods. They came upon a nice pond in the woods on a hot day and decided to take a swim. They took their clothes off and went skinny-dipping. Along comes a big bear. The two friends jump out of the pond and get ready to start running when one of the two stops and puts his sneakers on. The other one says, "Why are you doing that? We can't outrun the bear!" The one who put his sneakers on says, "I know, I just have to outrun you."

Salinas then told his team they were going to transform themselves and outrun their competition during the recession and will not only survive but thrive in the future. He stated that now was the time to take advantage of their weaknesses. He is doing this by investing in a transformation process to move his stores and bank in a new strategic direction.

The Elektra Transformation Process

The goal is to reposition the more than 1,200 stores in Mexico, Central America, Brazil, and Argentina to a new competitive level. The company is Latin America's leading financial services company and specialty retailer selling electronics, household appliances, motorcycles, furniture, cell phones, and electronic money transfers. Banco

Azteca is closely integrated with the retail stores so as to offer consumer credit, credit cards, car loans, mortgages, and personal loans.

Salinas launched a transformation process designed to enhance Grupo Elektra's competitiveness and profitability by improving efficiencies in customer services and delivery capabilities. It started in January 2009 with the launch of eight teams of leaders to work on projects dealing with supply and merchant issues as well as issues in the store and credit areas. The teams had a six-month four-phase process:

CURRENT PRACTICES & PROCESSES

> **Phase 1: Value Targeting**—Assess financial impact of improving key processes
>
> **Phase 2: Prototyping**—Prototype details and refine proposed process changes
>
> **Phase 3: Lowing Risk**—Reduce risk by proving execution in one hundred stores
>
> **Phase 4: Scaling**—Scale lowest risk, highest impact

THE PROJECTS: SETTING THE STAGE FOR IMPORTANT
STRATEGIC JUDGMENTS

This process will lead to an intensive transformation of Grupo Elecktra. Senior leaders from key functions will be actively involved so that they learn world class retail approaches and customize these for Elektra. Each team will require a financial person who is given a very clear charter and has regular checkpoint meetings with Salinas and the top team of Elektra leaders.

The charters for the teams are as follows: Each team should have six members who bring diverse talents and cross-functional skills. Team members should expect to spend 30 to 40 percent of their time on project work.

TEAM PROJECTS

> **Merchandise Effectiveness Projects**
>
> *1. Assortment Optimization* (GMROI)

This team will produce customer driven, compelling assortments with optimal returns on store space, display investment, return on inventory, and assortments that drive financing profits. The team must eliminate "clutter" and duplication in assortments and redeploy resources to growth product categories.

This should include a complete review of inventory/In Stock/turns. The team will improve the availability of products in the stores so that customers can find the merchandise they desire on store shelves, while driving unproductive inventory out of the pipeline. The team will work to improve supplier performance to fill the rate metric. Overall, the work should integrate supply chain inventory management and merchant teams leading to a reduction in overall lead time from order to store.

2. *Strategic Sourcing* (GMROI)

Implement a supplier performance program that optimizes end-to-end profitability. Review all SKU level pricing and profitability with assortment planning. Renegotiate overall vendor contracts and SKU level pricing with fact based data driven brief prepared in advance. Consider direct sourcing where net profits can be improved or use the data to improve existing vendor performance.

3. *Advertising (promotion) Effectiveness* (GMROAE)

Allocate advertising and promotional spend based on SKU and category responsiveness. Gauge overall spend level against productivity measures; eliminate nonproductive spending or promotional costs.

4. *Formats / Store Space / Plan-o-graming* (GMROI through display and remodel capital expenditures; GMROL through labor spend)

Upgrade overall image of existing store with a combination of cosmetic enhancements and merchandising disciplines. At an overall format level, define block plans for departmental utilization and then define "modules A, B, C" that will be set based on format and size of the actual store. Define signage and fact tags that make it easy for the customer, associate, merchandising and financing to execute defined strategies. Improve visual standards where the impact adds value to customer experience and profitability. Do all of this with a focus on ensuring execution of store Standard Operating Procedures (SOP); modules should be optimized so they are consistent with the store SOP recommendations.

Retail Effectiveness Projects
5. Retail/Credit SOPs

In many cases, we have left the details of the basic processes for operating a store to the store manager's discretion. Processes are learned and refined through experience or coaching as there has not been any documentation outlining exactly how to perform these basic tasks. One drawback of this approach is that it can waste time and store resources as mangers invent their own processes or replicate bad habits learned from others. Another drawback is that the lack of a standardized approach limits best practice sharing and ongoing process improvement.

This team will be responsible for identity detailing, documenting, and teaching the core store processes in the following phases:

Phase 1: Value Targeting

During the initial phase of the work, this team will start with those processes identified by leadership. The team will be responsible for:

- understanding the process work that has already been completed
- identifying the importance (in financial value) of each process to Elektra, starting with the customer and sales associate perspective
- identifying the current state of process implementation and estimating the financial value of improving each process in the short-, medium-, and long-term
- recommending a prioritization for which processes to improve in 2009 based on the stores' and credit's ability to absorb changes

Phase 2: Documentation and Prototyping

During this phase, the team will provide detailed documentation for the prioritized 2009 processes and work with stores to implement and assess these processes:

- Creating detailed process maps and teaching documentation for transferring knowledge of the proposed processes to ten or more stores
- Identifying process effectiveness and efficiency metrics and an appraisal process in partnership with the stores
- Work with the stores weekly to make adjustments based on learning
- After approximately one month, work with the stores to recommend a revised version of each prioritized process for implementation in one hundred stores across Mexico

6. *Store Communication*

The stores receive input, communication, and direction from multiple sources. This creates confusion and conflicting messages. The net result is that some store managers become overwhelmed in their attempts to deal with the communication while others ignore important directions. In order to hold our store managers accountable for implementation of key activities or campaigns, we must routinize and streamline our communication.

This team will be responsible for identifying all of the communication that stores receive and proposing a streamlined process in the following phases:

Phase 1: Value Targeting

The team will be responsible for:

- Identifying the sources, frequency, and volume of communication currently pushed to the stores
- Explaining the cost of this communication and the lack of coordination in financial terms
- Detailing communication needs that overlap with credit and how to streamline these to promote more efficiency and better teamwork
- Providing a vision and financial case for a streamlined, coordinated two-way communication process that could be used to inform the stores as well as learn and share best practices

- Identifying a RASI for how functional or other communication will be handled

Phase 2: Prototyping
The team will be responsible for:

- Working with a group of ten stores to prototype the communication process, potentially requiring IT support
- Coordinating the activities of staff functions so that regular communication intended for all stores is channeled separately to these ten stores
- Measuring in time and financial terms the value of improved communication
- Prototyping at least one interactive process with the store to drive learning or best practice sharing
- Revising the process and communication platform as needed in preparation for a one hundred store rollout

7. Labor Productivity (Profit/Labor $)
This team will be responsible for decomposing how sales associates spend their time and recommending how to improve the efficiency of labor dollars spent. This will include understanding how to optimize scheduling for different times and days, task assignments during low customer traffic times, and identification of unproductive bureaucracy that reduces sales efficiency.

Phase 1: Value Targeting
The team will be responsible for:

- Identifying opportunities for improving labor efficiency and sale effectiveness based on customer traffic (this may mean an increase in labor at peak times and a decrease in labor at other times)
- Recommending how labor scheduling should be managed for optimal performance (central scheduling, software based, store manager discretion, etc.)

- Creating a detailed breakdown of how store associates in different types of stores (consider A,B, C formats) spend their time and the financial cost of unproductive time spent or missed sales opportunities
- Recommending changes in how store associates should manage tasks and sales during a day, and which low value activities should be eliminated or changed

Phase 2: Prototyping
This team will either demonstrate its recommendation in the ten-store test or may be integrated with the Retail/Credit SOP work.

8. *Banking Products*

This team will identify how to exploit Banco Azteca's deposit base and generally increase sales of banking products. This will include identifying new opportunities such as credit cards and also how to drive cross-sales opportunities so that financial products per customers increases. The team must examine the role of the store manager in selling financial products. Does he or she have the knowledge and tools? The team should recommend where an investment in training or tools, or improved use of existing tools (e.g., electronic wall) will increase sales. The team must also understand how our offers and precuts relate to the competition.

There are a number of specific challenges to enable store managers to effectively sell:

- Headquarters must have a comprehensive product portfolio for individuals and micro-businesses, and be able to transmit this to each store
- Store managers must be able to detect segment financial needs and react immediately toward product placement (detect and close the sale; be able to understand and provide excellent long-term customer service)
- We must ensure that financial products (other than consumer credit) are properly placed in an economically viable compensation model

- We must ensure that all key areas (Sales & Credit specifically) are aligned from upper to lower management toward providing store managers and credit officers with the culture, knowledge, and leadership they need to successfully sell financial precuts of diverse nature and market segments
- Development or improvement of financial products or technology to improve accessibility and/or cost reduction

Banco Azteca is, and needs to continue to be, the expert at attracting entry level customers to banking. In addition, for those approximately 12 million customers with whom we have already broken the barrier and are now looking for options with potential competitors, what else can we offer? For entry level customers, we should maintain a simple and accessible product line and excellent communication. For those with growth potential, how do we identify them, what can we give them, and how do we communicate with them?

SETTING UP MODEL STORES AND THEN SCALING

Parallel to the project teams, work with the stores has begun. It started with creating very clear audit and improvement tools for assessing each store on the quality of store leadership, the quality of the overall talent in the store, and the adherence to standard operating procedures for both credit and retail. Starting in May, a team of internal change agents, acting as both auditors and coaches started working with a targeted group of stores to make them the role models for the total system. By the end of August one hundred stores strategically located around Mexico were the models in terms of the leadership, talent, and standard operating procedures. In addition, these stores had implemented the output of the eight project teams.

In September, the remaining eight hundred stores had until the beginning of the Christmas season to learn from the one hundred. They were charged with implementing the improvements modeled in the one hundred stores. The one hundred were used as learning models and laboratories. Each of the one hundred had eight stores in their region that they were to help transform. The eight stores in the region spent time in the model store to learn and see the changes in action.

The Judgment Process for Ricardo Salinas

PREPARATION PHASE

Salinas sensed the recession early in the middle of 2008 and quickly framed and named it as an opportunity to beat the competition. The bear story reflects his leadership mindset, namely, this was an opportunity whereas most of his competitors were framing it as an awful belt-tightening, hunker down and survive the storm situation. He modernized and aligned his whole organization. Salinas had a several thousand-person workshop in the fall of 2008 to prepare these leaders to go back to the 35,000 associates and get them properly mobilized and aligned for the transformation in 2009.

CALL PHASE

As the project teams, the change agents, and his own team came up with transformative ideas, Salinas and the top team made a series of leadership judgments in a number of areas, namely store format, labor models, and how credit and sales could cooperate better, etc. . . . These judgments were all made on a platform of a very clear teachable point of view on the part of Ricardo. He spent multiple workshops teaching his regional managers in charge of all the stores his business ideas—the business model as well as the values to support the ideas. The values came in two categories:

I. Indispensable (essential) conditions—you must have these or you cannot work at Grupo Salinas:

1. Honesty (to be honest is to be upright; it implies congruity between what one feels, thinks, says, and does. Honesty allows establishing a relation of confidence and respect, which is crucial for teamwork.)
2. Intelligence (the aptitude to understand, to learn, and to associate ideas. It requires dexterity and skill to adapt to new situations or to find solutions to problems.)
3. Execution (or implementation; the personal work must be

oriented to fulfill concrete goals and we must make ourselves responsible for them.)

II. Six Qualities That Allow Us to Stand Out:

1. Excellence (passion for doing things well, fast, and efficiently)
2. Learning (facing change and preparing for an environment of constant transformation)
3. Teamwork (it is indispensable to develop teamwork and to persevere as a team to achieve a common goal)
4. Fast and simple (accomplish tasks rapidly and in a simple way, eliminate unnecessary functions and processes)
5. Customer focus (the customer must be our center of attention)
6. Generosity (to love the community in which we live and improve the quality of its health, education, and ecology)

EXECUTION PHASE

During the execution phase, Salinas reviews the changes in the stores as well as reviews the leadership talent. Changes are made as the learnings come from the one hundred stores. There are redo loops when displays and new formats either work or do not work in stores. The leadership is continuously assessed on the values, both the indispensable ones and the six qualities, using 360 (data from above, below, and peers), survey data, as well as the judgments of the leaders. The execution phase goes on for years.

◆ ◆ ◆

This chapter provided two best-practice examples of leaders making crisis judgments. The Yum!Brands/Novak examples were food safety examples. In that industry, Yum! Brands has more risk exposure than any other fast food chain because of the diversity of the ingredients, even compared to the larger McDonald's. Every crisis that Novak has faced has led to good judgments. They have also given him the platform to keep developing other leaders who will be better and better at handling inevitable and unforeseen crises. The lesson for other leaders is to have mechanisms in place that enable a quick response to crises and that simultaneously develop the next generation of leaders.

Ricardo Salinas showed how a leader can and should take advantage of a crisis as a competitive advantage. The global recession hit the Mexican economy harder than most. Rather then go on the defensive, Salinas made the judgment to go on the offensive and use the recession to reposition his Elektra business against the competitors. His framing and naming of the recession as a transformational opportunity has enabled him to mobilize his 40,000-person organization. This is in contrast to Michael Dell who was unable to capitalize on the competitive onslaught of HP. A crisis is a terrible thing to waste.

11

KNOWLEDGE CREATION

■ **Leaders with Good Judgment Are Committed Learners**
- They constantly evaluate their own performance.
- They seek knowledge and build on experience.

■ **Knowledge Creation for All Constituencies Is an Explicitly Stated Goal**
- Operating mechanisms support teaching and learning.
- Judgment capacity is a key leadership development target.

■ **Customers, Stakeholders, the Larger Community Are Tapped for Input**
- Everyone teaches. Everyone learns.
- Front-line employees are the new knowledge workers.

◆ ◆ ◆

I want to know everything I can about leadership. Because I don't believe leaders are born. I don't believe you spring fully armored out of the head of Athena to slay Hector in battle. I believe leaders choose to lead at some point in their life. And it's because they have a call to action.

They have a calling. They have something they want to
make happen. They choose to be part of a change that
they want to see in the world going around them, and they
choose to step forward, and they choose to take the risk of
leadership . . . the key is to be yourself. Be who you are. Be
passionate about who you are and what you care about,
and have fun.

—A. G. Lafley, P&G CEO[1]

We have a very strong belief that the first imperative to being a good
leader who makes good judgments is a commitment to be a learner,
to keep building one's knowledge and wisdom. Leaders have two
imperatives when it comes to knowledge creation. First and foremost,
they must continuously strive to make themselves smarter and better
at judgments by the kind of self journey to improvement that Immelt,
Lafley, and other leaders profiled in this book have taken. In addition, leaders need to garner the support of their teams, their organizations, and their stakeholders in people, strategy, and crisis judgment
making. While striving to make themselves better with the support of
others, they must simultaneously invest in the development of leadership judgment in others: namely, their team, their organization, and
the organization's key stakeholder's. This duality, making yourself
better while teaching and developing others judgment capacity, is the
key to good leadership.

SELF-KNOWLEDGE CREATION:
A JOURNEY INTO YOURSELF

Good leaders are on a transformational journey starting with themselves, which carries over to their teams and organizations. To do
this, leaders need the paradoxical combination of self-confidence
and humility to learn. Twenty years of observing Jack Welch as GE's
leader provided deep insight into how a leader can create judgment
self-knowledge.

First, it has to be a central agenda item of the leader. It takes commitment to self-learning, significant time, and relentless willingness to "look in the mirror" and a paradoxical self-confidence and humility. These are not descriptors that some would give to a leader like Jack Welch, often seen as just a leader of action. However, we have observed them firsthand. His quest for self-knowledge was fascinating to observe. It came in many forms. He relentlessly benchmarked other leaders, looking for new ideas from anywhere. He would use his almost every other week visits to Crotonville, not as a platform to pontificate but as a setting to learn about how his leadership was doing, collect new insights, and figure out ways of improving the company and his team so they could make better leadership judgments.

When Noel was running Crotonville in the 1980s, it was fascinating to observe Welch in action. He would often arrive toward the end of the day, taking the fifteen-minute helicopter ride from GE headquarters in Fairfield to Crotonville, GE's leadership development institute, and walk into the "Pit" the 110-person tiered classroom where all those in programs at Crotonville would come to spend a few hours with the CEO. There might be first-time managers, twenty-eight-year-old engineers, executive program participants, twenty-year GE veterans who were pretty far up the hierarchy, all in the same session.

Welch would share ten or fifteen minutes maximum of what was on his mind, ranging from world events that might be impacting GE, to his Teachable Point of View on leadership, to challenges in some of the businesses, like the difficulty of integrating Yokogawa Medical Systems in 1987 with the Wisconsin headquarters. He would then tell the group, "I am here to discuss anything that is on your mind, from globalization to GE values, to why we made a particular acquisition." These were not straight question-and-answer sessions. They were often question and question and highly interactive conversations with Welch, who wanted to know how people in the group thought. He actively solicited their opinions, asked how they would solve a problem, probe at why bosses hadn't answered some question about the business. It was always a very interactive give-and-take mutual learning session, creating what we have called a virtuous teaching cycle: the teacher (Welch) shares his Teachable Point of View but then creates an environment where the learners become his teachers.

Virtuous Teaching Cycles

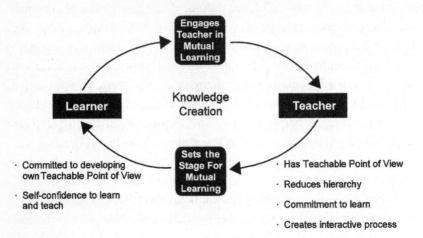

Welch engaged in two other activities to get him smarter. Before the 110 leaders broke for an informal cocktail session with Welch, each of the 110 filled out a feedback form that asked three questions: (1) As a result of this session, what has been resolved for me? (2) As a result of this session what is still unresolved or still troubles me? and (3) What is my biggest takeaway from the session? Welch would have these hand-written sheets either before he left in the helicopter or within twenty-four hours. He read them as the candor and insights kept him learning. People were overwhelmingly candid and most signed the forms and indicated where they were from in GE so Welch got regular feedback, which might include: What was resolved—"Now I understand why we sold the aerospace business." I am still troubled by "why we are still not settling the PCB controversy in the Hudson River when we are saying we want to be good environmentalists." The major takeaway might be "I learned things about my business that our leader should have taken the time to explain, and I am going to challenge him."

Welch would then use the cocktail time to work the crowd as another source of learning, getting into often heated conversations with three or four managers at a time. One time he was standing with five or six managers from his old business, Plastics, challenging them with why they messed up with a major customer.

The regular teaching and learning interaction described above is in addition to the action learning platforms that were created at Crotonville when Noel was heading it up in the late 1980s and continue today. Basically, the GE CEO uses the executive programs to have teams work on real issues for GE, ranging from having teams go to South Korea for a couple of weeks to reexamine the GE strategy in that region, to coming up with strategy ideas with Immelt for how GE needs to handle global citizenship issues, both environmental and human service (these are multiweek action learning task forces).

Welch chose Jeff Immelt to succeed him as CEO in large part because he recognized that Immelt was a leader with an insatiable thirst for being better, who invested himself in self-knowledge creation. Immelt told an incoming class of MBAs at the University of Michigan:

> The first part of leadership is an intense journey into yourself. It's a commitment and an intense journey into your soul. How fast can you change? How willing are you to take feedback? Do you believe in self-renewal? Do you believe in self-reflection? Are you willing to take those journeys to explore how you can become better and do it every day? How much can you learn? Can you look in the mirror every day and say, gee, I wish I had done that differently, boy I think I've got to do better here . . . you've got to be willing to do an intense journey into yourself. . . . I've been lucky, you know, because I've got to do things that I love with people that I love. But more than anything else, the burning desire inside me was to get the best out of what I could be and go on that journey.[2]

Immelt also uses the Crotonville platform for "dreaming sessions" with customers and suppliers to develop new CEO knowledge.

A. G. Lafley, Jeff Immelt, Jim Owen, David Novak, and Steve Bennett all use their leadership development platforms as knowledge creation processes as well. They all have extensive commitments to working real problems with their leaders, engaging in virtuous teaching cycles so that they and their organizations create knowledge collaboratively. This is counter to what the vast majority of companies do—outsourcing leadership development to business schools and consultants, reading case studies and not having the leaders of the company teaching and driving real action learning projects. The traditional management development both in companies and at business schools delivers a fraction of the return on the investment of those that fully engage in knowledge creation; this is the opposite of academic knowledge download (rather than a mutual learning approach).

Self-Knowledge Creation Requires Reflection as Well as Action

Action with no reflection does not create knowledge. Our bad judgment leaders often end up destroying knowledge through hip-shooting and acting out the same behaviors that got them to succeed in the past even as the world around them has changed.

A. G. Lafley makes it clear that to have good leadership judgment you have to

> first, know yourself. . . . You need to be in touch with what your aspirations really are; what your dreams really are. You need to understand your value system. You know, what is really meaningful to you? What do you really care about? What counts in your life?[3]

Knowledge creation for good judgment requires the leader to have a discipline to reflect and write. We have observed that leaders who get better and better at their judgments work at it not just in real-time interactive sessions, but then develop their Teachable Point of View as a work in progress. They also tend to write as a reflective tool, whether it is the twenty annual report letters Welch personally wrote, a tradition Immelt has followed at GE, or the curriculum that David Novak personally created for teaching his Yum! Brand leaders. Reflection, articulation, and then continuous improvement are the hallmarks of a leader continuously developing better judgment. This also includes a tough look at failures for learning.

Jeff Immelt describes how he works on improving his leadership judgment; it takes time and discipline to "wallow in ideas," as he describes it, before making a final judgment call.

You get these things by wallowing in them awhile. We had a few steps worked out in 2003, but it took another two years to finish the process. Jack was a great teacher in this regard. I would see him wallow in something like Six Sigma, where easily the first two years were tough. People would say, "Whoa, what the hell is this?" Still, he wouldn't move on to something else. He'd get the different businesses sharing ideas, and everything always crystallized in the end. He was a good initiative driver.[4]

The "wallowing" learning must ultimately get reflected in the leader continuously examining and improving his/her Teachable Point of View.

Self-Knowledge Creation and the Judgment Process

Developing judgment leadership capacity occurs during all phases of the process. A. G. Lafley has a well articulated Teachable Point of View that he uses not only to guide his own development but to develop judgment in his leaders at P&G. Immelt and the other good judgment leaders we have studied all share this common trait. It starts with facing reality, as Lafley states:

> the ability to see things as they are, not as I would like them to be . . . to see things as they are, to come to grips with reality, not to see the world through rose-colored glasses. One of the things that helped me is, I'm reasonably good at seeing things and accepting them as they are, and then dealing with them.[5]

The leader needs to be real clear about what it means to make judgment calls. Lafley reflects on his point of view and underscores the importance of action.

> Strategy, in my world, is critical, because strategy is the choice set. It's the set of choices that we make that guide the allocation of the human resource, and the allocation of the financial

resource, and frankly, place bets on what we're going to do, and more importantly, what we're not going to do.[6]

Lafley is on a continuous learning and knowledge creation journey. He is very clear that being able to make the tough judgment calls is critical to being a good leader; he shared what goes on in his mind when it comes to making judgment calls on strategy:

> But we chose to grow from our core—core businesses, core capabilities and core technologies that we know. We chose to create a portfolio for the first half of the twenty-first century that would grow faster, and hence, our move into beauty care, health care and personal care. We chose to commit to low-income consumers in developing markets, 'cause we knew the growth was going to be faster there. Demographics drive our business.
>
> We chose to focus on our core strengths and get better, in fact, best in class. So we want to be the best at understanding consumers, the best at creating brands and building brands, the best at innovating consumer products, the best at going to market through our channels of distribution and retailers, and the best at leveraging global scale. And then we wanted to be more productive than any other consumer products company in the world, and we wanted to attract the strongest talent and build the strongest cadre of leadership.[7]

It is obvious by now that our point of view on good judgment means the leader totally owns execution. If it does not happen and if the leader does not continuously monitor and learn and adjust, good judgments turn into bad judgments. Again, A. G. Lafley has a very clear point of view:

> The power of execution. And execution is what really happens, what you really do. And execution, in fact, is the only strategy that your consumer . . . it's the only strategy our retailer . . . it's the only strategy our competitor . . . it's the only strategy anybody else on the outside ever sees. They don't see the strategy we wrote down. They don't see the choice set.[8]

The leader's knowledge creation journey is the necessary condition for then focusing on knowledge creation at the social network, organizational, and contextual levels where the leader not only mobilizes these domains to support the judgment process but builds their capacity to develop judgment knowledge capacity.

SOCIAL NETWORK/TEAM KNOWLEDGE CREATION

It is up to the leader to build knowledge creation processes for his/her team and to ensure that they get executed. Bill George, former Medtronic CEO, reflects on this critical element of judgment capacity building at the team and social network level:

> Every job I had been in in my life, including all my jobs at Medtronic, I never knew a fraction about the business as much as my team did at Litton. So what I did was just learn how to form a team around the people that I could rely on intimately, close. And I developed very professionally intimate relationships with my subordinates. I've always believed in separating my friendships in my personal life from my business life. So I don't want all my friends to be the people I work with because I need to get away and I want to have different types of friends. But I developed very intimate, professional relationships so we could talk openly about anything.

Virtually every leader relies on a group of trusted advisers. Throughout history, whether Kennedy's kitchen cabinet or Nicholas II's Rasputin, these individuals or groups have influenced key leadership judgments; some good, some bad. For most leaders, their team is the group with which they spend the most time. When there are difficult judgments to be made, they convene their team to debate and deliberate. Making choices about who we surround ourselves with and from whom we take counsel is perhaps the biggest judgment that any leader can make. Building a social network that keeps developing knowledge creation capacity is central to the success of a leader.

Who Is on Your Team

The first component of this is making a conscious judgment about each individual on your team. You must ask the question: Does this person help the team to make better judgments? Organizations are littered with technically competent people who possess poor judgment. Rather than contribute to the judgment process, they encumber their teams with false assumptions, opaque judgment processes, or indecision. There should be no "neutral" ratings in your assessments. Saying that someone is neutral is equivalent to that person's failing to impact the judgment process. There is a tremendous opportunity cost to having someone who is not trusted or incapable of offering good advice as you make judgment calls.

Assuming a team and social network that has a solid level of trust, it is then important to look at what each person brings to the team. Again, this is not a question of whether or not they are capable of doing their job; rather, it is whether they personally exercise good judgment and have a positive impact on the team's judgment process.

If a team has been well formulated, there are diverse skills, perspectives, and relationships that can help the leader as he or she prepares to make a judgment call. Some of the assets that team members bring may include:

- *Domain expertise:* Deep understanding of a technical area such as a functional specialty or technology.
- *Industry knowledge:* The ability to diagnose industry trends or help place changes in historical context that is predictive of possible future outcomes.
- *Organizational knowledge:* Understanding of the organization's competencies, talent, networks, processes, and culture that suggests execution capability or receptivity to change.
- *Constituent knowledge:* Up-to-date information and relationships about one or more key constituents such as regulatory agencies, key customers, or suppliers that predict how these actors will respond to your organization's moves.

- *Access to information:* Personal networks, relationships, and know-how that enable the person to get reliable answers to questions even if they do not have the answers themselves.
- *External experience:* A different perspective based on experiences outside the company or industry that helps to identify best practices or alternate approaches.
- *Unconventional problem solving:* A differentiated thought style that can generate creative solutions not likely to come from standard analyses or the industry's conventional wisdom.

Team Dynamics for Good Judgment

Throughout the book we have portrayed judgment as a dynamic, emotional process that must account for the human actors who are involved. As a leader, you establish a social architecture—how people interact and the energy generated by those interactions—that directly influences the quality of the judgment process.

At each stage (preparation, call, execution), you must manage the process for your team. The framework on the next page provides the leader with guidelines and diagnostic questions to build team judgment capacity.

ORGANIZATION KNOWLEDGE CREATION

Building judgment capacity at scale in a global organization the size and complexity of GE, Yum! Brands, Walmart, or Toyota requires the leader to be a large-scale social architect. It means creating processes that engage thousands of leaders in judgment muscle strengthening activities.

In chapter 10, we saw how Ricardo Salinas at Grupo Elektra created an organization level knowledge creation process at scale during a crisis. The challenge for Salinas will be to create steady-state, noncrisis, ongoing knowledge creation processes for thousands of his associates, which will need to encompass a new operating system for how they do strategy, budgeting, and succession planning.

Building Team Judgment Knowledge Capacity

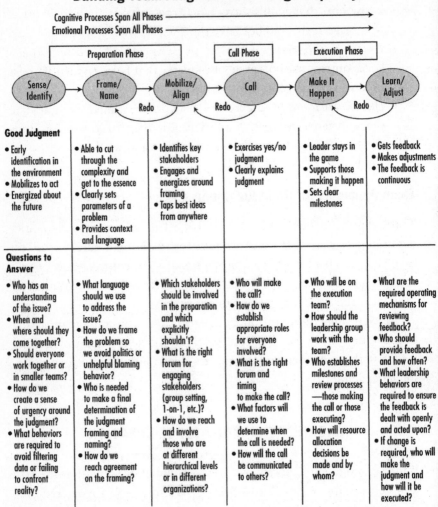

Cognitive Processes Span All Phases →
Emotional Processes Span All Phases →

	Preparation Phase		Call Phase	Execution Phase	
Sense/ Identify	Frame/ Name	Mobilize/ Align	Call	Make It Happen	Learn/ Adjust
		Redo	Redo		Redo
Good Judgment					
• Early identification in the environment • Mobilizes to act • Energized about the future	• Able to cut through the complexity and get to the essence • Clearly sets parameters of a problem • Provides context and language	• Identifies key stakeholders • Engages and energizes around framing • Taps best ideas from anywhere	• Exercises yes/no judgment • Clearly explains judgment	• Leader stays in the game • Supports those making it happen • Sets clear milestones	• Gets feedback • Makes adjustments • The feedback is continuous
Questions to Answer					
• Who has an understanding of the issue? • When and where should they come together? • Should everyone work together or in smaller teams? • How do we create a sense of urgency around the judgment? • What behaviors are required to avoid filtering data or failing to confront reality?	• What language should we use to address the issue? • How do we frame the problem so we avoid politics or unhelpful blaming behavior? • Who is needed to make a final determination of the judgment framing and naming? • How do we reach agreement on the framing?	• Which stakeholders should be involved in the preparation and which explicitly shouldn't? • What is the right forum for engaging stakeholders (group setting, 1-on-1, etc.)? • How do we reach and involve those who are at different hierarchical levels or in different organizations?	• Who will make the call? • How do we establish appropriate roles for everyone involved? • What is the right forum and timing to make the call? • What factors will we use to determine when the call is needed? • How will the call be communicated to others?	• Who will be on the execution team? • How should the leadership group work with the team? • Who establishes milestones and review processes —those making the call or those executing? • How will resource allocation decisions be made and by whom?	• What are the required operating mechanisms for reviewing feedback? • Who should provide feedback and how often? • What leadership behaviors are required to ensure the feedback is dealt with openly and acted upon? • If change is required, who will make the judgment and how will it be executed?

Leaders have three major levers for large-scale knowledge creation. First, there are the operating systems of the organization, including strategy formulation, budget processes, and succession planning. Second, there are the leadership development activities spread over one's career, job experiences, rotations, and formal development experiences at different career stages. Third, there are the large-scale, total company knowledge creation platforms, such as training the whole workforce in Six Sigma quality, or cascade teaching to everyone in the company.

Knowledge Creation Through Operating Systems

Immelt inherited from Welch a totally revamped operating system of GE, one that was transformed into a learning and judgment creation set of mechanisms carried out throughout the year. The GE model has become the benchmark for many other companies including Best Buy, Intuit, 3M, Boeing, Yum! Brands, and Honeywell, to name a few. The true essence of what Welch accomplished was a radical transformation of what was purely a set of traditional bureaucratic processes into a learning/teaching judgment building set of activities.

"The GE Operating System" that follows is the actual diagram used to teach Welch's organization about the operating system. The written portion in the right margin is in his own words and underscores the learning system aspect of the processes.

Immelt inherited the operating system and made significant additions, including a "session T," which is a technology process for knowledge creation. The heads of businesses and key team members go to the Global Research Center four times a year to immerse themselves in interaction with the researchers to stimulate growth from new technology platforms.

As was discussed in chapter 8, "Strategy Judgments at GE," GE leaders are generating new knowledge regarding technology growth platforms that set the stage for new strategic judgment while simultaneously building the organization's judgment capacity.

These knowledge creation operating systems are always a work in progress and require the leader to keep redesigning them as interactive virtuous teaching cycles, or else organizational inertia and dry rot will set in to turn them back into bureaucratic knowledge blockers and destroyers.

Developing Leadership Judgment

All leadership development, from new hires through senior leaders, needs to be geared toward knowledge creation for better leadership

The GE Operating System

Operating Managers Meeting ("Boca")
600 Leaders
INITIATIVE LAUNCH
- Case for New Initiative
- Outside Company Initiative Experience
- One Year Stretch Targets
- Role Model Presentations
- Re-Launch of Current Initiatives

JANUARY

- Intense Energizing of Initiatives Across Businesses

FEBRUARY

Corporate Executive Council: (CEC at Crotonville)
35 Business and Senior Corporate Leaders
- Early Learning?
- Customer Reaction?
- Initiative Resources Sufficient?
- Business Management Course (BMC) Recommendations

MARCH

Anonymous Online CEO Survey:
11,000 Employees
- Do You "Feel" Initiative Yet?
- Do Customers Fee
- Sufficient Resourc to Execute?
- Messages Clear and Credible?

APRIL

Globalization
Six Sigma Quality
Product Services
e-Business

GE Values

DECEMBER

Corporate Executive Council: (CEC at Crotonville)
35 Business and Senior Corporate Leaders
- Agenda for Boca
- Individual Business Initiative Highlights
- Business Management (BMC) Course Recommendations

NOVEMBER

Operating Plans Presented:
All Business Leaders
- Initiatives Stretch Targets
- Individual Business Operating Plans
- Economic Outlook

OCTOBER

Corporate Officers Meeting: (Crotonville)
150 Officers
- Next-Year Operating Plan Focus
- Role Models Present Initiative Successes
- Executive Development Course (EDC) Recommendations
- All Business Dialogue: What Have We Learned?

SEPTEMBE

Corporate Executiv Council: (CEC at Cro
35 Business and Se Corporate Leaders
- Business Manage Course (BMC) Recommendations
- Clear Role Models Identified
- Outside Company Practices Present
- Initiative Best Pra (All Businesses)
- Customer Impact Initiatives

dership Performance
iews at Business
ations:
  Business Staffs
  itiative Leadership
  eview
  vel of Commitment /
  uality of Talent on
  itiatives
  ifferentiation
  .0% / 70% / 10%)
  romote / Reward /
  emove

A Y

Second Quarter

Corporate Executive Council:
(CEC at Crotonville)
35 Business and Senior
Corporate Leaders
• Initiative Best Practices
• Review of Initiative
  Leadership
• Customer Impact
• Business Management
  Course (BMC)
  Recommendations

J U N E

U G U S T

nformal Idea
xchanges at
orporate and
usinesses

J U L Y

Session I: 3 Year Strategy
• Economic / Competitive
  Environment
• General Earnings Outlook
• Initiatives Update /
  Strategy
• Initiative Resource
  Requirements

Third Quarter

The GE
Operating System

The Operating System is GE's learning culture in action—in essence, it is the operating software of the Company.

It is a year-round series of intense learning sessions in which business CEOs, role models and initiative champions from GE as well as outside companies, meet and share the intellectual capital of the world: its best ideas.

The central focus is always on raising the bar of Company performance by sharing, and putting into action, the best ideas and practices drawn from our big Company-wide initiatives.

The Operating System is driven by the soft values of the Company—trust, informality, simplicity, boundaryless behavior and the love of change. It allows GE businesses to operate at performance levels and speeds that would be unachievable were they on their own.

What may appear in the diagram to be a typical series of stand-alone business meetings is in reality an endless process of enrichment. Learning at each meeting builds on that of the previous, expanding the scope and increasing the momentum of the initiatives.

Globalization has been enriched through more than a dozen cycles, Six Sigma is in its fifth cycle, Services is in its sixth, and e-Business its third. The GE Operating System translates idea to action across three dozen businesses so rapidly that all the initiatives have become operational across the Company within one month of launch, and have always produced positive financial results within their first cycle.

judgments, both to support real-time judgments and to develop the next generation's capacity for leadership judgment.

One platform for this was described in chapter 7, "Strategy Judgments," at Best Buy. The shift to customer centricity was developed off an action learning platform, six teams coming up with the new segments for Best Buy to focus on. Over the six-month action learning process each of the leaders not only worked on solving the strategic segment challenge but received personal leadership feedback and development around business acumen, leading change, and team dynamics, all aimed at growing their judgment capacity. At the end of the process every leader was assessed by the CEO, Anderson, and the top team on their judgment performance and their leadership behaviors in the action learning process, which consumed about 30 percent of their time over the six months while they continued to have to manage their regular job. The action learning process not only framed and created the segments, but provided the development and selection platform for the leaders of these new segments. The leaders were selected for both their demonstrated leadership judgment in the process and their future potential to lead the building of the segments and thus their people, strategy, and crisis judgment as it would apply to their new segment.

This same action learning platform was used at GE Medical Systems in the early 1990s as it globalized and integrated two acquisitions, Yokogawa Medical Systems (two thousand Japanese) and Thomson-CGR (six thousand Frenchmen), with GE's twelve thousand Wisconsin-based makers of CAT scanners, MRIs, and X-ray equipment, and at Royal Bank of Canada to drive their shift to customer centricity, and at Royal Dutch Shell, Intuit, and Intel.

JUDGMENT CAPACITY BUILDING
AT THE FRONT LINE

When Peter Drucker presciently introduced the world to the concept of knowledge workers, he urged managers to treat knowledge workers as assets rather than as costs. Drucker's line of thinking has been popularized to the point at which it can be found in an enormous volume of corporate reports and management writing. Drucker asked a fundamental question that, despite the increased attention, organizations still struggle with: What is needed to increase (knowledge workers') productivity and to convert their increased productivity into performance capacity for the organization?

In their bid to create a differentiated customer experience, Best Buy and Intuit are realizing that the key to answering Drucker's question lies in enabling knowledge workers at the front lines to make good judgment calls. The process starts with the CEO and senior leaders setting clear direction for the organization and defining the role and scope of contribution expected of frontline leaders. The senior leadership is ultimately responsible for setting the strategy, reinforcing desired values, energizing the organization, and making tough calls on resource allocation and staffing. In short, the senior leaders are responsible for developing a Teachable Point of View, which is taught throughout their organizations. Our work at both Intuit and Best Buy started with helping the senior teams develop such a Teachable Point of View.

Trilogy Software, an Austin, Texas, company founded by Stanford dropout Joe Liemandt, is a prototypical company for the knowledge economy. Selling complex enterprise software, Trilogy is an extremely successful private enterprise that partners with many *Fortune 50* companies. Since its founding, it has relied on hiring the best and brightest computer scientists from top campuses. In a *Harvard Business Review* article, we chronicled how Joe Liemandt created Trilogy University, a three-month orientation "boot camp," to simultaneously indoctrinate these hotshot new hires while creating the next generation of products. Today, Trilogy runs its university in Bangalore, India, because the bulk of its hiring is at the top Indian and Chinese universities, and new recruits create products for a global market.

Trilogy's workers fit the old stereotype of the knowledge worker— the highly trained engineering and computer science graduate. The importance of knowledge workers such as these cannot be disputed, but we see the emergence of a new breed of knowledge workers.

Intuit, the Mountain View, California, company, also produces software. Its TurboTax, Quicken, QuickBooks, and other software solutions serve both small enterprises and individual consumers. As with Trilogy, computer scientists play a vital role in developing its products. Unlike Trilogy, however, Intuit relies heavily on specialists to support accountants and retail customers. These knowledge workers don't necessarily hail from top universities or write complex computer code. They are frontline leaders and agents working in call centers, often paid an hourly rate. Intuit has learned that these call service agents can have a critical impact on customers and sales by both identifying customer needs and solving after-sale problems.

At Intuit, frontline leaders take responsibility for sharing best practices and creating new knowledge about customer needs. For example, one frontline manager developed a process in which customer service agents now meet several times a week to discuss common customer problems and role-play responses. By doing so, they not only share knowledge but also creatively come up with newer and more innovative ideas to enhance the customer experience. As a result, there has been a nearly 40 percent increase in the measure of customer satisfaction.

Intuit demonstrates how knowledge creation increasingly is shifting to the customer interface. Best Buy is another example. A frontline associate in one of Best Buy's California stores knew that the area surrounding his store had a large number of real estate agents. After several failures to sell digital cameras to real estate agents, the associate researched their needs. Having been trained to diagnose customer problems and empowered to create his own solutions, he realized that real estate agents needed to take pictures and then e-mail or print them on the spot, often from their cars. He assembled a bundle of products and software that would enable an agent to snap a digital photo, produce the photo with a mobile printer that fit easily in any backseat, or e-mail the picture from a laptop or PDA. After the product bundle became a hot seller in the area, one of the agents invited the Best Buy associate to present to the real estate agents at a monthly meeting at the local Chamber of Commerce. The associate's innovation resulted in thousands of dollars of incremental sales and a group of new customers who continued to shop at Best Buy.

The stories at Best Buy and Intuit demonstrate the impact that frontline associates have when they exercise good judgment and come up with innovative solutions to customer opportunities. We have collaborated with these companies in developing frontline leadership capacity for customer-centric knowledge creation. The specific solutions these frontline leaders provided their customers could not be anticipated in advance. Instead, leaders had to be adaptive, weigh their options, and figure out how to please their customers.

As companies strive to differentiate themselves with inundated consumers, more and more are realizing that knowledge is created at the customer interface, not at headquarters or in isolated development groups. This requires the full engagement and intellect of frontline associates. It can only happen with top-down support, a clearly articulated strategy with strong enablers at all levels of the organization, and intensive training and development of frontline leaders and their associates.

Stories like this are not uncommon at Best Buy. They could not have happened, however, if the company had not invested in the judgment capability of its frontline leaders. These leaders were able to read their store profit-and-loss statements, calculate return on invested capital, and understand their net operating profit targets. In contrast to the company's traditional policy of handing down only operating targets without explanation, business acumen gave frontline leaders a new capability on which to base their judgment calls. The material in "Pocket Guide for Financials" is an example of frontline knowledge creation. A team of hourly associates in one of the stores developed teaching materials to teach their colleagues about customer centricity. They worked on their own time to create a booklet that was originally called "Customer Centricity for Dummies" until the store manager very supportively explained to them that they were violating both trademark and copyright laws. They quickly learned and changed the cover. The booklet walks through examples, such as creating a "T-shirt" stand, how to get capital, how to measure capital turns, and how to calculate return on invested capital. They then go from case example to application in their Best Buy store. The point is to unleash the knowledge-creating capability in people, and it is amazing how smart they can become and make others around them as well.

Pocket Guide for Financials

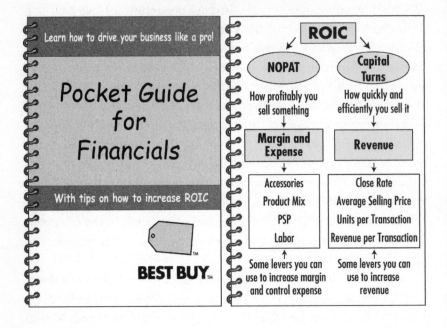

Best Buy also had to build new operating mechanisms to support knowledge creation in the stores. This included a morning forty-five-minute "chalk talk" with twenty to thirty associates before the store opened. They reviewed daily P&Ls, close rates, what happened with their segment the day before, and ideas for improving the performance for this day. The sessions were highly interactive, with the store manager and team fully engaged with the hourly associates. They were all generating new knowledge.

At Best Buy, there are now hundreds of stories describing how frontline employees dynamically created customer solutions. Innovative approaches to problems as diverse as ethnic marketing programs, tailored product displays, and new product introductions have been identified and implemented directly by frontline associates. This could only happen because Brad Anderson, Best Buy's CEO, defined the organization's strategy around "customer centricity," a concept that we helped Best Buy's leadership team frame in partnership with Larry Selden from Columbia University.

In Brad's judgment, the strategy that had made Best Buy the leading consumer electronics seller in North America and a top-performing stock would not sustain the company's success. Anderson had to create the conditions for enabling frontline leaders to fully implement a customer-centered strategy. The Best Buy transformation is still a work in progress as it has required a massive revolution. The company historically was built on strong centralization, with employees at its Minnesota headquarters setting strategy and passing down "knowledge" and direction for the troops to follow. Today, the "troops" are expected to act as local field generals, generating solutions and new knowledge. Best Buy continues to invert the organizational pyramid, empowering employees to turn customer hypotheses into business cases that can then guide headquarters to provide support for what was traditionally process controlled.

The transformation at Best Buy has required massive change of information, skills, and tools to make good judgments. The company is also providing each store with a local profit-and-loss statement, good customer data, and performance management tools. Similarly, the career paths, compensation systems, merchandising programs, and numerous other facets of the business have had to be entirely rethought.

Intuit's Knowledge Creation in Call Centers

At Intuit the focus is on simplifying the technical challenges call center agents face in trying to find information, execute company processes, and share knowledge with one another. Intuit has engaged frontline associates directly in identifying and changing how the company works to support better customer interactions. Intuit is reducing the bureaucracy that stands in the way of letting customer agents focus on customers and make good judgments.

As a result of CEO Steve Bennett's driven effort, the call center managers now create virtuous teaching cycles with their associates when examining the success metrics their teams use. One example was a manager who worked with her team to identify the vital metrics to measure team effectiveness and now assembles the team weekly to diagnose progress and share practices for improving each agent's customer impact.

Teaching Frontline Managers to Teach

Best Buy, Intuit, and Trilogy all make the enormous investment of teaching frontline managers how to coach and teach their associates. At Best Buy, thousands of employees have participated in workshops teaching everything from financial basics to customer segmentation approaches to frontline leadership.

Intuit has required its call center managers to become teachers. We launched the process with a rigorous three-day process designed to prepare frontline managers to be more effective teachers of frontline agents. Following the workshop, each frontline manager conducted his or her own disciplined, highly interactive workshop for groups of frontline leaders. No consultants or staff personnel were allowed to teach. At the end of the three days the frontline leaders had new concepts and tools for enhancing the effectiveness of their call center agents. The frontline leaders identified how they could better structure their work to deliver the business strategy, how they could eliminate unnecessary activities, and how they could reshape goal setting and performance management. The frontline leaders also engaged the agents to provide input on companywide initiatives to streamline operational processes. As knowledge creation increasingly moves to the front lines, Intuit recognizes that its managers must be more skilled than ever in leadership fundamentals.

Intuit's Frontline Leader Process

Intuit's investment in developing the judgment capability of frontline leaders requires them to attend two workshop sessions, teach their own teams, implement new work routines, and execute a knowledge-creation project. The "Intuit Frontline Program" provides an overview of the Intuit process for the front line.

Intuit Frontline Program

Step 1: *Three-Day Workshop*
- Frontline leaders are immersed in the strategy, values, and vision and taught how to translate them to their area.
- Frontline leaders are immersed in business acumen.
- Frontline leaders are taught to focus on creating a team-teachable point of view and using operating mechanisms as virtuous teaching cycles.
- Frontline leaders are taught how different employee styles and capabilities may be deployed.
- Frontline leaders are prepared to teach.

Step 2: *Frontline Leaders Teach*
- Frontline leaders who attended the three-day workshop are required to teach—they personally re-create the workshop they attended, doing all of the teaching themselves.
- The process develops their ongoing teaching and coaching capability.

Step 3: *Knowledge-Creation Project*
- Frontline leaders work with their team of frontline associates to share knowledge and implement a project with measurable business impact.

Step 4: *Two-Day Follow-Up Workshop*
- Frontline leaders share results and best practices with one another.
- Frontline leaders continue learning on business acumen, company support processes, frontline leadership, and performance management.

When most people picture knowledge workers, they think of engineers, scientists, or service professionals, not hourly sales people or call center agents. However, as numerous companies increasingly attempt to differentiate themselves through their service, they are recognizing that the best strategy is creating judgment capability at the front lines.

The paradox of shifting power to the front lines is that it requires senior leaders to use their authority to overcome the technical, political, and cultural barriers that often stand in the way. Companies must actively invest in creating the support systems that enable frontline leaders to make good judgment calls. When they do, they realize that frontline leaders are those most skilled in making local decisions to simultaneously delight customers and protect the bottom line and continuously create knowledge.

CONTEXTUAL KNOWLEDGE CREATION

The final knowledge creation arena is how to work with key stakeholders, the board, the suppliers, the customers, and the communities in which the organization operates.

Immelt personally hosts customer dreaming sessions at Crotonville with his team and teams from key customer groups. Immelt describes a session as follows:

> We hosted what we call a dreaming session in the summer of 2004 with the 30 biggest utilities. Some of the top players in the industry—CEOs like Jim Roberts and David Rutledge—came to Crotonville and heard Jeff Sachs from Columbia talk about global warming. There were other speakers who were pretty compelling on different topics, and breakout sessions. I floated the idea of doing something on public policy on greenhouse gases, and we had a good debate.[9]

This interactive virtuous teaching cycle process helped Immelt frame and name "ecomagination" as a way "to show the organization that it's OK to stick your neck out and even to make customers a bit uncomfortable." Leaders need to develop customer and supplier interactive processes for developing new knowledge.

Board Knowledge Creation

In the defensive post–Sarbanes Oxley age of boards of directors, all too many publicly traded companies are not partnered with their boards as knowledge creators. The paranoia and procedures imposed on boards due to the fallout from the Enron, Tyco, ImClone, World-Com, and other ethical meltdowns is undermining the very real potential for boards to partner in knowledge creation.

Best Buy Board Engagement in Customer Centricity

Early on in the launch of customer centricity at Best Buy, the board was present and engaged with the 164 officers in the first big multi-day workshop. Board members sat in with the teams and worked side by side with the leaders on what this meant for Best Buy. The preparation for leaders to teach thousands of Best Buy leaders was with the board members working with the executives. For half a day of the workshop, board members were mixed into groups of five or six Best Buy leaders, helping them work on their Teachable Points of View to take back to their teams.

During the transformation and action learning process to come up with the Best Buy segments and to move the organization forward to a new strategic platform, the board was engaged every step of the way. Larry Selden and Noel worked with the board and teams in three different sessions. These sessions involved having members of the action learning teams work interactively with the board on ideas they were developing for different segments, the value propositions. The board also spent time in the stores, walking them and interacting with the associates who were driving the transformation at the customer interface. Boards can and should be partnered in knowledge creation.

Community Engagement: Global Citizenship

The final contextual dimension is the wider societal community in which the organization operates. Over the past decade Noel has worked with Best Buy, Circuit City, Ameritech, U.S. West, Intuit, Genentech,

HarperCollins, Ford, Royal/Dutch Shell, Royal Bank of Scotland, and Covad to incorporate corporate citizenship, dealing with both environmental and human capital challenges and blending them into the mainstream of leadership development. The leaders of the company are required to have a Teachable Point of View on "citizenship" and to engage their own teams in community work as a way to develop them, give back to the community, and also generate new knowledge.

At Best Buy, for example, all the leadership development programs would as a group spend half a day in the downtown Minneapolis Boys and Girls Club working one on one with the children. At Genentech, hundreds of leaders, as a regular part of the leadership development programs, work with Opportunities Industrialization Center West, a job retraining program in East Palo Alto.

GE's Global Citizenship efforts have truly become large scale and mainstream to being a leader in the company. There are large-scale partnerships in Ghana to develop a community with both GE products and volunteers. In Stamford, Connecticut, there is a partnership to work with the school system that also exists in Louisville and Cincinnati.

The point of these efforts is that with the right leadership, the CEO drives their workforce to be a part of what Immelt has challenged his organization to be: namely, a company—that gives back globally to the communities in which the company operates.

12

JUDGMENT FOR

FUTURE GENERATIONS:

THE NEW YORK CITY

LEADERSHIP ACADEMY

▎**Mayor Bloomberg Judgment to Transform New York City Schools**
- Judgment to appoint Joel Klein as chancellor.
- Judgment to partner with Jack Welch, Dick Parsons, and the business community.

▎**Joel Klein and Mayor Bloomberg Judgment to Centralize the School System**
- Focus on 1,200 school principals as key change agents.
- Set up a Principals' Leadership Academy.

▎**Judgment to Have Bob Knowling to Head Principals' Academy**
- Bob Knowling and Sandra Stein lead the Academy.

◆ ◆ ◆

By any yardstick, a higher percentage of New York City high school students are graduating now than at any time in decades. The rate has risen every year during this administration and is an important validation of our

reforms, Chancellor Klein's leadership, and the hard
work of our students, principals, and teachers. The
rate obviously remains far too low, but the gains
demonstrate that our hard work to raise student
achievement is paying off, and we are beginning to
turn around a failing system.

—Mayor Michael Bloomberg[1]

Mayor Bloomberg's quote above is not a declaration of victory but a
realistic assessment of progress being made in the Herculean effort
to transform the failing New York City school system. Society's
most important social institution is the public school system. It is the
shaper of the next generation's capacity for exercising good judgment.
This is not to underestimate the role of family, church or synagogue,
or institutions like Girl Scouts, Boy Scouts, and Boys and Girls Clubs
in shaping the next generation, but public schools are by far the biggest opportunity for society to create individuals and leaders with the
judgment to make a difference in the world. Failing school systems
fail our society's future. Joel Klein, the chancellor of the New York
City school system, views the role of the school system in shaping
children's judgment in the following terms:

> We give kids real-world sorts of working challenges, and then
> they have to exercise their judgment. I mean, to me that's a
> good part of it. Judgment is like muscle capacity. You develop
> it. You exercise . . . we will give them a real-world scenario.
> We'll put them in teams to figure it out and those are the kinds
> of things we hope over time will get them to exercise good
> judgment. . . . Judgment is a product of the people you interact
> with—they learn from mistakes and consequences.

Bloomberg and Klein want to help shape good judgment in 1.2
million New York City children. To do that it takes leadership in the
New York City schools, where there are eighty thousand teachers and
fourteen hundred principals. To deliver on the Bloomberg and Klein
strategy judgment, the focus had to be on the principals. This is the
leadership role that has the maximum impact on the children; a good
principal is the key to good teachers.

THE NEW YORK CITY TRANSFORMATION JOURNEY

When Michael Bloomberg changed careers, from a very successful entrepreneur to mayor of New York City, he took his well-honed leadership judgment capability and applied it to New York City. He sensed and identified the need for revitalizing the human capital side of New York, namely, its schools and the next generation of young people.

The schools were a mess and run in a maze of local fiefdoms, forty local superintendencies, all with their own agendas, local patronage, and with little real leadership from the center. The chancellor had minimal impact on these loosely based local units. The performance of the more than twelve hundred schools and the impact on the 1.1 million students were highly variable and overall subpar in terms of graduation rates, test scores, and the performance of graduates.

Judgment number one was to frame and name the issue: "We have a leadership problem in our school system and schools and it needs to be fixed to impact outcomes." Bloomberg did not buy the conventional wisdom that some new curriculum dreamed up by the schools of education would transform the schools. He had witnessed years of emphasis on curriculum and teacher education but very little on who was leading the schools. Schools of education train aspiring teachers, but have no track record of developing principals, other than taking academic coursework.

Bloomberg's Teachable Point of View included an assumption that organizational performance was dependent on a good leader. He had certainly seen that in business and clearly assumed it was true in education. The key leader was the one closest to the students, namely the principal. For these frontline leaders to succeed, the top leaders needed to provide the context and the selection and development pipeline; that was the challenge for Bloomberg, who needed a leader who could execute his judgment to tackle the public education problem in New York.

That is how Mayor Bloomberg framed it. He made a bold people judgment call and recruited Joel Klein, a noneducator, to be school chancellor. He wanted Klein to be his partner in transforming public education in New York. He also realized that Klein would need tremendous political support from the Mayor's Office if he was going to succeed in transforming the school system. It was also clear that he and Klein would have to consolidate power and break up the forty-three fiefdoms to be able to drive the transformation.

THE BURNING PLATFORM

Bloomberg was clear that the hand he had been dealt was pretty grim and that the stakes were high.

> We spend enormous amounts, far more than any other nation. But we're not getting a sufficient return on our investment. The fact is, our education system looks a lot like the U.S. auto industry in the 1970s—stuck in a flabby, inefficient, outdated production model driven by the needs of employees rather than consumers.
>
> For instance, we have built too many bureaucracies that lack clear lines of accountability, which means that mediocrity and failure are tolerated, and excellence goes unrewarded. We recruit a disproportionate share of teachers from among the bottom third of their college classes. Then we give them lifetime tenure after three years, and we reward them based on longevity, not performance. We fail to help struggling students in the early years, when costs are lower, and then, in the upper grades, we pay for expensive remediation programs, which have very limited success. And we allow vast funding inequalities to exist between school districts, with poor students, who are disproportionately black and Hispanic, paying the price.
>
> We can continue to invest enormous sums of money in this failing system—and remain like Detroit in the 1970s, slipping further and further behind our international competitors. Or, we can put our famous American ingenuity to work and build a better system—and become like Silicon Valley today, which is leading the world in innovation and technology.
>
> The choice is clear, but the challenge will not be easy. It

will require a top-to-bottom rethinking of our school system, one that insists on a performance-based culture of accountability that is oriented around children, not bureaucracies. It will require us to offer higher teacher salaries to attract more of the best and brightest, and to offer financial rewards to the most successful teachers. It will require us to set and uphold high standards, encourage innovation and competition, and end social promotion—the harmful practice of advancing students to the next grade despite their poor academic performance. And it will require us to invest in early childhood development and distribute funding more equitably.[2]

This assessment was the burning platfom for a massive transformation of the New York City school system. It needed a massive transformation of the New York City school system. It needed a transformational leader to make it happen.

JOEL KLEIN ENTERS

Joel Klein grew up in Astoria, a kid from a working-class family who made it to Columbia as an undergraduate and then to Harvard Law School. He ran his own law firm, was a prosecutor and deputy counsel to President Clinton and then assistant attorney general in charge of the Justice Department's antitrust division, as well as CEO of Bertelsmann in the United States. He had a very successful career in business and law, but no experience at all in public education except as a student growing up in New York. Bloomberg tapped a psychological vein in Klein and gave him the biggest leadership challenge of his life. When we asked Klein why he took the job he told us:

This one I can explain with psychology, not economics. So I mean, so I took it for a couple of very fundamental reasons. I think it's the greatest domestic issue that the nation faces. I think it's a crisis that people don't really perceive, and the reason they don't perceive it is their own kids aren't typically affected. Second, I believe that the American dream and the

relationship of education to the American dream is what makes
this country different and great. And frankly I think that the
dream's being lost on lots of kids, kids of color in particular,
and the sense that education allowed them a ticket out of poverty is something I worry about. And third and most importantly, because of what the mayor did by gaining control, it
seemed to me you had a really good shot at trying to do the
hard work, the transformation.

He knew he had some important judgments to make, the first of
which were people judgments, who he would have on his team. He
made some good ones and some bad ones. One of the best was to partner with the business community, reaching out to Jack Welch and Dick
Parsons, CEO of Time Warner, to help him with developing leadership
capacity at the school level. In addition he drew in a social network
that included Carolyn Kennedy (daughter of John F. Kennedy) to help
raise almost $100 million to support the New York Leadership
Academy for school principals.

Klein's background had taught him that the way to change a system was through key leaders, namely school principals.

If the organization that matters is the school, then the school
leader matters. That's the game. I can't do it with all 1,400 principals at once but I basically I'm going to do what I can. I didn't
think the ed schools had the right cultural view of this thing that
I wanted to inculcate in order to have a chance at change.

Therefore, Klein and Bloomberg knew that if change was going to occur,
the leadership of the New York City public school system had to gain
control of the selection and development of its principals. This simple
strategy had eluded the New York City system throughout history and
was made worse by the decentralization of the school system in the 1970s
under the banner of community control. What was meant to be a move
to empowerment turned out to be a bad judgment. It led to forty-three
separate and consequently disempowered local school systems. There
were no clear standards across the city and no meaningful community
involvement in the vast majority of cases. Each of the forty superinten-

dents had their own board of education and their own political patronage system. Many of the local school systems struggled with corruption.

Bloomberg and Klein took on these political fiefdoms, dismantling them and centralizing the system under Klein. This judgment was necessary but obviously not sufficient to transform the system. It gave them control over the selection, development, and management of the principals. Next they needed to build a new leadership pipeline for future principals. Klein had a vision of a leadership academy for principals, but he needed the right leader to build it.

JOEL KLEIN JUDGMENT
TO RECRUIT BOB KNOWLING

I was actually at a dinner one night with Jack and I said to him, I said, "Look, you know, here's my concept." He said, "You're absolutely right on," and he wanted to get involved and help, and he did. In the business community the partnership raised $30 million. I went out and found Knowling.

Klein needed a leader to build and run the New York City Leadership Academy, a concept that was directly influenced by Jack Welch and the vision of a "Crotonville" Leadership Development Institute concept for New York City principals. Klein admired Welch's transformation of GE and the role that Crotonville played in supporting it and developing leaders at GE. Now he needed to find the right person to build and then lead the "principal academy."

Michael Brimm, a professor at the French business school INSEAD, was a friend and coach to Ron Beller, a former Goldman Sachs partner. Beller was working with Klein's team pro bono, and when he told Brimm about the principal leadership academy, Brimm suggested Bob Knowling. Brimm had worked with Knowling since the early 1990s, when Noel brought Brimm into a Crotonville-style leadership development program at Ameritech that Bob Knowling was heading up.

Brimm knew that Knowling, who had gone on from Ameritech to be the number two executive at U.S. West, the CEO of Covard,

CEO of SimDesk Technology, and on the boards of HP, Heidrick and Struggles, and Ariba, was highly committed to citizenship and giving back to society. As an African American who embodied leadership development, he had a commitment to giving back and was a very successful business executive. Brimm felt it was worth trying to get Knowling for the principal academy and talked to Klein about him. Klein discussed Knowling with Jack Welch, who in turn called Noel on the matter. In early January 2003, Noel and Patti Stacey met with Knowling, who agreed to seriously consider taking the New York City challenge. Knowling had one condition, which was that Patti Stacey had to agree to work with him through the whole process. She agreed.

Klein and Knowling met and hit it off. Joel Klein's judgment call to appoint Knowling was influenced by his conclusion that Knowling's experiences in the regulated phone industry, with both Ameritech and U.S. West, gave him relevant experience. Also, Knowling's experience with entrepreneurial start-up companies made him a lot more than a traditional "Bell head," as the old phone company executives were often called. Klein said, "Knowling would have to deal with unionized, entrenched bureaucracy while being a start-up entrepreneur, while being driven by a passion for the kids," a unique combination that Knowling embodied. As Klein explained:

> He knows Monopoly, right? He understands organizations that exist to perpetuate the staff entitlement and the organization rather than the delivery and service of the product and that's what he had to do. I had met him when he was at U.S. West and Covad. I called a good friend of mine, Michael Powell, [former Chairman of the Federal Communications Commission], who knew Bob. Michael was my chief of staff at the Justice Department. I talked to Michael about him. I asked Jack Welch to go talk to some people. I talked to Carly Fiorina about him because he was on the Board of Directors of HP. Fundamentally I sensed he had the right background, the right qualifications.
>
> Then I talked to him and I found his heart. His heart—kind of my heart, right? He cares about kids who look like him. And that matters to me, because most of my New York kids look like him or have a similar background, they grew up like him and families—you know, a lot of kids didn't go to college and

parents didn't go to college. So I thought he's got the right skill set, he's got the right background and he's not—he doesn't need a job here. Right? I'm not gonna give him the best salary he ever got, right? So why is he coming? He's coming because he believes in the mission and he totally gets it—I mean, in the first 30 seconds I knew that he got the importance of our principals, and I thought it was a powerful statement that somebody of Bob's background, of his economic opportunity was willing to leave Denver to come to New York and say, "We're going to create great school leaders so kids in high poverty communities can have options that currently don't exist in those communities."

Klein was then relentless at making sure that Knowling became the CEO of the New York City Leadership Academy, which at this point was a concept with no design, no curriculum, no staff, and almost no funding. A social entrepreneur was needed. The Klein judgment to appoint Knowling was one of the keys to launching the transformation of the New York City public school system.

PEOPLE JUDGMENT BY KLEIN

Klein made another very important people judgment. He knew Knowling had no educational background and wanted to make sure that his team had depth in this area, so he appointed Sandra Stein to be a key member of his team. Klein told us:

The first one was actually what was an arranged marriage. I brought in Sandra Stein. That was hard for Knowling because normally, you know, you like to put your own team together, and I thought she had done a lot. She would bring credibility when doing change. You have mister outside and miss inside, working together. So that was key on the academic side, because he didn't have the academic background to do principal training.

This is how the academy framed the roles of Knowling and Stein:

The Chief Executive Officer of the Leadership Academy is Bob Knowling, the former CEO of Covad Communications and

SimDesk Technologies Inc., who also created and managed leadership academies at both Ameritech and U.S. West. Mr. Knowling is working with a team of experienced, world-class educators and business experts to provide practical training programs that combine organizational change management, leadership development, and instructional leadership training. Sandra Stein, the former director of the Aspiring Leaders Program at Baruch College, serves as the Academy's Academic Dean. The Leadership Academy's Advisory Board is chaired by Jack Welch, the former Chief Executive Officer of General Electric. The Academy is an independent 501(c) (3) non-profit corporation and is funded by corporate and philanthropic giving. In addition to the strong financial support of The Wallace Foundation, the Leadership Academy has also received a $30 million commitment from the Partnership for the City of New York. The fundraising efforts for the Academy are being coordinated by the Office of Strategic Partnerships, led by Caroline Kennedy.[3]

BOB KNOWLING'S JUDGMENTS

The cascade of judgments from Bloomberg, to Klein, to Welch, to Knowling resulted in Knowling becoming CEO of the New York City Leadership Academy in February of 2003. Knowling spent the first several months visiting schools, working with several of his staff to start designing the Academy. Noel and Patti Stacey spent several days in multiple design sessions occurring in the winter and early spring. Knowling was clear that he was coming as a change agent, a self descriptor he had used since the early 1990s, a role about which he said in a discussion with Noel, "until you are comfortable with having no fear of being fired, you can't be a change agent." He has been willing to put his job on the line since that time. Therefore it was not bluster for Knowling to tell us:

Because of the change agenda I'm bringing in here, I will disturb the status quo. I'm going to build huge barriers for these ed schools who have feasted on this system. I'm going to be an executive coach to the chancellor and be in his ear about what he needs to do to drive change.

Knowling expected resistance, but he wasn't prepared for the New York City press; to this day it drives him crazy, as he stated:

> I'm a catalyst and I wasn't quite sure that I had the stomach to be able to turn the cheek to this very biased media that just preys on the school system. In fact, my disdain for a certain number of the media reached an all-time high being here. I think that they are the worst forms of whores that I've ever encountered in my life. They don't seek the truth. They seek sensationalism. And I'm so disappointed in the media. Right now I wouldn't give you a nickel for them. I mean, if we could, if we could reincarnate the *Titanic* I'd load 'em all up.

Knowling launched the New York City Leadership Academy with the partnership with Sandra Stein, who has succeeded him as CEO. Sandra led a major initiative of the Academy that was aimed at ninety aspiring principals. This was a full-time program for carefully recruited and selected educators who wanted to be principals. The Leadership Academy had them full-time on their payroll and engaged them in an intense total-immersion development program that included extensive workshop time as well as internship work with practicing principals in the schools.

Knowling then had the 1,200, now 1,400, principals to develop. There were 250 new principals, about the same number each year, who had a very intense series of workshops starting in the summer, before they took over their schools, backed up by four multiday workshops during the school year.

CROTONVILLE WORKSHOP
TO LAUNCH THE ACADEMY

In the spring of 2003, after dismantling the forty superintendencies, Klein had selected his ten regional superintendents and some of their staff, and he had his own staff as well. To get them aligned and supportive of the New York City Leadership Academy, he brought the team of about sixty up to GE's Crotonville, by now renamed the John F. Welch Leadership Center, for a three-day workshop that Noel and Patti Stacey facilitated with Knowling. Jack Welch also helped launch the first day. The purpose was to align the regional superintendents and board of education staff with a common Teachable Point of View for transforming the New York City school system, the principals' academy being a key element. The symbolism of doing this workshop at Crotonville was huge, as was having Welch help kick it off, with Carolyn Kennedy in attendance as well.

Welch opened up the session in the famous Crotonville "Pit," a 112-person amphitheater setting where he and now Jeff Immelt have dialogues with GE leaders several times a month. Welch started off very humbly. He let them know that as educators, they had a much tougher job than he did as the CEO of a business, and that they were dealing with the most important leadership challenge of all: developing the next generation.

Welch then turned on the "tough love." He got in the educators' faces about the importance of their being better leaders. He bemoaned the dismal failure of our schools and told them they needed to annihilate bureaucracy. He also shared his views on leadership. One of his messages was a page out of his last annual report in which Welch wrote:

> Annihilating Bureaucracy: We cultivate the hatred of bureaucracy in our company and never for a moment hesitate to use that awful word "hate." Bureaucrats must be ridiculed and removed. They multiply in organizational layers and behind functional walls—which means that every day must be a battle to demolish this structure and keep the organization open, ventilated and free. Even if bureaucracy is largely exterminated, as it has been at GE, people need to be vigilant—even paranoid—because the allure of bureaucracy is hard to resist, and it can return in the blink of an eye. Bureaucracy frustrates people, distorts their priorities, limits their dreams and turns the face of the entire enterprise inward.[4]

The group clearly recognized how they had become victims of the bureaucracy and needed to be the leaders, like Welch, who took it on for the benefit of the students. Over the next several years, Welch attended as many principal academy sessions as he could fit in, usually one every month, along with board meetings and one-on-one coaching sessions with Knowling and Klein. All in all, he gave a lot to the Academy.

The three-day workshop was designed to help the group develop a collective Teachable Point of View and vision for the transformation of the New York City school system. Klein shared his vision and challenged the group to take on the all-important transformation agenda. The remainder of the workshop had small groups wrestle through how they would execute the audacious transformational challenges. They came up with a set of values that would guide their behaviors and started crafting a vision for how they would work. There was a very complex set of political forces at play: Joel Klein and Bob Knowling were outsiders to the school system, facing many skeptics and lacking an established power structure. They faced central office administrators with their own decision-making authority and lifelong educators, many of whom were former superintendents in the decentralized system who were now forced to give up their autonomy and report to Klein. In retrospect we all underestimated the fluidity of the political environment and the difficulty of coalescing this leadership group with its multiple power bases.

By the end of the three days, it became clear that the biggest political challenge would be getting the deputy chancellor on board regarding Klein and Knowling's agenda to build leaders. The ten new superintendents reported to her, so on paper she controlled a lot of what would go on in the system. She was worried about her turf, especially with regard to the Leadership Academy; she was focused on curriculum as the answer to an improved school system, not leadership, and she was also antibusiness. This was an early warning that was not dealt with and reflected bad people judgments by both Klein and Knowling.

In Klein's case it was a bad judgment call to hire her in the first place. Ultimately, she was dismissed, but only after a lot of momentum was lost and political capital wasted. Klein reflected on some other bad people judgments and what he learned from them, stating, "I need a traditional educator. That was probably the hardest position for me to fill, and as it turned out it didn't work out."

Then Klein wanted to get additional talent to help transform the system and get discipline in the culture, so he filled another key position from outside with a very successful general from the U.S. Army. However, the general could not adjust to the school system and political environment. In Klein's words, "I went out and found a former army general and she was terrific, but not for this. She just didn't get how you transform an organization." Klein reflected on why these bad judgments occurred. The bottom line was inadequate preparation:

> What I think I did right is conceptualize the things. The things that I think I did wrong were fundamentally trying to make snap judgments. I mean, while I'm a big believer in Blink, it's hard work. But you see, I was under enormous pressure.

In discussions with Welch, Klein picked up some important wisdom: "Hire slow and fire fast," a lesson he has successfully built on over the last several years.

Knowling dealt with the deputy chancellor problem by avoiding her, and this turned out to be a bad judgment as well. This led to Knowling misjudging the importance of the superintendents who worked for her and their impact on the principals. In spite of this bad political backdrop, the New York City Leadership Academy had a huge impact, but it could have had more sooner with aligned leadership at the top. Knowling too learned from his bad people judgment. He told us:

> I needed to do a little political mapping and get her involved. Now, interestingly with the next deputy chancellor, Carmen Tariña, I went out of my way to build those bridges and to build that alliance, and I have got to tell you it was smooth sailing.

Both Klein and Knowling were nondefensive learners and took ownership for their judgment mistakes and learned from them. This takes self-confidence and clarity of purpose.

TEACHING SCHOOL PRINCIPALS LEADERSHIP JUDGMENT

Knowling did his homework as he entered the school system. First, he needed to understand how his bosses saw the situation. It was pretty clear when he talked with Bloomberg and Klein what they saw:

> When the mayor and chancellor sit and talk about these bad decisions that these principals were making and how we're on the front page of the news all the time, it's because leadership judgment is not applied. And by the way, they don't teach that in education schools.

Knowling knew that principals needed to learn to be leaders. They had all grown up in the highly bureaucratic school system and needed help framing their role as true leaders of their schools, with a responsibility to keep developing the teachers and shaping the education experience in the schools, not merely being survivors or caretakers.

Knowling developed a very clear Teachable Point of View on judgment. He went out into the schools, observed principals, and interviewed them to analyze why they made good and bad judgments. He concluded, "Folks weren't steeped in a process. People didn't understand the decision-making process. That was the problem they were trying to fix. It just never was—it was never . . . explained that way."

Principals had to be transformational leaders, those who could "creatively destroy and remake their schools" to deliver for the kids. Knowling wanted the principals to be able to make transformational judgments, including firing bad teachers even though they were highly protected by the teachers' union. Each principal needed to make strategic judgments for his or her school and be ready to make crisis judgments. That is how Knowling framed and named his strategy judgment for the New York City Leadership Academy:

> What is the manner in which principals get their input or data collection as they look at situations or problems? Are they seeking

facts? Do they understand when they have invested enough time to gather data? We learned that most principals don't understand that decision making is a process and absent a process, they make poor or bad calls. We knew we had to address situational leadership and work overtime to help principals improve the quality of their decisions.

NEW PRINCIPAL PROGRAM:
A LEADERSHIP JUDGMENT SUPPORT SYSTEM

The 250 new principals each year are part of an intensive yearlong leadership development process that starts with a five-day workshop in the summer and four multiday workshops during the academic year and includes ongoing mentoring and support from both the Academy and business partners. All of the experiences were designed to help develop good people, strategy, and crisis judgment in the principals.

Leading a school had all of these elements. Historically the new principals were so overwhelmed with taking over a school, with little more than academic classroom coursework on administration, that many failed outright, while others muddled along and a few—through trial and error—emerged as good leaders. The yearlong process was designed with an action learning framework, in which principals would learn new capabilities, apply them, learn from the judgments, and drive measurable results with consequences.

Workshop 1: Preschool Five-Day Workshop

The first step in the process was a workshop for thirty new principals at a time. These thirty were a cohort who would work with one another throughout the year, coming together in each workshop. The first five days set the platform for the principals to become transformational leaders of their new school with the capacity for people, strategy, and crisis judgments. Knowling describes the workshop as:

> high-octane sessions that allowed the principals to retrace their steps and to learn from each other. There was never a short-

age of current problems and challenges that they brought with them to the workshop, either. In fact, many of them couldn't wait to get to the session to get some free consulting help. The Academy facilitators were relentless in making the prinipals slow the music down and getting the facts as quickly as possible. And once they had the facts, to make the call. Often they don't have time to go find the superintendent, so they needed to get comfortable in making the call.

The five-day session focused on helping them develop their Teachable Point of View for their school. The ideas component included their strategy on curriculum and on working with parents and the community. The participants got expert input on curriculum and working with stakeholders, including the teachers' union. They worked with one another to develop written action plans for the strategy and ideas for their new school.

In addition, they each developed a set of values for their schools that would support the ideas. Emotional energy focused on how to be transformational leaders and how to build the operating systems for their schools, how to engage stakeholders, how to run effective meetings that energize and teach. The edge component dealt with handling crisis, hiring and firing, and allocating limited resources.

The session was highly interactive, with principals engaged throughout in coaching one another. The overall design is presented in the table "Academy for New Principals Workshop." The final exercise was to have each principal videotaped giving his or her own version of the Martin Luther King "I Have a Dream" speech for his or her school. They were all challenged to take their Teachable Point of View and create the storyline for their schools. This was first done in written form by having them each write a *Time* magazine cover story on their school three years in the future, what they want written about their leaders, the judgments they have made, and the impact they have had on their students and community. After sharing their *Time* stories, they each prepared their storyline for a five-minute video. The purpose of this was to help them practice the storyline that they would have to repeat at least a hundred times in all different contexts, with their teachers, their students, parents, and the union.

ACADEMY FOR NEW PRINCIPALS WORKSHOP

Day 1	Day 2	Day 3	Day 4	Day 5
• Opening	• Hand You've Been Dealt	• Opening Your School	• Building a School Leadership Team	• Union–Management Relations
• TPOV				
• Leadership Is Autobiographical	• Curriculum	• Budget Dialogue	• Power and Conflict	• Storyline
	• Resistance to Change	• People Edge	• Vision	• Action Planning
• Envisioning	• GRPI/PAL	• Operating Mechanisms	• Transformational Leadership	• Chancellor Session
• Values	• Action Planning			
• Team Building/ Dinner		• Action Planning	• Emotions of Change	
			• Team Building/ Dinner	

It became the platform for helping them make better people, strategy, and crisis judgments.

One very interesting "crisis" that loomed for the new principals was all new books for students to be delivered prior to school opening. Never in the New York City school system had there been a massive turnover of texts. None of the new principals had ever experienced anything like this and they were in near shock at the thought of hundreds of books being dropped off at their schools a week before school opened, needing to be cataloged and distributed. Knowling loved this opportunity. One of the many tools the principals were taught was process mapping: how to systematically lay out a process and execute it with maximum effectiveness and efficiency, a tool well used in companies doing quality improvement, Six Sigma or lean manufacturing, but almost never used by educators to manage their organizations.

Knowling used the textbooks as the "living case" to learn process mapping, and the result was the principals all had a way of handling the "textbook crisis." They planned where the books should arrive, be staged, who would catalog them, how they would get to classrooms, and so on. This was illustrative of what occurred throughout the year, concepts, tools, and coaching in real-time to improve school performance.

Workshops II, III, and IV

These were multiday clinic sessions. The same thirty principals reconvened for several days, each coming to the session with prework accounts of what happened in their schools as well as coming with "judgment problems" they were wrestling with and wanted to get help from the cohort group.

PRINCIPALS AND TEACHERS SHAPE OUR FUTURE

Through their commitment to take on public education in New York City, Bloomberg and Klein mobilized a social network of leaders including Bob Knowling, Jack Welch, Dick Parsons, and Carolyn Kennedy, among others, to join in the very difficult execution phase of their yet-to-be completed strategic judgment. Execution required organizational processes, namely the establishment of the New York Leadership Academy and a mechanism to drive large-scale development and transformation of the schools by focusing on the principals as the key to better schools.

Klein is very clear that the Academy is all about developing good leadership judgment in the principals. He describes it as follows: "I think part of it is your life experiences. We try to teach judgment and I think the value add . . . is really trying to role-play and demonstrate, and also to put you next to people with good judgment."

Klein is also very clear about what he wants to see as the output of his academy and how he knows whether or not he has a good principal. Klein visits schools all the time to assess firsthand the execution phase of the Academy's work. He told us, "I can tell in half an hour if I got a good principal. . . . If they start telling me all the reasons why it's not working and oh, the woe is me tale, you know, people who are excuse makers fundamentally don't succeed."

Klein ends with a philosophical view of judgment:

> In the end it's what life is about . . . you set some criteria and
> people, at least if they give you an intelligent way to think about
> how to get from here to there, you think, okay. Then the second
> thing you say to yourself is, Did they get from here to there?
> They fooled me once; they're not gonna fool me twice. Right?
> It's just that simple.

The stakes are high; leadership judgment in schools is about shaping the capacity for good judgment in our children.

13

CONCLUSION

We have made a strong assertion in this book that the leader's most important role is making good judgment calls in three domains: key people, strategy, and crisis. Great leaders have a high percentage of good judgment calls; they are good only if the execution is successful. The second most important role you play is to develop other leaders who can make good judgment calls.

The book sets out to help leaders in their roles to make better judgment calls while also developing other leaders to do the same. We don't pretend to have all the answers—or to have asked all of the possible questions—but we have watched hundreds of leaders making thousands of judgment calls. We have seen good calls and bad ones. We have seen leaders make so-so initial calls and then manage and retune them in midair to produce brilliant results. And we have seen leaders make spot-on, inspired decisions and then end up in the ditch because they didn't follow through on execution, or they looked away and missed a critical context change. We have learned a lot. And by putting our brains and experiences together, we have come up with our framework.

We hope that our contribution to leaders and to academics is a framework for improving leadership judgment. The process of judgment begins with the leader recognizing the need for a judgment and continuing through successful execution. Leaders are said to have "good judgment" when they repeatedly make judgment calls that turn out well. And these calls often turn out well because they have mastered a complex process that unfolds in several dimensions:

- **Time:** We have identified three phases to the process. *Pre*—what happens before the leader makes the decision. *The call*—what the leader does as he or she makes the decision that helps it turn out to be the right one. *Execution*—what the leader must oversee to ensure the call produces the desired results.
- **Domain:** The elements of the process, the attention that must be paid to each of them, and the time over which the judgment unfolds varies with its subject matter. We have identified three critical domains in which most of the most important calls are required: (1) judgments about people; (2) judgments about strategy, and (3) judgments in time of crisis.
- **Constituencies:** A leader's relationships provide the information and the means for executing the call. A leader must interact with these different constituencies, consider their various interests, and manage those relationships to make successful calls. And to improve judgment making in the firm, the leader must use these interactions to help others learn to make successful calls.

We have identified four types of knowledge needed to do this: *self-knowledge*—personal values and goals; *social network knowledge*—regarding those who surround you daily; *organizational knowledge*—people at all levels; and *contextual knowledge*—the myriad other stakeholders (customers, suppliers, government, stockholders, competitors, and interest groups).

We offer this framework to help you improve your judgment-making faculties, to do a better job of developing good judgment in others, and to encourage a more vigorous conversation about judgment. We need more leaders with better judgment.

HANDBOOK FOR

LEADERSHIP JUDGMENT

Chris DeRose and Noel M. Tichy*

Handbook for Leadership Judgment

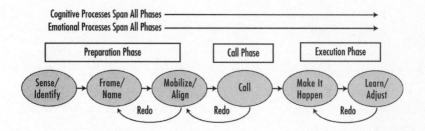

*We want to acknowledge the substantial intellectual contributions to the Handbook made by Warren Bennis.

INTRODUCTION

Judgment is the essential genome of leadership. Ultimately, a leader is judged by others on the performance of his or her organization. That performance is reliant on many factors; some are large—such as who to put in key jobs—while others are smaller—such as how to manage a product introduction or policy change. Each of these performance factors, whether big or small, requires judgment. That is, they demand that a leader use however much data is available to determine when to act and what to do.

This handbook deals with the big leadership judgments: people, strategy and crisis. These are the ones that determine leadership success or failure. While this handbook will help you apply the leadership judgment lessons discussed in the main text, it can also be treated as a stand-alone guide to improving your own judgment capabilities.

A DYNAMIC PROCESS

We make a distinction between judgment and decision making. Much of the academic literature and popular notions of decision making culminate in a single moment when the leader makes a decision. In this handbook, we focus on judgment as a process that unfolds over time. Analysis of this process has either been absent, leaving leaders to unconsciously pick a course of action, or has been unrealistically linear. In our experience, the judgment process is actually more like a drama with plotlines, characters, and sometimes unforeseen twists and turns. A leader's success hinges on how well she manages the entire process, not just the single moment when a decision is made.

Key leadership judgments encompass several dimensions:

Time: We have identified three phases to the process. These phases do not always happen in a clean linear fashion; good leaders self-correct by using "redo loops," repeating earlier phases to correct errors or adjust for oversights.

Preparation: What happens before the leader makes the decision.
The Call: What the leader does as he or she makes the decision that helps it turn out to be the right one.
Execution: What the leader must oversee to make sure the call produces the desired results.

Domain: We have identified three critical domains in which most of the most important calls are required:

Judgments about *people*
Judgments about *strategy*
Judgments in time of *crisis*

Constituencies: A leader's relationships are the sources of the information needed to make a successful call. They also provide the means for executing the call, and represent the various interests that must be attended to throughout the process. A leader must interact with these different constituencies and manage those relationships to make successful calls. In addition, to improve judgment making throughout the organization, the leader must use these interactions to help others learn to make successful calls.

The diagram on the next page shows how these dimensions play out in the judgment process:

IT'S WHAT HAPPENS THAT COUNTS

A leader's report card is ultimately a reflection of how he or she fared on the major judgments that impacted the well-being of the institution. The diagram on the next page lists factors that contribute to good or bad leadership judgment. The leader can make mistakes and still have a good judgment outcome by using the redo loops to continuously self-correct. The test of leadership is how well the leader adapts during the process to drive a successful outcome. There is no such thing as a strategy that's good in theory but lousy in execution. A leader sets his or her organization on a course based on the premise that it will lead to success. Recognizing execution limitations during the judgment process is as vital as having intellectual clarity about a potential breakthrough strategy. Similarly, people judgments rest on whether people put in leadership positions are able to do the job with integrity and courage as they deliver results.

Bill George, former CEO of Medtronic and currently a Harvard professor, shared a story during an interview that encapsulated this sentiment. Reflecting on a wildly successful career that included growing

LEADERSHIP JUDGMENT PROCESS

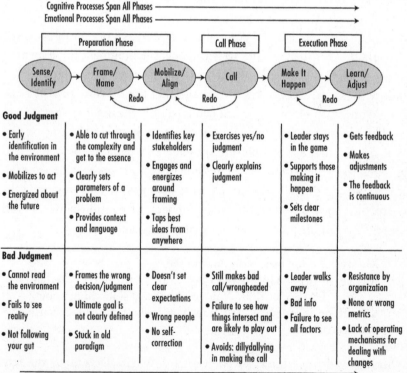

| Cognitive Processes Span All Phases ⟶ | | | | | |
| Emotional Processes Span All Phases ⟶ | | | | | |

Preparation Phase			**Call Phase**	**Execution Phase**	
Sense/ Identify	Frame/ Name	Mobilize/ Align	Call	Make It Happen	Learn/ Adjust
	Redo	Redo		Redo	

Good Judgment

• Early identification in the environment	• Able to cut through the complexity and get to the essence	• Identifies key stakeholders	• Exercises yes/no judgment	• Leader stays in the game	• Gets feedback
• Mobilizes to act	• Clearly sets parameters of a problem	• Engages and energizes around framing	• Clearly explains judgment	• Supports those making it happen	• Makes adjustments
• Energized about the future	• Provides context and language	• Taps best ideas from anywhere		• Sets clear milestones	• The feedback is continuous

Bad Judgment

• Cannot read the environment	• Frames the wrong decision/judgment	• Doesn't set clear expectations	• Still makes bad call/wrongheaded	• Leader walks away	• Resistance by organization
• Fails to see reality	• Ultimate goal is not clearly defined	• Wrong people	• Failure to see how things intersect and are likely to play out	• Bad info	• None or wrong metrics
• Not following your gut	• Stuck in old paradigm	• No self-correction	• Avoids: dillydallying in making the call	• Failure to see all factors	• Lack of operating mechanisms for dealing with changes

Not Following Gut Can Span All Phases ⟶

the company from $1.1 billion in market capitalization to over $60 billion, and the market introduction of lifesaving technologies along the way, George shared what he called his "greatest failure." Prior to his years at Medtronic, George had been a promising senior executive at Litton Industries. While there, for three years George actively groomed someone to ultimately be his replacement. "Every year I would present him as my successor and everyone said, 'Yes, yes, yes!'" But when George left Litton, the CEO stepped in and selected a different production leader with less experience. George still blames himself for Litton's poor performance and eventual closure after his own departure.

George's self-assessment is candid, honest, and, in our view, correct. His succession judgment was a failure. Although George's succession candidate likely would have been better than the CEO's choice—it's hard to imagine much worse—George wasn't able to make it happen. It would have been easy for George to let himself off the hook on this judgment call, even to have felt smug about the correctness of his analysis. After all, the CEO intervened and George had no real ability to campaign after he left the company. However, George holds himself accountable for his inability to get his people judgment implemented and realizes that the eventual closure of the business was related to that failure. In short, George knew long ago that the measure of a successful judgment isn't how well-reasoned it is; only the outcome matters.

This doesn't mean that a leader must make the right call on the first try. Rather, as the diagram on page 289 depicts, the leader can go back to earlier stages of the judgment call process to correct mistakes. We call these "redo" loops. This openness to learning and self-correction should not be mistaken for lack of commitment. As Bill George said of his many later successful judgments,

> My style is I don't second-guess myself. . . . I may be wrong and we may have to change it but I don't say, 'Why didn't I do that' or 'Why did I go for that.' You don't know if something's going to work until you go. . . . You just have to hang in there because you don't know.

Another leader we interviewed, General Wayne Downing, the late four-star commander of the Special Operations Forces, described a "redo" loop he experienced on the battlefield. After a year and a half of planning, in 1989 a stealthy force was infiltrated into Panama to topple the illegal and corrupt regime of Manuel Noriega. Less than five hours before U.S. forces were prepared to strike, covert surveillance lost sight of the Panamanian leader. As Downing told us,

> "We're in a crisis, a major crisis . . . and the clock is ticking. We have the duly elected government under protection, which we planned to install as soon as we get Noriega and his regime out of there. Our forces are preparing to move to their attack positions as soon as it gets dark. The 75th Ranger Regiment and the 82nd Airborne Division were in the air flying down to jump in at 1 A.M. And we cannot find this guy."

One response to the chaos of the situation would have been for General Downing to execute the plan as it had been rehearsed. This would have enabled the United States to stabilize the situation so that the elected government could have taken control. However, in the process Noriega likely would have eluded U.S. forces and escaped to Cuba or Venezuela. The long-term strength of the democratically elected Panamanian government would have been jeopardized. Downing described his team's response:

> It was me and my operations officers. We sat down and started peppering each other back and forth. In fifteen minutes, we turned that thing—changed something that we'd been working on for a year and a half—and changed it just like that because the situation had changed. . . . You're prepared for this because on a battlefield the enemy always has a vote. You can have all these great plans, but you know things are going to change.

The new plan that Downing and his team came up with was to find the top 100 people that Noriega was associated with and from whom he would likely seek assistance. In the hours that followed the preplanned raids, U.S. forces found 95 of the top 100 people. As Downing recalled, "We dried up his support network to a point where he had to seek refuge with the Papal Nuncio, and then later surrendered to us."

Downing's story is a vivid example of a "redo" loop in action. Rather than hope his original plan would somehow still work and rather than completely abandon the mission, Downing created space for him and his team to deliberate, debate, and adjust.

The following chart reflects some of the key differences between popular notions of decision-making and how we frame the judgment process:

DECISION MAKING AND FRAMING THE JUDGMENT PROCESS

Characteristic	Traditional View	Judgment Process View
Time	Single moment, static	Dynamic process that unfolds
Thought Process	Rational, analytic	Recognition that rational analysis happens alongside emotional, human drama
Variables	Knowable, quantifiable	Interactions among variables can lead to entirely new outcomes
Focus	Individual—heroic leader persona who makes the tough call	Organizational—a process that the leader guides but is impacted by many actors and subsequent judgment calls
Success Criteria	Making the best decision based on known data	Ability to act and react through judgment process that guides others to a successful outcome
Actors	Top-down, leader makes the key decisions	Top-down-up, execution influences how judgments are reshaped
Transparency	Closed system in which decision-makers hold information and rationale for judgments not explained	Open process in which mistakes are shared and learning used to adjust
Capability Building	Unconsciously happens through experience or luck. Reserved for top leadership	Deliberate development at all levels

JUDGMENT BUILT UPON DEEP KNOWLEDGE

Great leaders have a high percentage of good judgment calls. Every leader makes some bad judgments but great leaders learn from these and don't repeat them. They manage the judgment process so that outcomes are successful while people are involved and developed along the way. Doing this requires the leader to have knowledge that spans beyond a "just the facts" analytical capability. It requires deeper knowledge in four areas:

- **Self-Knowledge:** Awareness of one's personal values, goals, and aspirations. This includes recognition of when these personal desires may lead to a bias in sensing the need for a judgment or interpreting facts. It also includes the ability to create a mental storyline for how judgments will play out and the results they lead to.
- **Social Network Knowledge:** Understanding of the personalities, skills, and judgment track records of those on your team. This includes how they supplement or bias your judgment process.
- **Organizational Knowledge:** Knowing how people in the organization will respond, adapt, and execute. This also includes personal networks or mechanisms for learning from leaders at all levels in the organization.
- **Contextual Knowledge:** Understanding based on relationships and interactions with stakeholders such as customers, suppliers, government, investors, competitors, or interest groups that may impact the outcome of a judgment. This entails anticipating not only how they will respond directly to a judgment but how they will interact with one another throughout the judgment process.

DEVELOPING JUDGMENT

Too often judgment is viewed as one of those ineffable leadership qualities that a person either has or doesn't have. Obviously, judgment is built upon life experience. Most of us prefer the experienced doctor who has seen thousands of cases to the newly minted resident who will use our case to develop knowledge. Certainly, some people do seem to possess inherent leadership characteristics that enable the judgment process. To name only a few of these: they develop broader and deeper relationships, they empathize with others, they are future-oriented, or they have courage to act in the absence of full knowledge. Nonetheless, judgment is a capability that can be developed and improved when it becomes a conscious process.

This starts with the extent to which judgment as a capability is discussed and developed within your organization. Take the following test to assess where you stand:

Building Blocks

	Not at all		To a	great extent	

1. **Process Orientation:** Judgments are conscious, deliberate processes rather than single-moment decisions.

1	2	3	4	5

2. **Involvement:** Judgment calls involve the team, organization, and stakeholders in an open, transparent process.

1	2	3	4	5

3. **Teaching Environment:** The judgment process helps everyone understand how, when, and why a judgment call is made so people can learn from the experience.

1	2	3	4	5

4. **Learn and Adjust:** Knowledge comes from all levels of the organization to help assess and adjust to drive a successful outcome.

1	2	3	4	5

5. **Development Process:** Judgment capability is an explicit part of the assessment and development processes.

1	2	3	4	5

6. **Succession Planning:** Leadership roles go to those who consistently demonstrate good judgment capability.

1	2	3	4	5

Implications for my organization:

_____

_____

_____

_____

_____

PLAN FOR THIS HANDBOOK

Now that you have reflected on the characteristics of successful leaders and the judgment processes they create, this handbook will help you to develop your leadership judgment capability. The organizing principle for the handbook is to examine the four bases of knowledge that lead to good judgment. Each section will focus on one of these and guide you through a series of exercises to assess your judgment and plan for improvement.

Section Two: Self-Knowledge
- Experiences that have shaped your judgment capability
- Evaluating your judgment track record
- Identifying your judgment pitfalls and development opportunities

Section Three: Self-Knowledge—Developing a Storyline
- Outlining your storyline
- Imagining alternate endings
- Knowing when you need to make judgments

Section Four: Your Team
- Evaluating your team's judgment capability
- Recognizing how individuals affect judgment processes
- Building mechanisms for improving your team's judgment process

Section Five: Organizational Knowledge
- Identifying your network for organizational knowledge creation
- Developing mechanisms for engaging the organization
- Judgment-building processes for all levels

Section Six: Contextual Knowledge
- Outlining your stakeholder network and relationships
- Determining when, where, and how to involve key stakeholders
- Developing processes that engage stakeholders

Section Seven: Make the Right Call
- Turning your learning into action

SECTION TWO

SELF-KNOWLEDGE

Any successful career in leadership is built on a foundation of self-awareness. Leaders rarely have the ability to engage others, set direction, and make good judgments if they are not introspective enough to realize how they affect the organizational processes and actors around them. As Bill George, a former CEO of Medtronic and current Harvard professor, says:

> Becoming an authentic leader is not easy. First you have to understand yourself, because *the hardest person you will ever have to lead is yourself*. Once you have an understanding of your authentic self, you will find that leading others is much easier.[1]

JUDGMENT FROM EXPERIENCE

We established earlier that leadership success is a function of a leader's judgment track record. Successful leaders not only have a better batting average, they are successful on those key judgments that shape their organizations and define their legacies. In short, they not only make more good judgments, they also get the big ones right.

Jim Owens, CEO of Caterpillar, made this observation during an interview with Noel. Reflecting on his own career and how leadership judgment is developed, he said:

> I think I've been fortunate in my career. I've been thrust into situations that were in somewhat crisis and where we needed to make radical change. I had an opportunity to evaluate the business situation and make recommendations that turned out

to be good judgments. In many cases, there are brilliant people who don't get thrust into situations where they are given that opportunity.[2]

Fortunately, our judgment capability is also a product of making thousands of judgments. Although we may not all have experiences that prepare us for a CEO role, our judgment is shaped over our lifetime. Some judgments are personal while others are professional. Some are monumental—who to marry, which job to take, whether to have children—while others are as trivial as which cereal to eat. Some are planned but many are, as the saying goes, things that just happen while you are making other plans. Our judgment capability is the cumulative experience of these many judgments. The lessons we learn are a reflection of our ability to tell the big judgments apart from the inconsequential, and to consciously learn when we do well or fail.

Kathy Gallo, chief learning officer and senior vice president of North Shore–Long Island Jewish Health System, explained what is required to become an excellent triage nurse. Kathy was not only a nurse herself but instrumental in designing the emergency response system used by hospitals across New York. As Kathy told us, in a hospital, it is the triage nurse who often determines which part of the hospital sees an emergency room walk-in and how quickly a patient gets service. In many cases, the triage nurse literally makes on-the-spot judgments that can mean life or death for a patient. This judgment capability is honed through experience and reflection that enables learning. As Kathy told us:

> Those people that cannot learn from their success or their mistakes fail miserably at triage. . . . You know, going back into that loop to see how your judgment call turned out, whether it was correct or not correct. Reflection is considerable. You reflect and then you say, "Well, that was a good one," or "I shouldn't have put the patient back out in the waiting room because they had x." But you actually go and hunt out that piece of information that you were missing.

Reflection is a critical capability for developing good judgment. Use the following space to chart your judgment journeyline. That is, identify those key judgments you made, when you made them, and what you learned. The horizontal axis reflects time, or years of your life. On the vertical axis, plot positive or negative judgment calls. Remember, a positive call is something that had a good outcome and generated positive emotional energy.

Leadership Judgment Journeyline

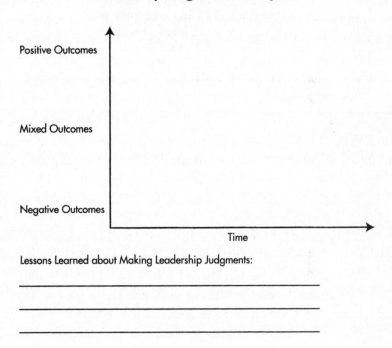

Positive Outcomes

Mixed Outcomes

Negative Outcomes

Time

Lessons Learned about Making Leadership Judgments:

_____

_____

_____

Judgment Experience in Different Domains

The judgments we face as organizational leaders are often dictated by our roles and the scope of our responsibilities. As noted above, they are also dictated by the number of years we have spent occupying leadership positions, as judgment capability is a function of experience. We also have unique, personal experiences that we can reflect upon to assess how well we handled them at the moment we were asked to make a judgment call.

For example, Jim Owens had a moment of deep personal reflection when he was passed over for the CEO role at Caterpillar in 1999.

Although Owens went on to win the CEO position in 2004, at the time he wasn't sure he would have another shot at the job. "I knew that might have been my last chance," said Owens. He immediately went on the head-hunters short list and began fielding recruiting calls to take over as CEO of another company. Owens listened for a few weeks before making a defining personal judgment call.

> I made a decision that being a CEO wasn't the most important thing in life to me. I enjoyed my job here, respected the company and [the CEO]. . . . I thought I could help make things more successful. . . . I thought, if it's meant for me to be a Chairman someplace, I want it to be where I've come through the ranks, know the key players, like the culture. So I opted to stay.[3]

Ultimately, Owens was one of three contenders for Glen Barton's job in 2003 and became CEO at the start of 2004. The self-knowledge Owens demonstrated—reflecting on what was important to him and under what circumstances he wanted to be in the top job—no doubt has contributed to his success.

Use the matrix below to determine which types of judgments you have faced. For each cell of the matrix, fill in one significant judgment you have made. Don't be surprised if you can't fill in every cell. For those that you can identify, rate the outcome. Use a scale of 1 for a bad judgment to 5 for a flawless judgment and execution.

Use the chart on page 301 for reference, then complete the blank chart that follows.

TYPES OF JUDGMENTS

	People	Strategy	Crisis
Self	Personal judgments about your ambitions, role, and capabilities	Personal judgments regarding your career and life strategy	Personal judgments made during times of crisis and introspection
Social Network	Judgments about who is on your team and off your team	Judgments about how your team evolves to meet business demands	Judgments about how your team operates and with whom you operate during crisis
Organizational	Judgments about organizational systems for ensuring quality and capability of people in the organization	Judgments about how to engage and align all organizational levels in strategy execution	Judgments about how to work with the organization through times of crisis
Contextual	Judgments about which stakeholders are important and how to engage them	Judgments about engaging stakeholders to frame, define, and execute strategy	Judgments about dealing with key stakeholders during times of crisis

	People	Strategy	Crisis
Self	My Judgment: Rating (1–5):	My Judgment: Rating (1–5):	My Judgment: Rating (1–5):
Social Network	My Judgment: Rating (1–5):	My Judgment: Rating (1–5):	My Judgment: Rating (1–5):
Organizational	My Judgment: Rating (1–5):	My Judgment: Rating (1–5):	My Judgment: Rating (1–5):
Contextual	My Judgment: Rating (1–5):	My Judgment: Rating (1–5):	My Judgment: Rating (1–5):

Learning about My Judgment Experience

Reflect on your responses on page 302 and consider the following:

1. Areas Where I Consistently Make Good Judgments:

2. Areas Where Judgments are Difficult or Results are Poor:

3. Areas Where I Have Little or No Experience:

Understanding Judgment as a Process

The judgment domains provide an easy framework for understanding where we are called upon to make judgments as leaders. However, every judgment we make is part of a dynamic process that is guided by our life's experiences, personal values, and the actions of others. The diagram on the next page depicts this process, revealing some of the potential judgment pitfalls along the way. Review the diagram, then select one judgment you have made in the people, strategy, and crisis arenas for further review.

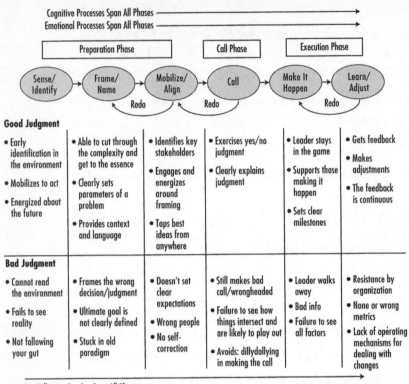

	Cognitive Processes Span All Phases

Good Judgment

Sense/Identify	Frame/Name	Mobilize/Align	Call	Make It Happen	Learn/Adjust
• Early identification in the environment • Mobilizes to act • Energized about the future	• Able to cut through the complexity and get to the essence • Clearly sets parameters of a problem • Provides context and language	• Identifies key stakeholders • Engages and energizes around framing • Taps best ideas from anywhere	• Exercises yes/no judgment • Clearly explains judgment	• Leader stays in the game • Supports those making it happen • Sets clear milestones	• Gets feedback • Makes adjustments • The feedback is continuous

Bad Judgment

• Cannot read the environment • Fails to see reality • Not following your gut	• Frames the wrong decision/judgment • Ultimate goal is not clearly defined • Stuck in old paradigm	• Doesn't set clear expectations • Wrong people • No self-correction	• Still makes bad call/wrongheaded • Failure to see how things intersect and are likely to play out • Avoids: dillydallying in making the call	• Leader walks away • Bad info • Failure to see all factors	• Resistance by organization • None or wrong metrics • Lack of operating mechanisms for dealing with changes

Not Following Gut Can Span All Phases

People Judgment: Select a people judgment you've made in the recent past. Assuming this was not a perfect judgment, identify what you did well and areas for improvement at each stage.

	Preparation	Call	Execution
Positive—things I did well			
Areas for Improvement			

Strategy Judgment: Select a strategy judgment you've made in the recent past, and repeat the exercise below.

	Preparation	Call	Execution
Positive—things I did well			
Areas for Improvement			

Crisis Judgment: This time select a crisis judgment.

	Preparation	Call	Execution
Positive—things I did well			
Areas for Improvement			

Character and Courage

By this point, you should have a good feel for your judgment track record. You have identified those judgments that shaped your leadership capability and the domains in which you've made judgment calls, and considered areas you can improve based on recent judgments.

Underlying all judgment calls are two foundations: character and courage. The former is composed of your personal values while the latter is a willingness to act and accept consequences in an imperfect situation.

Few leaders have survived a career without having deeply held values challenged. How we respond at those moments defines our character: those things that we stand for and those that are central to our self-identity. Character is also rising above self-interest and putting the interests of others ahead of your own. Bill George labels leadership as authentic when personal values line up to support such judgment calls.

Your ability to make good judgment calls rests on your character. Use the space below to write down the values that guide you in making judgments. For each value, identify a time that you have used that value to help you make a specific judgment.

My Values	When I Used This Value	How It Helped My Judgment
1.		
2.		
3.		
4.		
5.		

If the values that make up our character set the standard for our behavior, then courage is the ability to act in accordance with that personal standard. Some of the failures of leadership courage are based upon the fears listed below. For each, identify the extent to which you think this item impacts your judgment. Rate each item on a scale of 1 to 5. If it is not a problem, rate it a 1. Give it a 5 if it is a big challenge for you.

Exercising Courage in Judgment

1. **Fear of action**—inaction even when
   the need to act is known; preference
   for the status quo over change

1	2	3	4	5

2. **Fear of criticism**—concern that a
   key stakeholder will be critical of a
   judgment or the required execution

1	2	3	4	5

3. **Fear of defiance**—worry that others
   will not follow your leadership
   judgment, thereby undermining
   your leadership authority

1	2	3	4	5

4. **Fear of personal loss**—concern
   that something of value or a career
   opportunity may be lost by taking
   the necessary action

1	2	3	4	5

5. **Fear of insufficient or imperfect
   information**—self-doubt and
   concern that in the absence of
   perfect information, your
   conclusions are wrong

1	2	3	4	5

Insight into Self-Assessment

The preceding pages have asked you to look at your judgment track
record and personal character. Self-knowledge resulting from reflection is a vital ingredient in good judgment. However, we all have a
limited ability to perceive ourselves. While only the individual can
know his or her innermost thoughts and secrets, the mind is also
capable of deluding conscious self-perception. We create images of
ourselves as we would like to be, not as others experience us. Feedback from others helps us to balance our self-assessment.

To help you generate more self-knowledge, follow the steps below:

1. Select a people judgment, strategy judgment, and crisis judgment you have recently made. (If possible, use the same ones as
   for the exercise above.)
2. For each judgment, select three to five people who were also
   involved in each of the judgment processes. Distribute pages

304 to 307 to each person. Ask them to provide you with feedback on what you did well or can develop for each of the judgments.

3. Ask people to write down what they believe your personal values would be and to answer the five questions on page 307.

4. After everyone has returned their assessment to you, compare their answers with your own. Look for the degree of overlap or feedback that will help you adjust your self-perception. Use the space below to make notes.

Areas of Overlap/Shared Perceptions:

Areas Where Others' Perceptions Differ from My Own:

What I Will Do as a Result:

SECTION THREE

SELF-KNOWLEDGE—

YOUR STORYLINE

FOR THE FUTURE

In the preceding section, you were asked to reflect on the judgments you have made. This is your judgment track record, the experiences that have shaped your leadership capacity for making judgments.

Making judgments about the future requires you to use your past experiences to help you anticipate the future. To do so, leaders develop a storyline for what their organization will do, how their team will act, and the role that they will personally play. When leaders possess this capability, it plays out as a drama in their imagination. They envision the actions that they will take, imagine how competitors might respond and dialogues between key actors in the drama, and they write themselves into the script.

Like the director's cut on a DVD, however, the story often includes multiple endings. As the leader writes his storyline, he can see the twists and turns that may lead to different outcomes, some desirable and some less so.

As a leader, you likely have your own storyline for your organization. A critical component of self-knowledge is conscious awareness of this storyline. For many people, the storyline is their vision of the future: a reflection of their hopes and dreams for what their organizational, team, and personal accomplishments will be. In some cases, leaders have vivid storylines that run like movies in their heads. These minidramas are only bounded by our imagination. They may enable us to visualize the moment that we'll beat out our competitor and close the big deal with our customer, or the newspaper headline announcing an anticipated acquisition.

For others, the storyline is a vague notion of where they would like to be, more directional than definitive. Some people experience the storyline on an emotional level without the imagery. They may not be able to put it into words but they have a sense of what they want—or at least a gut reaction when they feel they are off course.

This storyline, whether consciously or otherwise, can propel us toward action and sometimes cloud our judgment. That is, we often make judgments that try to preserve the storyline we desire. This can lead to conforming data to fit prejudices or it can lead to selectively neglecting data that may contradict our desired storyline. For those who are not conscious of the storyline they have written, they may fail to sense and respond to critical changes in the world around them.

On the positive side, a storyline can also prepare us to make challenging judgments by helping us anticipate potential outcomes and interactions between the many actors and factors that may affect us. Those leaders who are able to imagine a dynamic storyline for themselves and their organizations are able to shape the living drama that plays out over the course of a judgment call.

STARTING WITH YOUR TEACHABLE POINT OF VIEW

The first step is making your personal storyline explicit. This starts with having a Teachable Point of View about where your organization is going in the future. Simply put, a Teachable Point of View is an articulation of the ideas that will help your organization be successful, the values required to be on your team, and how you will energize people along the way. These components—ideas, values, and emotional energy—become your guideposts for making judgments. The ability to face reality and make such judgments is what Jack Welch, General Electric's former CEO, called "edge."

Leadership judgments are made in the context of the storyline based on the building blocks of a Teachable Point of View as illustrated in the figure below.

A Teachable Point of View Shapes Your Judgment Storyline

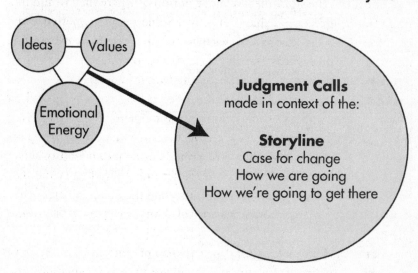

The elements of a Teachable Point of View form an interactive system that helps you lead your organization. Each element reinforces the other elements:

Teachable Point of View Element	What It Is	Systemic Effects
IDEAS	• Your beliefs and strategies for winning in the marketplace. For business organizations, it includes assumptions about customers, products, distribution channels, supply chains, pricing, and technology. • Ideas are the underpinning of organizational success; without a winning idea, your organization will be bankrupt.	• *Ideas–Values Link:* Values should reinforce execution of your ideas and subsequent strategies. • *Ideas–Emotional Energy Link:* The ideas should be compelling and emotionally energize people at all organizational levels.
VALUES	• Behaviors required of leaders to remain in the organization and receive rewards such as higher pay or promotion. • Values should lead to operational definition of behaviors. These behaviors form the foundation of your organizational culture.	• *Values–Emotional Energy Link:* If values resonate with employees, they will be emotionally energizing and provide a moral compass for the organization.
EMOTIONAL ENERGY	• Methods for engaging employees and exciting them about the organization. • Methods may be formal (e.g., reward systems, mission), systemic (e.g., meeting structures and rhythms), or informal (e.g., praise, stretch goals.)	• Noted above

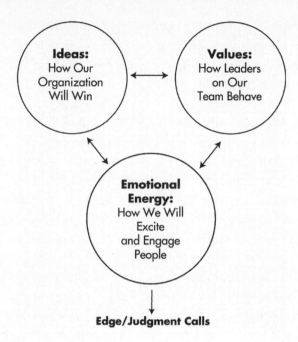

Use the space below to outline your Teachable Point of View:

Ideas	Values	Emotional Energy
_____	_____	_____
_____	_____	_____
_____	_____	_____
_____	_____	_____
_____	_____	_____

LEADER AS WRITER/ACTOR/DIRECTOR

The Teachable Point of View is based on our analysis and assumptions regarding what it will take for our organization to be successful. It guides the activities we undertake and how we engage with others as we lead. However, while the Teachable Point of View provides a foundation for action, it does not provide us with the detail of *how* we will achieve success. Implementing the Teachable Point of View will require alignment of many individuals inside and outside your organization. It will also be highly dependent upon the evolution of your industry, moves made by your competitors, or your customers' response. As a leader, you must have a vision for how these forces will work together, the role you play, and what will be required of others to be successful.

In its most effective and compelling form, this vision becomes a storyline for the future. By building upon the analytical content of a leader's Teachable Point of View, the storyline takes it one step further to describe the human drama that will play out.

The leader has a key role in this storyline. First, by composing the storyline and sharing it with others, he or she works to align the team around a vision of success. The leader also plays a key role: his or her actions are determinants of how the narrative unfolds. Finally, the leader makes key judgments along the way. He or she compares events in the real world to the storyline he or she had composed and makes judgments that keep the organization on track with the original storyline. The leader may also decide to rewrite the story, thereby changing the vision of success. In this capacity, the leader is similar to a writer who directs and stars in his or her own movie, making changes to the script along the way as the plot unfolds.

As noted above, you must be aware of your own storyline. Use the space on the next page to outline your story:

Imagine that your organization will be on the cover of a leading publication. The story will feature the success of your organization and your team over the next two years.

1. What company or marketplace metrics did you achieve?

2. Which competitors did you beat and how did you do it?

3. What were the critical cultural changes that took place and how did they happen?

4. What role did others play and why were they energized to perform?

5. What challenges or resistance did you face along the way and how did you overcome them?

6. How did you know you were successful, and how did it feel to you, your organization, and your customers?

FRAMING JUDGMENTS TO SHAPE THE STORYLINE

The elements of the storyline that you outlined above form a vision of how you would like your organization to succeed in the future. As a leader, your role is to make judgment calls along the way that help you get to your desired ending. This requires you to be aware of both how you need different actors in the drama to behave and ways that they can potentially derail your success. Your job is to anticipate the "derailers" so that you can sense and respond to these in ways that keep you on course.

Looking at the storyline elements above, consider how different people or events may influence the outcome of your story. Think of who could influence your future—competitors, customers, suppliers, internal leaders—as well as industry, regulatory, or other forces that may impact you. Using the space below, identify who could change your storyline, what they could do, and how it would positively or negatively impact your story's outcome.

Actions Others May Take		
Who	**Action They Could Take**	**Impact on Outcome**

SENSING THE NEED FOR JUDGMENT CALLS

Now that you have composed your storyline and considered the individuals or events that may impact it, you are able to identify potential judgment calls. In other words, you can anticipate the events that may change your story. This anticipation enables you to pick up on weak signals in the environment so you proactively make judgment calls, rather than being surprised or ending up in crisis.

Phil Schoonover, former CEO of Circuit City, attempted to help his company recover from a surprise move by one of its key vendors. For Circuit City, the North American consumer electronics retailer, the 2006 holiday season was supposed to edge pricing on popular flat-screen televisions down by 10 to 20 percent. Unexpectedly, a manufacturer teamed up with Walmart to provide an opening price point on its most popular plasma television that was 40 percent lower than it had been the previous year. In the twenty-six days following the announcement, the margins in flat-panel televisions nearly evaporated, leading to one of the fastest single-product price declines in consumer electronics history.

While no single variable ever spells the demise of a company, the flat-panel disaster may have been the coup de grâce for Circuit City. For starters, the company sold more televisions than its direct competitors, with the fat margins offsetting its lower sales in other departments. Additionally, the company had just launched Firedog, a services brand geared toward home installation of televisions and converging electronics technology. This multimillion dollar investment relied on increasing sales of flat-panel televisions to spur consumer demand for installation. Unfortunately, the dramatic drop in television prices made Circuit City's services pricing seem disproportionately high. A $300 installation and setup fee appears very different to a consumer spending $1,000 versus $2,000.

Under Schoonover's leadership, the company attempted a recovery but never regained its footing. Despite efforts to overhaul its supply chain, retail operations, and inventory management, the surprising overnight decay of its flagship business made the company vulnerable. Activist investors and take-over groups agitated the situation and Circuit City filed for bankruptcy in November 2008.

Kathy Gallo described the process that nurses go through when screening patients in the hospital emergency room. Expert nurses who have years of experience start assessing patients "as soon as they walk through the door," Kathy told us. "You start looking at how they're dressed. Are they dressed appropriately for the weather? How is their gait as they walk? Do they look like they're in pain? What does their color look like?"

In response to these questions, triage nurses make quick judgments regarding where patients should go within the hospital. Kathy explained that good nurses never discount the signals they pick up. "We will over triage. We'd rather assume you have a bleed than say, 'Ahh, we'll wait and see.' Over-triaging keeps everybody safe as we learn and get feedback on a call."

The notion of "over-triaging" is a good metaphor. Kathy's experience points to the need for being extremely sensitive and responsive at the first signs of trouble. Organizational leaders may not receive the kind of observable, physical symptoms that nurses do; they must be hyper-attentive to environmental cues that suggest a judgment will be required.

Use the space below to consider the big judgment calls you may need to make and how you will know when a call is needed:

Judgment Call I May Need to Make	Signals That May Indicate a Call Is Needed

"WHEN" CAN BE AS IMPORTANT AS "WHAT"

A key component of any judgment call is timing—knowing when you need to make a call or when a call can be deferred. There is a vital difference between indecisiveness and deliberate deferral. The former is an inability to confront a critical judgment; it is inaction at a time of urgency. The latter is recognition that the benefits of waiting—more data, more deliberation, more stakeholder engagement—outweigh any potential loss.

The importance of timing is perhaps nowhere more evident than on a chaotic battlefield. General Wayne Downing, the late four-star commander of the U.S. Special Operations Forces, described how timing can be a life-or-death matter.

For example, in Vietnam as brigade operations officers, we often had to reinforce units in contact. We were in a very volatile area with an active enemy force and when a contact began we often did not know how serious it would become. From experience, we knew that our light infantry units generally had the least staying power in an intense fight because they had to carry all their ammunition, food, and water on their backs. We also knew our mechanized and armored units could move long distances quickly and fight for several days before resupply. But these heavy units also had missions we did not want to take them from unless absolutely necessary. The secret to maximizing our options was something we call the warning order. We simply alerted a reinforcing unit that it might have to reinforce a contact in another area. We always told them what the mission would be, who was to be reinforced, what the enemy looked like, what support we could give them, and how soon they would have to move if directed. We would adjust that reaction time as the situation developed: shorten it to minutes if things worsened or extend it to an hour or more if things appeared to be settling down. The unit alerted was to continue with their current mission but mentally they could start planning how they would execute a reinforcement if ordered to move. When the crisis had passed we would rescind the warning order. If, however, the crisis worsened (and it often did), the warning order allowed us to save hours of reaction time in moving the reinforcements to the place they were needed most in time to influence the outcome.[4]

General Downing's example demonstrates the need for a well-thought-out time line of when judgments will need to be made. The leader must have a time frame in which the storyline will unfold. Although few organizational leaders are faced with such high-stakes judgments, the essence of Downing's point is instructive: take too long and you will miss an opportunity, move too quickly and you deprive yourself of the opportunity to learn more.

You have identified some of the key judgments you will need to make above. Draw a timeline of key events from your story. Then label the key events and potential judgments you will make along the way.

Today ———————————————————▶	Vision Accomplished
	____ months

When	Key Event	Potential Judgments

ALLEGORY NOT ALGORITHM

Note that the process outlined in this section applies linear logic to a distinctly dynamic process. Any judgment is the outcome of potentially hundreds, if not thousands, of variables. Let's face it, whether a customer buys something or a partner accepts a business deal can often be contingent on their mood at the moment. Likewise, your performance may be the result of unforeseen personal factors—stress at home, a health condition, or that slice of pizza you had at 1:00 A.M. The point here is that by crafting a storyline you are building your muscle to dynamically react to circumstances as they unfold. View this as an exercise to build your leadership judgment capability, not a paint-by-numbers process.

SECTION FOUR

YOUR TEAM

Virtually every leader relies on a group of trusted advisers. Throughout history, whether Kennedy's kitchen cabinet or Nicholas II's Rasputin, these individuals or groups have influenced key leadership judgments. For most leaders, their team is the group with which they spend the most time. When there are difficult judgments to be made, they convene their team to debate and deliberate. Making choices about who we surround ourselves with and from whom we take counsel is perhaps the biggest judgment that any leader can make.

In today's world, it is a given that the people on your team need to be business savvy, technically competent leaders. Every role on your team should have a job description, and there should be core requirements that set minimum expectations for someone in a leadership role. In this section, we start from the assumption that those on your team are up to the required performance standards. We would like to focus instead on how those on your team individually and collectively impact your judgment.

The first component of this is making a conscious judgment about each individual on your team. You must ask the question: Does this person help the team to make better judgments? As Bill George told Noel,

> Every job I had in my life, including all my jobs at Medtronic, I never knew a fraction about the business as much as my team did. . . . So what I did was just learn how to form a team around the people that I could rely on intimately. . . . I think you really have to know the character and inner being of the people you're

dealing with. What are their motivations? Are they playing it straight with you? What are their strengths?[5]

Organizations are littered with technically competent people who possess poor judgment. Rather than contribute to the judgment process, they encumber their teams with false assumptions, opaque judgment processes, or indecision. There should be no "neutral" ratings in your assessments. If someone is neutral, he or she has failed to impact the judgment process. There is a tremendous opportunity cost to relying on someone who is not trusted or incapable of offering good advice as you make judgment calls.

Use the space below to evaluate the judgment contribution of each of your team members.

Team Member	Extent to which I trust the person's judgment (1 = Very Little, 5 = Very Much) *Write the number and explain your rating*	Extent to which the person positively influences the team's judgment process (1 = Negatively, 5 = Very Positively) *Write the number and explain your rating*

Once you have evaluated the judgment impact of each individual team member, it is important to look at what each person brings to the team. Again, this is not a question of whether or not they are capable of doing their job; rather, it is whether they personally exercise good judgment and have a positive impact on the team's judgment process.

If a team has been well formulated, there are diverse skills, perspectives, and relationships that can help the leader as she prepares to make a judgment call. Some of the assets that team members bring may include:

JUDGMENT: KNOWLEDGE SOURCES

- *Domain expertise:* Deep understanding of a technical area such as a functional specialty or technology.
- *Industry knowledge:* The ability to diagnose industry trends or help place changes in historical context that is predictive of possible future outcomes.
- *Organizational knowledge:* Understanding of the organization's competencies, talent, networks, processes, and culture that suggests execution capability or receptivity to change.
- *Constituent knowledge:* Up-to-date information on or relationships with one or more key constituents such as regulatory agencies, key customers, or suppliers that predict how these actors will respond to your organization's moves.
- *Access to information:* Personal networks, relationships, and know-how that enable the person to get reliable answers to questions even if they do not have the answer themselves.
- *External experience:* A different perspective based on experiences outside the company or industry that helps to identify best practices or alternate approaches.
- *Unconventional problem solving:* A differentiated thought style that can generate creative solutions not likely to come from standard analyses or the industry's conventional wisdom.

Consider each of your team members again. Based on the list above and your own observations, identify what each person brings to your judgment process. By looking at what each team member brings, you will start to form a composite view of the knowledge base that your team uses to make judgment calls.

Team Member	What the Person Contributes

	Little Extent				Great Extent
1. Extent to which my team's composition offers diverse perspectives, knowledge bases, and problem-solving approaches	1	2	3	4	5
2. Extent to which my team's composition provides deep knowledge or access to required expertise	1	2	3	4	5
3. Extent to which my team is able to effectively utilize the depth and diversity of knowledge as we make judgment calls	1	2	3	4	5

Conclusions about my team's judgment depth and diversity:

Actions to take:

Making the Team Work

Now that you have examined the composition of your team members, it is important to consider how you work with them to make judgment calls. There are two simultaneous dynamics that you must balance as a leader. First, you must engage your team in an open, energizing way that leads to candid discussion and provides you input to name, frame, and make the correct call. Second, you must engage the team in a way that commits them to execute the judgment and does not dilute your authority to make a call.

Procter & Gamble's CEO, A. G. Lafley, demonstrated the importance of team engagement when he made a key people judgment regarding who would head P&G's baby care division. Baby care was the company's second largest business after laundry but had been flagging in recent years. P&G had two powerful brands in Pampers and Luvs but was still suffering from a strategic blunder in the mid-eighties that allowed Kimberly-Clark's Huggies brand to beat it to market with a new product shape and capture more than 30 percent market share.

Lafley was appointed CEO in 2000 and knew the background of the business intimately. He could have named the baby care division's struggles as a marketing or technology issue but knew better. In his estimation, it was a business model issue. "I felt that we were technically competent in baby care," Lafley says, "but that the machine guys and the plant guys and the engineers were running the show. And our problem was on the consumer and market side."

Lafley framed the core issue as a people judgment call. To change the business model, the baby care business needed someone who could build a good team, align people throughout the organization, develop a smart new strategy, and pull the unit out of its current crisis. Lafley conferred with his head of human resources, Dick Antoine, and together they reviewed a slate of candidates. They settled on Deb Henretta. Lafley concluded: "She was a laundry person, but I knew what she really was, which was a tough and decisive leader. She was great at understanding consumers and great at branding and great at building innovative programs. And that's what we needed."

By failing to consult with his team during the process, however,

Lafley failed to mobilize and align the people who would be required to support Deb in her new role:

> I announced Deb's appointment at the morning management meeting. It was before the announcement went out to the company. It was to go out in a day or two. By three o'clock the revolt was well underway. Every one of the vice chairs and group presidents were ticked off because they had their own candidates ready for promotion.

As a result, Lafley had to "redo" the mobilize-and-align phase of the judgment call. Although he had come to a judgment in his own mind, the negative energy from his team required him to step back, listen, and be open to changing his selection. With everyone sitting around he invited each one to make their case against Henretta or for someone else. Lafley recalls saying, "I want you to take your list. I want you to make the best case you can for why your candidate or candidates are a better choice than Deb. So, we went around the table and I listened . . . sequentially, publicly in front of everybody else. Then I said, 'Okay, you know there were a couple of good cases. But let me tell you why I chose Deb.'"

Lafley knew that even if the powerful vice chairmen and business heads were not transformed into supporters of Henretta, they were no longer justified in any visible resistance to the call. The important thing here is that he did not try to slam dunk his decision. While Lafley had made a mistake by moving independently where team involvement was called for, he made time before moving on to set the stage for success. Lafley also stayed close during the execution phase, knowing that Henretta may face initial resistance to her change efforts, and he "supported her every step of the way."

Consider a recent judgment call you made with your team. Look at the preparation phase and assess how well your team worked together.

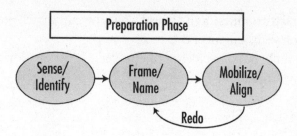

Sense and Identify					
1. Ability to read the environment	1	2	3	4	5
2. Mobilizes to action	1	2	3	4	5
3. Willing to confront reality	1	2	3	4	5
Frame and Name					
4. Ability to cut through complexity	1	2	3	4	5
5. Set the appropriate scope for the problem	1	2	3	4	5
6. Can provide context and language for the issue	1	2	3	4	5
Mobilize and Align					
7. Identified all the needed stakeholders	1	2	3	4	5
8. Engaged and energized the correct stakeholders	1	2	3	4	5
9. Worked across organizational boundaries and hierarchy	1	2	3	4	5

Any item that is less than a 3 should be a cause for serious concern. Judgment is a dynamic process. Missing one of the required elements will often cause you to enter a "redo" loop in which you must repeat an earlier step to correct your mistake. Consistent shortcomings in your judgment routines may prevent you from ultimately getting to execution on your judgment call.

Use the table below to identify improvement actions for how you work with your team:

Typical Judgment Errors	My Action
Sense and Identify	
Inability to read the environment • Not actively seeking environmental cues • Failure to think outside-in/bias toward internal thinking • Underestimate the importance of trends • Seek input from too few people	
Not mobilized to act • Fail to detect gradual changes until they become crises ("boiled frog" phenomenon) • Complacent with current success • People protect resources and turf at the expense of preparing for an external threat	
Unwilling to confront reality • Magnitude of problem motivates avoidance ("ostrich syndrome") • Politics get in the way of open dialogue or confrontation • Cannot break with conventional wisdom of your industry	
Frame and Name	
Inability to cut through complexity • Become mired in data and analysis • Connect the wrong data points	

Typical Judgment Errors	My Action
Set the appropriate scope for the problem • Goal is not clearly defined • Goal is too broad or too narrow • Goal conflicts with other organizational objectives	
Cannot provide context or language • Fail to see the background and history that necessitates the judgment call • Do not find language that captures the essence of the judgment to be made	
Mobilize and Align	
Failure to identify the necessary stakeholders • Flawed assumptions about who will be required to approve or execute the judgment • Lack of peripheral vision to see nontraditional constituents (e.g., regulatory agencies)	
Do not engage or energize stakeholders • Unclear roles in the process • Fail to make a case for change or paint a compelling vision • Leader sets up a false sense of empowerment or inauthentic democracy	
Stymied by boundaries and hierarchy • Political correctness keeps people from crossing turf lines • Fail to understand how parts of the organization work together • Naive about organizational politics	

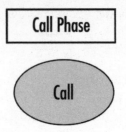

The call phase is when the leader must manage the team dynamics to go from analysis and dialogue to judgment. As Jeff Immelt describes this process, he gets input from everywhere and spends time wallowing in debate with his team, then "boom, I make a decision." It is incumbent on the leader to establish the rules of engagement for the process: who will make the call, based on what, and when. If the leader fails to be transparent about who has the authority to make the final call or fails to articulate why a call is made, he risks being viewed as an autocrat by his team.

Using the same judgment that you examined above, consider how your team fared at making the actual call.

Making the Call

1. Clear, well-articulated rationale for making the judgment call

1	2	3	4	5

2. The judgment call is timely— neither premature nor overdue

1	2	3	4	5

3. The judgment call accounts for all of the necessary variables and stakeholders, including how these interact

1	2	3	4	5

4. There is a clear judgment that is well understood by everyone involved in the process

1	2	3	4	5

5. The judgment accounts for all of the information gathered during the preparation phase, not just the most recent input

1	2	3	4	5

Use the table below to identify improvement actions in how you work with your team:

Typical Judgment Errors	My Action
Making the Call	
Unclear judgment criteria • Lack of framing regarding the fundamental definition of the problem and data needed to come to a judgment • Shifting criteria across multiple dialogues gives people different impressions about requirements for making a judgment call • Lack of role clarity regarding who gets to make the call and others' roles in the process	
Bad timing • Self-created sense of concern or crisis drives someone to make a judgment before needed, depriving the team of opportunity to continue framing and naming • Dillydallying or arrogance leads to making the call reactively and after the optimal time	
Failure to see interactions • Criteria for making the call were insufficient and failed to consider one or more critical variables • Lack of consideration for how different stakeholders may interact, collude, or confront the judgment call	
Unclear call • Leader equivocates when making the call, giving some the impression that it is optional or negotiable • Time is not taken to clearly state the judgment call and determine how this will be communicated to others	

(continued)

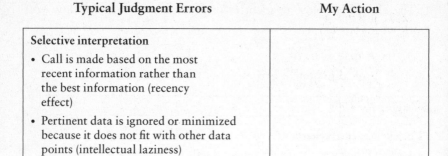

Typical Judgment Errors	My Action
Selective interpretation • Call is made based on the most recent information rather than the best information (recency effect) • Pertinent data is ignored or minimized because it does not fit with other data points (intellectual laziness)	

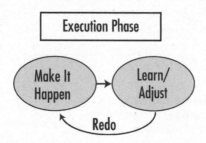

The execution phase is where the rubber meets the road. Many discussions of judgment and decision making have ended with making the call. In reality, a call is made only to get to a desired end point. Like looking at a map and deciding which city to visit, it only gets interesting once you are on your way.

The leader's responsibility is to see the judgment through to execution. This requires personal selling, engaging directly with stakeholders, facilitating smaller judgments to make the call stick, and constantly assessing progress. As the leader learns more, he or she adjusts the execution plan to keep the judgment on track. There can also be a "redo" loop between the execution and call phases if the leader determines that a wrong call has been made and execution is infeasible or damaging.

Make It Happen

1. Those involved in making the call stay close to the execution and actively monitor implementation

1	2	3	4	5

2. Clear milestones have been defined and are consistently reviewed

1	2	3	4	5

3. Implementation plan accounts for the necessary people, time, and resources to get the job done

1	2	3	4	5

Learn and Adjust

4. Feedback loops for evaluating speed and quality of execution are established

1	2	3	4	5

5. Leaders welcome feedback and are willing to make changes along the way

1	2	3	4	5

6. There is a process for assessing and implementing needed changes

1	2	3	4	5

Typical Judgment Errors	My Action
Make It Happen	
Abdicate responsibility • Leaders who don't like to get their hands dirty and avoid the details ("hands-off" mentality) • No routines for linking those making the call with those who will execute/overreliance on ad hoc communication	
Unclear milestones • No defined metrics or milestones for evaluating progress along the way • Too many or wrong milestones to assess execution	
Inappropriate structure • Assumption that normal organizational processes will provide needed funding and people for implementation • Unwillingness to create implementation plan or structure on grounds that it is "bureaucracy" • Burden execution with too much structure and process that it impedes execution	
Learn and Adjust	
Weak feedback • Mistaken assumption that people will provide feedback through informal or ad hoc mechanisms • Feedback is filtered through hierarchy or intermediaries who dilute and distort the feedback	

Typical Judgment Errors   My Action

Mishandling feedback • Leaders become hostile when confronted with negative feedback • Leaders ignore, rationalize, or fail to act on feedback • Leaders under- or overreact to feedback, causing them to make unnecessary or unhelpful changes	
No change process • There is no established process for escalating issues and changing the implementation plan • The change process is bureaucratic and fails to implement changes in a timely manner	

BUILDING AN OPERATING MECHANISM FOR JUDGMENT

So far, this section has asked you to review previous judgments you've made with your team so that you can assess whether you have fallen into any of the judgment pitfalls. Next you will have the opportunity to apply your learning to a current judgment.

As mentioned earlier, judgment is a dynamic, emotional process that must account for the human actors who are involved. As a leader, you establish a social architecture—how people interact and the energy generated by those interactions—that directly influences the quality of the judgment process.

At each stage (preparation, call, execution), you must manage the process. The questions below ask you to consider some of the factors that will define the social architecture you create around the judgment process. Use the questions to help you plan the judgment process and social architecture required for a current judgment you are facing.

Designing Your Judgment Process

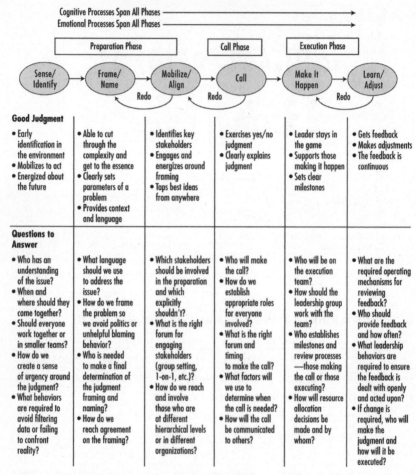

Cognitive Processes Span All Phases ⟶
Emotional Processes Span All Phases ⟶

	Preparation Phase		Call Phase	Execution Phase	
Sense/ Identify	Frame/ Name	Mobilize/ Align	Call	Make It Happen	Learn/ Adjust
		Redo	Redo		Redo

Good Judgment

• Early identification in the environment • Mobilizes to act • Energized about the future	• Able to cut through the complexity and get to the essence • Clearly sets parameters of a problem • Provides context and language	• Identifies key stakeholders • Engages and energizes around framing • Taps best ideas from anywhere	• Exercises yes/no judgment • Clearly explains judgment	• Leader stays in the game • Supports those making it happen • Sets clear milestones	• Gets feedback • Makes adjustments • The feedback is continuous

Questions to Answer

• Who has an understanding of the issue? • When and where should they come together? • Should everyone work together or in smaller teams? • How do we create a sense of urgency around the judgment? • What behaviors are required to avoid filtering data or failing to confront reality?	• What language should we use to address the issue? • How do we frame the problem so we avoid politics or unhelpful blaming behavior? • Who is needed to make a final determination of the judgment framing and naming? • How do we reach agreement on the framing?	• Which stakeholders should be involved in the preparation and which explicitly shouldn't? • What is the right forum for engaging stakeholders (group setting, 1-on-1, etc.)? • How do we reach and involve those who are at different hierarchical levels or in different organizations?	• Who will make the call? • How do we establish appropriate roles for everyone involved? • What is the right forum and timing to make the call? • What factors will we use to determine when the call is needed? • How will the call be communicated to others?	• Who will be on the execution team? • How should the leadership group work with the team? • Who establishes milestones and review processes —those making the call or those executing? • How will resource allocation decisions be made and by whom?	• What are the required operating mechanisms for reviewing feedback? • Who should provide feedback and how often? • What leadership behaviors are required to ensure the feedback is dealt with openly and acted upon? • If change is required, who will make the judgment and how will it be executed?

◆ ◆ ◆

Use the questions above to design your own process:

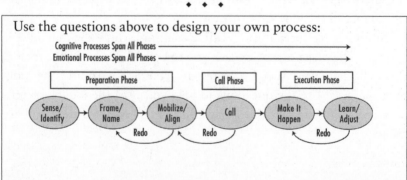

Cognitive Processes Span All Phases ⟶
Emotional Processes Span All Phases ⟶

	Preparation Phase		Call Phase	Execution Phase	
Sense/ Identify	Frame/ Name	Mobilize/ Align	Call	Make It Happen	Learn/ Adjust
		Redo	Redo		Redo

ORGANIZATIONAL

KNOWLEDGE

Miles's law famously states that "where you stand depends on where you sit." Coined by Rufus Miles in 1948 to describe how government administrators shifted opinions based on which agency employed them at the moment, it reminds us that our points of view are often a reflection of our organizational roles. These roles dictate the information that we can access, what we prioritize, who we listen to, and how we spend our time. This is no less true for a CEO than for an entry-level employee.

Whatever a leader's role, Miles's law is a good reminder that the leader's judgment is likely to be skewed from the start. Any successful judgment process must enable the leader to connect with multiple perspectives at many different levels and positions of an organization. Similarly, most judgments will not be implemented by an individual. Judgments that cause strategic shifts or people changes will require implementation and support from others. In the case of a fundamental strategic move, this could require thousands of people to realign their activities.

Every leader must carefully assess his or her network and the mechanisms he or she has for formulating, executing, testing, and modifying judgment calls.

BUILDING A PERSONAL NETWORK

The concept of "six degrees of separation" asserts that we are closely connected to everyone around us. The basic idea is that, if you are one step removed from someone you directly know and two steps removed from someone that person knows, you are only six steps away from any other individual on the planet. This reference, likely based on Stanley Milgram's small-world experiment at Harvard, and still the topic of much debate and research, is illustrative of our ability to access knowledge through the people we know.

We each have a personal network that spans beyond others on our work team or even in our department or company. Our inner circle may be filled with people we see on a routine basis, but most have a larger network of people that they call on occasion for information, help, or just the latest gossip. Research into how people get access to critical knowledge or resources shows that often this comes from "weak links" in a leader's network, meaning that acquaintances, rather than an individual's closer colleagues, often provide differentiated perspectives or support.

The impact of this is that "individuals with few weak ties will be deprived of information from distant parts of the social system and will be confined to the provincial news and view of their close friends."[6] Simply put, leaders must not only be aware of their networks, they must also actively populate them with people who can provide access to diverse perspectives.

However, it is not enough to have a network that spans organizational boundaries and hierarchical layers. These networks must be constantly revitalized as the organization changes to ensure that the leader's judgment does not become entrapped by input from the same actors.

For example, we knew a CEO of a geographically dispersed business with more than fifty thousand employees. He actively cultivated relationships with people that represented diverse and sometimes deviant perspectives for his organization. His network penetrated organizational layers, functional boundaries, and most definitions of diversity. With a phone call, he could get an accurate view of how the strategy was being executed or of his leadership team's credibility. This was great initially.

Over time, however, the CEO failed to add to his sources of information and build alternate relationships in his outer circle. Eventually, others in the organization caught on and the CEO's information sources were treated as political players in their own right. After a while, they had their own agendas for what they thought the CEO should hear and they were, in turn, politically manipulated by the CEO's senior team. What started as a benign attempt to avoid Miles's law ultimately turned into a political cancer.

This is a cautionary tale reminding us that we must know who to tap and under what circumstances. Maintaining networks requires a deliberate investment of time and personal energy to ensure that relationships are genuine, reciprocal, and honest.

Use the space below to identify some of the people you commonly tap in your network. In the inner circle, identify those people on whom you most often rely before making a significant judgment call. Note how they contribute to your judgment capability. In the outer circle, identify people who you call on occasionally. Consider how you cross organizational boundaries or hierarchy lines to get better or different information. Then answer the questions below.

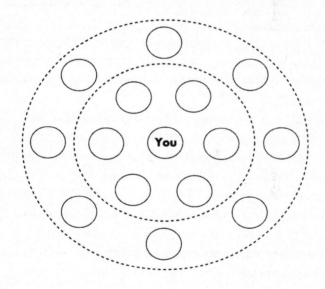

How My Organizational Network Contributes to My Judgment Capability:

	Little Extent			Great Extent	
1. Extent to which my network enables me to sense and identify the need for judgments	1	2	3	4	5
2. Extent to which my network provides timely, accurate information across boundaries to make judgment calls	1	2	3	4	5
3. Extent to which my network enables me to assess and adjust during execution	1	2	3	4	5
4. Extent to which I refresh and renew my network on an ongoing basis	1	2	3	4	5

Action Items:

OPERATING MECHANISMS FOR ENGAGING THE ORGANIZATION

As networked as any leader may wish to be, there is a limited amount of time for one-on-one or small group interactions. A leader must actively create opportunities to interact with new and different groups of people that add to his or her perspective and relationships.

The best leaders not only are open to ad hoc, informal interactions but also thoughtfully orchestrate where, how, and from whom they seek input. They do so not only with the intent of getting help in formulating judgment calls but also to test execution of calls that have been made. Jack Welch was a master of this.

When Welch was CEO of General Electric, he taught at GE's management development center on a monthly basis. This was an operating mechanism for him to skip levels, share ideas, and get unfiltered perspectives from people in different parts of GE's diverse businesses.

During one session, one of the attendees challenged Welch's famous strategy for the company to be number one or number two in market share in an industry or to get out of the business. Welch's logic, which served the company well and led to tens of billions in market capitalization growth, stated that the dominant player in any industry captured an outsized share of profits and was better able to withstand a downturn. However, the attendee told Welch, senior executives were treating the number one or number two mantra as a dictate. They felt they had to show Welch data that supported that their division was indeed one of the top two players. The effect, the attendee continued, was that GE divisions were underinvesting in growth opportunities so they could narrowly define their industries to support their conclusion that they were number one or number two. As a result of this learning, Welch turned GE's conventional wisdom on its head. He asked his senior team to define their businesses as no more than 10 percent of their industry to spotlight growth opportunities.

Welch's operating mechanism brought him into contact with people that he may never have run across as CEO. In the case above, the information caused Welch to reassess a strategy judgment that had been historically successful but had the potential to constrain the organization's long-term opportunities. Welch is hardly alone in his desire to build bridges directly to people in different parts of his organization. Many organizations have similar mechanisms.

One of the important characteristics of leaders with good judgment is that they actively foster an environment of learning and teaching. They come to these operating mechanisms with a Teachable Point of View. They have beliefs about what should be happening in these organizations but do not allow these to overpower others' ability to contradict or debate them. In a prior book, Noel called this approach a Virtuous Teaching Cycle because everyone is involved in reciprocal learning and teaching.

Virtuous Teaching Cycles

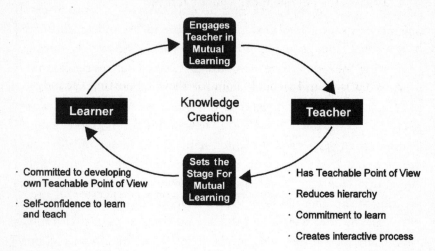

Some of these operating mechanisms are also deliberate people assessment processes. At Caterpillar, for example, CEO Jim Owens noted that executive officers visit every major facility at least once per year and at least two executive officers are involved in every major business plan review. This puts Caterpillar's senior team in direct contact with leaders two to three levels below them. As Owens commented, this systematic involvement "gives us a chance to observe the whole leadership and their strategic thinking—where they are, what they hope to deliver, and to take a measure of that team."[7] This operating mechanism simultaneously helps the leaders of key facilities make better judgment calls by getting top executive involvement and alignment, and also prepares the senior team to make better people judgment calls throughout the year.

Use the questions on the next page to help you design your own operating mechanism for testing a judgment call.

1. What is the judgment call you are testing?

2. What is your Teachable Point of View supporting the judgment call?

3. Who can provide you with a real-world perspective on the judgment call?

4. What questions would you ask this person(s)?

5. What firsthand observations would you like to make?

6. Where should this happen? What is the right setting for this?

7. When is the right timing for this to happen?

BUILDING JUDGMENT CAPACITY

Before making a judgment call, it is incumbent on the leader to assess his or her organization's execution capability. Most significant judgments will require others throughout the organization to do more than implement blindly. The leader can issue a decree but execution is successful only if those who are implementing can make supporting judgments.

Take the example of David Novak, CEO of Yum! Brands, who attempted to implement a multi-branding concept. Yum! Brands, which owns Pizza Hut, Taco Bell, KFC, and other restaurants, typically would build a restaurant with only one brand serving only one kind of food. Novak saw the opportunity to co-locate two or more of Yum!'s famous brands. As he told us, the vision was that "mom could have chicken while the kids had pizza." Many months after making the call to move forward with multi-branding, Novak attended a franchisee meeting. This was an operating mechanism he used to learn from Yum!'s franchise operators and for Novak to get insight into his judgment calls. One of the franchisees told him that despite the rhetoric, Novak's team was dragging its heels on implementation. This forced Novak into a "redo" loop with his team.

Today, multi-branding has proven to be an insightful, highly profitable strategy. However, it was impossible until operators below the CEO made their own judgment calls regarding how to integrate logistics, revise construction procedures, and modify franchise policies. At first, leaders ignored such judgments or made them with a mindset of minimizing change to the status quo. Only after Novak took the time to ensure they were onboard and truly understood the strategy were they willing and able to make the needed calls.

Building judgment capacity is a core leadership requirement. Leaders must take responsibility for ensuring that those who they will rely on for execution have the necessary knowledge, skills, and operating mechanisms to do the job. This process starts with driving alignment around the Teachable Point of View—ideas, values, emotional energy—that is guiding the organization and should enable everyone's judgment calls. It then requires leaders to consider the knowledge and skills required to implement, as well as the operating mechanisms that those who are implementing will need to do the job. Finally, the leader must build operating mechanisms so those who made the original call are involved in execution and can help adjust.

The story of Best Buy, the largest North American retailer with over six hundred stores and 100,000 employees, demonstrates how these steps come together to create judgment capability throughout an organization. In 2004, Brad Anderson took over as CEO from the company's founder, Dick Shultz. Brad had a personal Teachable Point of View that encompassed the need to serve customers better and engage the frontline retail associates to do so. However, with the company's stock ranking among the best performers on the New York Stock Exchange and a strong mind-set of headquarters-based centralization, people didn't want to hear or understand Brad's perspective.

Making matters worse, Brad sensed and identified the need to change the strategy. Wal-Mart, which had dominated the grocery and toy sectors once it entered those markets, had just announced the intention to make consumer electronics one of their top five profit areas. Meanwhile, Amazon had succeeded in generating higher revenues in electronics than in books and Dell was consistently sucking the margin out of the computer category. Brad sensed the need for a judgment call and framed the issue as "Customer Centricity." This was the need to serve customers on a differentiated, personalized basis rather than treating them all alike as the mass merchant had traditionally done.

In October 2004, Brad gathered his top 150 leaders and his board of directors for an off-site meeting in a remote location in Maddens, Minnesota. Along with our colleagues Patti Stacey and Larry Selden, we designed and facilitated the session with Brad, enabling him to share the Teachable Point of View and introduce Customer Centricity. The 150 leaders identified how they could support the strategy, live the values required to support it, and build high-quality teams that were ready to execute. These leaders were then required to teach the Customer Centricity values and strategy throughout the organization by the end of the year.

Now that the company had started aligning behind the need for change, Brad needed to make a judgment call: What would Customer Centricity look like when implemented? We built a judgment platform for Brad to engage thirty-six high-potential leaders from around the company to answer this question. The thirty-six were divided among six teams, each of which was charged with identifying the most profitable current or potential customer segments.

Over a three-month period they came up with more than fourteen viable segments, six of which were selected as the core focus for the company. The next step was to design a value proposition for each. These value propositions included changing store layouts, refining color palettes, customizing store merchandise, and adapting staffing to each store's specific customer needs.

By March 2005, Brad and his top team had made the call based on the input from the high-potential 36 leaders. Customer Centricity would require a massive transformation that would touch every function and every store in the chain. Over the next several months, Brad brought together the top 150 leaders twice to mobilize and align them, including having them teach the new strategy and supporting tools throughout the organization.

Brad had made the call but execution would require more than two years of hard work. To be successful, associates on the retail floor would need to make the right judgment calls on a daily basis so they truly served customers rather than abiding by headquarters policy. We worked with Brad and his team to design a process that taught thousands of associates, from district manager to store manager to floor associate, the fundamentals of business acumen and Customer Centricity. This enabled them to make local judgments about which products to display on valuable end-cap areas, how to adjust pricing, and how to create product and service bundles that targeted specific segments.

As a result, Best Buy was able to target customer groups it had never taken seriously before. Associates came up with plans to target real estate agents, developing mobile digital photography and printing solutions, as well as builders, bar owners, and Vietnamese immigrants, to name only a few.

Perhaps the most radical transformation came in stores serving the customer segment the company called "Jill," a suburban housewife who came to Best Buy at the behest of her kids or husband. In the past, Jill was almost always treated poorly; when she came to the store she was ignored or the associates would talk to her husband even if she asked the questions. If they did answer her, Jill usually heard techno-babble about a product's specifications rather than how it would help make her busy lifestyle easier. Consequently, Jill's goal was to get in and out of Best Buy as quickly as possible, hoping to avoid insulting interactions with store personnel.

As a result of Customer Centricity, stores hired personal shopping assistants who provided concierge service to Jill. They kept databases of Jill's prior purchases and were able to recommend products for her and her family. Best Buy associates also devised some clever programs, such as the kid's birthday gift card. Since the company now had a birthday database, local shopping assistants would send a complimentary $10 gift card in the mail. The associates had calculated the return on this: based on purchase patterns at multiple stores, a $10 gift card usually translated into a $50 purchase. The gift card made Jill's family happy and Best Buy pocketed a nice profit margin.

DEVELOPING JUDGMENT AT THE FRONT LINES

The Best Buy story features a population that we believe is particularly important; namely, frontline leaders. This group leads the people on the front lines that interact daily with an organization's customers, assemble a company's products, or deliver services. This group is vital because the judgment calls they make, although individually minor, amount to an organization's ability to execute strategy on a sustained basis. The answer a customer service representative provides from a call center or the service level of a retail delivery person may seem relatively inconsequential. Poor judgment calls on the front line, however, lead to inconsistently executed strategies, frustrated customers, and missed profit opportunities.

Better still, frontline associates can translate their direct customer contact into innovative programs. A part-time associate in one of Best Buy's stores spotted the emerging category of voice-over-Internet protocol, VOIP, or Internet telephony, as an underserved customer need. He had a passion for the product so he went to his store manager to ask if he could try moving product displays to create product and service bundles he thought would sell better. Armed with business acumen training, both the manager and the associate were able to calculate the cost and potential return of the associate's proposals. They made a judgment: try it for two weeks and evaluate the results.

The experiment drove VOIP sales by more than fourfold, so the associate, who seemed uniquely skilled to sell the products, was asked to teach his colleagues. Senior executives took notice. The store consistently beat not only its own VOIP sales targets but every other store in the chain by a wide margin. The learning from this store was disseminated and drove double-digit increases in Best Buy's sales in this category.

Stories like this were not uncommon at Best Buy. They could not have happened, however, if the company had not invested in the judgment capability of its frontline leaders. These leaders were able to read their store profit-and-loss statements, calculate return on invested capital, and understand their net operating profit targets. In contrast to the company's traditional policy of handing down only operating targets without explanation, business acumen gave frontline leaders a new capability on which to base their judgment calls.

Best Buy also had to build new operating mechanisms. For example, it transformed the thirty-minute morning meeting held at every store into a forty-five-minute "chalk talk." The chalk talk was an opportunity for the store managers to review the prior day's results, learn from their execution hits or misses, and teach floor associates about the customer and the business metrics. Adding an extra fifteen minutes to six hundred stores' payroll cost millions of dollars, but Best Buy felt it was a fantastic investment.

Other companies have made similar investments in frontline capability. Intuit, based in Mountain View, California, produces Turbo Tax, Quicken, QuickBooks, and other software for both small enterprises and individual consumers. Intuit employs computer scientists, PhDs, and many highly trained technical specialists. However, the company also relies heavily on frontline leaders and agents working in call centers, often paid an hourly rate. Intuit has learned that these call service agents can have a critical impact on customers and sales by both identifying customer needs and solving after-sales problems.

At Intuit, frontline leaders take responsibility for sharing best practices and creating new knowledge about customer needs. For example, one frontline manager developed a process in which customer service agents now meet several times each week to discuss common customer problems and role-play responses. By doing so, they not only share knowledge but also creatively come up with more innovative ideas to enhance service. As a result, the customer satisfaction metric has gone up by more than 40 percent.

Like Best Buy, Intuit made an enormous investment in its frontline managers. Intuit has required its call center managers to become teachers. We worked with Steve Bennett, the company's former CEO, to develop a rigorous process in which frontline managers are taught the company's strategy, operating metrics, leadership fundamentals, and customer expectations. Those who go through the process are required to teach their teams. As part of this, the frontline leaders identified how they could better structure their work to deliver on the strategy, making judgment calls with their team on how to reshape their goals and eliminate unnecessary activities.

Best Buy and Intuit share some commonalities in their approaches to building judgment capability. They invested heavily on the front end of the process to align everyone with their Teachable Point of View, they invested in developing their employees' skill base to help them make supporting judgment calls, and they built new operating mechanisms.

Use the space in the following table to apply these principles to support the judgment calls you are making.

JUDGMENT BUILDING PROCESS   HOW I CAN APPLY THIS

Step 1: Clarify the Teachable Point of View	
What: The senior leadership team must take responsibility for outlining the core ideas, values, and emotional energy required to win in the marketplace. Key judgment calls regarding people, strategy, or crisis may result. *Who:* Senior leadership team. The Teachable Point of View will be formulated based on individual experience and input from key constituents. *How:* Typically a 2–3 day off-site.	
Step 2: Teach, Learn, and Align the Organization	
What: The Teachable Point of View and key judgment calls are taught, debated, and localized by leaders below the senior team. *Who:* Those who are 1–3 layers below the leadership team are taught by the senior team. Ultimately, the entire organization should be engaged in this experience. *How:* A multiday workshop session led and taught by the senior team. Those who are taught should be expected to teach their own teams.	
Step 3: Build Specialized Knowledge and Skills	
What: Knowledge and skills required for layers below the senior team to make judgments are taught. The teaching is tailored to the individuals or teams involved and the specific circumstances. *Who:* Will vary based on the judgment calls required. This can be loosely affiliated individuals, work teams, or entire departments/divisions.	

JUDGMENT BUILDING PROCESS	HOW I CAN APPLY THIS
How: Customized curriculum must be developed and taught. The effectiveness of the teaching should be evaluated as one component of judgment execution.	

Step 4: Develop Implementation Operating Mechanisms

What: Operating routines must be changed or developed to drive execution in some cases. New operating mechanisms are designed and implemented at the operator level to support implementation and judgment calls operators must make. *Who:* These are implemented by those who are doing the work to implement the judgment. They should be designed by those who understand the judgment call, those who are doing the work, and those who are one level above those implementing. *How:* Operating mechanisms should be designed by the group listed above and then iteratively tested and refined.	

Step 5: Develop Operating Mechanisms for Assessing Execution

What: Operating mechanisms for those who made the call to assess and adjust their judgment call as execution unfolds. *Who:* Should involve those who made the call and those who are implementing. *How:* Meetings, workshops, field visits, or other mechanisms that occur at formally scheduled execution milestones are spontaneously based on execution needs.	

DEVELOPING JUDGMENT CAPABILITY IN THE PIPELINE

Thus far, we have dealt with building judgment capability in the organization to support execution of a judgment call. This has included
building the judgment capability of those who will implement the call.
There is also a need to systematically assess the judgment capability
of leaders throughout the organization and promote those leaders
who demonstrate good judgment.

Judgment is an area that has been largely ignored in most succession planning processes. Despite the fact that a leader's track record
on key judgments is a measure of leadership effectiveness, few leadership appraisals seriously evaluate the quality of a leader's judgments.
In our work with clients, we find that a historical review of key judgments gives unparalleled insight into a leader's judgment capability,
as well as the systemic enablers and barriers to making good calls.

A *Fortune* 500 global manufacturing company we worked with provides a case in point. The company had made many significant judgment calls over a five-year period that had fundamentally transformed
many of its core logistics, manufacturing, and IT systems. The company
had also made big bets by changing the business portfolio, increasing
its stake in a partner, selling a large piece of one business unit, and
divesting its stake in an industry consortium. As if this weren't enough,
the structure had been through a radical overhaul. As the leaders went
through this massive change, they noted that the organization lacked
an ability to make timely judgment calls. Over the prior five years, it
seemed to be getting worse. They wondered whether this was a failure
of leadership, excessive bureaucracy, or a combination of the two.

With our colleague Professor Charles Kadushin, we worked with
a team of cross-functional, high-potential leaders to analyze the company's judgment process. This started by polling the senior leadership
team and a cross section of key leaders to determine the most important judgments made by the company amid the change. While no lists
matched exactly, a few judgments, such as a massive investment in
South America, made most of the lists.

We then surveyed and interviewed the key players for each of
the five most significant judgments. This included people at a vari-

ety of hierarchical levels and across various organizational units. An exhaustive qualitative analysis, along with calibration on numerical survey items, yielded consistent themes about what was getting in the way of making judgment calls. Overall, many of the calls suffered from at least one flaw in the judgment process and, of those, nearly all had to enter a "crisis" state before adjustments were made that put the call back on track.

As it turned out, the company's leadership team was right: it had both a failure of individual leadership and lousy organizational systems to support good judgment calls. On an individual level, leaders displayed personal behavior that prevented good judgment and impeded the ability of others to make good calls. Additionally, the company lacked effective HR systems, suffered from a finance-imposed numbers culture, and lacked operating mechanisms to effectively follow up on execution. The list on pages 354–55 shows just some of the themes that emerged from the study.

Judgment Theme	Negative Behaviors Impacting Leader's Judgment Calls	Negative Behaviors Toward Others Who Are Making Judgment Calls	Systemic Issues Negatively Impacting Judgment
Risk Aversion	• Put personal reputation and career self-preservation above making a courageous call	• Excessively punish failure	• Performance evaluation systems are weak so there is no reward for risk taking
Lack of Accountability	• Allow committees on groups to collectively take responsibility rather than personally accept accountability	• Use committee structure inappropriately, even when a leader is willing to accept personal responsibility for making a call	• Operating structures do not recognize who is entitled to make the judgment call; consequently judgments drive toward consensus or compromise
No Urgency	• Inability to create a burning platform	• Fail to respond or provide necessary resources/support for judgment execution	• Large staff bureaucracy and multiple approvals required for most judgments
Credibility Only Comes from Data	• Succumb to political pressures for excessive analysis and facts	• Expect others to come to meetings with data to answer any question, even most unlikely scenario	• Finance dominance—finance hurdle rates that veto or severely delay judgments

Judgment Theme	Negative Behaviors Impacting Leader's Judgment Calls	Negative Behaviors Toward Others Who Are Making Judgment Calls	Systemic Issues Negatively Impacting Judgment
Lack of Institutional Knowledge	• Focus on making one's mark quickly by implementing something new, even when the current strategies or structure are effective	• Leading staff to abandon execution of previous judgment calls without due consideration	• People are rotated through jobs every 18–24 months— perception that more than 2 years in a job is a sign of failure
Weak Strategic Integration	• Small-scale vision that fails to account for impact of judgment calls on other parts of the enterprise	• Encourage narrow silo mind-set and devalue benefits that will accrue to other departments	• Infrequent cross-functional rotation leads to limited silo view

While the breadth of the issues were disconcerting, in truth they were surprising to very few people inside the organization. Most people had suffered the pain of trying to drive a judgment call. Fortunately, some of the judgments we analyzed were successful and the difficulty of the judgment process had developed strong skills in some leaders:

- **Personal selling**—The financial controls and bureaucratic barriers required some to put their own credibility on the line when making a judgment call. Those who were successful had developed the ability to create a case for change, mobilize, and align key stakeholders.

- **Networking**—The number of stakeholders required across multiple divisions to approve a judgment call meant that success required extensive personal networks and the ability to know how to get to people in different parts of the organization.
- **Personal commitment**—Success was often a direct function of an individual's passion and resolve. Those who implemented judgments refused to back away from their agenda.
- **Self-confidence**—Since making big calls was viewed as risky and career threatening, doing so showed tremendous self-confidence. It also showed the ability not to waiver or succumb to political pressure when challenged by peers or superiors.

These traits were evident in nearly all of the successful judgments. While there was no doubt that the judgment process and supporting systems needed to be seriously overhauled, success in the face of these barriers had revealed tremendously talented leaders. Two of the leaders who emerged as having a positive judgment track-record throughout our study went on to become heads of the company's largest divisions.

Our study of the judgment process for this client also taught us something about developing judgment capabilities in others. The high-potential leaders we worked with personally conducted the interviews and worked side by side with us in analyzing the data and formulating recommendations. To a person, they said they were shocked at the learning that came from this process.

Never in their careers had they interviewed multiple leaders involved in the same judgment. While the company had conducted postmortems on judgment failures in the past, these had been limited in scope and structured through meetings rather than gathering individual perspectives.

By contrast, from the interviews a *Rashomon* effect emerged in which each individual interviewed had a subjective view of the judgment process that differed from others involved. Conducting the analysis and doing the interviews gave the high-potential leaders rare insight into disconnects in the judgment process. There was a visible paradox:

as the team members were identifying shortcomings in the development of judgment, they were simultaneously deeply developing their own capability. They took this development back to their own jobs and judgment processes.

The type of analysis we conducted with this manufacturing company is a good starting point for any organization to assess its overall judgment capability. One of our key findings as we work with companies has been that HR systems must support making good judgment calls but are often poorly equipped to do so.

The diagram below shows the fundamental components of any HR system and how they interact with one another.

Human Resources: Creating Judgment Capability

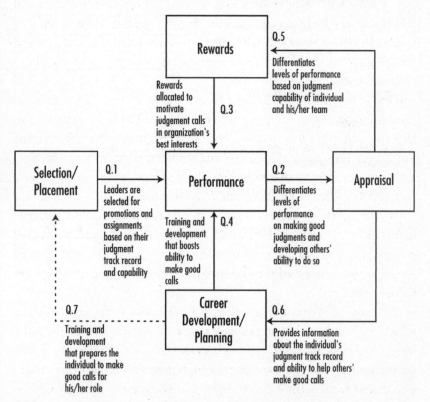

- **Rewards**

  Q.5 — Differentiates levels of performance based on judgment capability of individual and his/her team

  Q.3 — Rewards allocated to motivate judgement calls in organization's best interests

- **Selection/ Placement**

  Q.1 — Leaders are selected for promotions and assignments based on their judgment track record and capability

- **Performance**

  Q.4 — Training and development that boosts ability to make good calls

- **Appraisal**

  Q.2 — Differentiates levels of performance on making good judgments and developing others' ability to do so

- **Career Development/ Planning**

  Q.6 — Provides information about the individual's judgment track record and ability to help others' make good calls

  Q.7 — Training and development that prepares the individual to make good calls for his/her role

Use the questions below to evaluate how well your company's HR system supports good judgment.

	Little Extent				Great Extent
1. Leaders are selected for promotions and assignments based on their judgment track record and capability	1	2	3	4	5
2. Performance evaluations differentiate levels of performance on making good judgments and developing others' ability to do so	1	2	3	4	5
3. Rewards are allocated to motivate judgment calls in the organization's best interests	1	2	3	4	5
4. There are training and development that boost the ability to make good judgment calls	1	2	3	4	5
5. Appraisal process differentiates levels of performance based on the judgment capability of individuals and teams	1	2	3	4	5
6. Career development and planning provide information about the individuals' judgment track records and ability to help others make good calls	1	2	3	4	5
7. Career development and planning prepare the individual to make good calls for his/her role	1	2	3	4	5

SECTION SIX

STAKEHOLDER

KNOWLEDGE

All of a leader's judgments happen in the context of the stakeholders who surround the individual or organization. Failure to anticipate how a key stakeholder will react can threaten the success of any strategy or people judgment and force a leader into crisis mode. However, leaders can also proactively work with stakeholders to build relationships that provide new knowledge and assist in mobilizing action.

HOW STAKEHOLDERS RESHAPE YOUR STORYLINE

Any organization is impacted by myriad stakeholders; a partial list must include customers, suppliers, partners, investors, industry associations, regulatory agencies, interest groups, and communities. The actions and reactions of each of these constituent groups can make a shambles of any well-considered judgment.

Many crises are, in fact, the result of stakeholder actions. In the Circuit City example cited earlier, the company's profitability model was devastated by the move of a supplier working in tandem with a competitor. At Yum! Brands, David Novak had to contend with the possibility of *E. coli* in his supply chain at Taco Bell and with demonstrations by People for the Ethical Treatment of Animals (PETA) over the treatment of chickens by KFC. Royal Dutch Shell was forced into a defensive position on deep-sea oil drilling by Greenpeace.

Sometimes stakeholder actions don't create directly observable moves and countermoves, but rather change the assumptions used to make a call in the first place. A financial institution with which we worked had a small competitor attempt to sell itself to a larger competitor. This was a clear signal that industry consolidation was starting earlier than expected and forced the financial institution into a hostile takeover attempt.

Another client fell victim to investor pressures. The company had been the target of an unsuccessful takeover attempt. It had convinced institutional investors that it was better to go it alone despite the massive transformation effort that would be required. When the company missed its earnings one quarter, it put investments for key strategic efforts on hold. At a time when the company should have been investing for future growth, it was forced into cost containment, effectively trading future opportunity to reassure today's investors that they had made the right choice.

The commonality among these companies is that they were forced by others into a "redo" loop on major judgments. In some cases, the companies noted above responded quickly and effectively, while in others their judgment was deferred or derailed. While leaders can't build a contingency plan for everything, anticipating stakeholder moves that may threaten your big judgment calls is vital.

For example, at Caterpillar Jim Owens shared his thought process around a recent acquisition. Owens was concerned that the company Caterpillar wanted to acquire was being courted by its bankers to issue a public offering. Owens knew that the senior management team had big equity positions in the company and concerns about being assimilated by a company as large as Caterpillar. The combination could be enough to sway the company's CEO, a key decision maker for the company to be acquired, toward an IPO. "Get him back to Peoria," Owens told his group president. "I want him to see what a wholly owned stand-alone subsidiary looks like, feels like, how it operates, because I want him to be comfortable with that."

Owens had assessed the senior leadership team dynamics to know that the CEO would be key in influencing any outcome. He foresaw a scenario in which the CEO opted for an IPO, forcing Caterpillar to either lose the deal and have a hole in its strategy, or be forced into higher bids by the company's bankers. Owens also knew that words could not substitute for the impact of having the CEO see for himself how Caterpillar operated and hear testimonials from the leaders of other stand-alone divisions. As a result of Owens's attention to this key stakeholder in the acquisition process, Caterpillar completed the deal and has been able to enter a new line of business as a result.

In the Storyline section, you were asked to identify how various actors could change the Storyline you have written for your organization. In the space below, concentrate on the external stakeholders who could force you into "redo" mode.

Stakeholders	What They Could Do	My Redo
Customer	How could buying patterns, pricing expectations, brand preferences, purchase frequency, or other factors change?	
Supplier	How could disruptions to the supply chain, pricing changes, or industry consolidation impact you?	
Partner	How could the actions of an investment partner, channel partner, or alliance affect you?	
Investor	How could investor expectations change and what impact would that have on your access to capital or execution plans?	
Labor Union	Are there union policies, contracts, or roles that are in flux and could influence organizational support?	
Industry Association	How do industry consortiums affect standards, safety policies, purchase costs, or other factors?	
Regulatory Agency	Is regulatory approval required for a product or can regulators shut down your plans?	
Interest Groups	Which interest groups may target you?	
Community Groups	Are there any groups that protest your presence in their community, dislike your policies, and are prone to raise legal or other concerns?	
Other?		

STAKEHOLDERS AS KNOWLEDGE SOURCES

While stakeholders can create disruption, a leader who has thoughtfully considered the judgment process knows how to engage them as a source of knowledge and help. Working with stakeholders can assist any part of the judgment process.

Jeff Immelt, General Electric's CEO, introduced "customer dreaming sessions" in which senior leaders from among their customers are invited to discuss and debate market trends and how these could impact potential investments. Dreaming sessions have spanned alternate energy sources, health care, and cleaner coal supply.

Immelt and other senior GE leaders have gathered customer CEOs, government officials, NGO leaders, and academics for one- or two-day sessions in which participants visualize the future and discuss trends. Immelt may pose a question, as he did with a group of railroad CEOs, asking them how they would prioritize GE's $200 million to $400 million R&D spending in their sector. In short, dreaming sessions are vehicles that help GE leaders to sense and identify, name and frame, and in some cases mobilize and align support. Stakeholder input helps Immelt shape his judgments, not define them. As he said:

> I've spent my lifetime working with customers, and I love customers. I get great insight from them—but I would never let them set our strategy for us. But by talking to them, I can put it in my own language. Customers always pay our bills. But they will never pick our people or set our strategies.[8]

We helped Best Buy design a session with its vendors to mobilize and align support for its strategic judgment call to implement its segment-based approach called Customer Centricity. More than forty of its key vendors were invited for a one-and-a-half-day session in which they learned about Best Buy's strategy, shared input on customer segmentation, and met with key leaders. Similarly, David Novak held a session for his largest franchisees in which he discussed how their multibranding strategy was being implemented. Novak was at the "learn and adjust" phase of the judgment process when the franchisees told him the execution was slow and Novak's key lieutenants weren't aligned with him.

One trait all of these sessions shared is that the various company leaders created an environment of open and honest debate. As the quote above from Jeff Immelt demonstrates, they came with a Teachable Point of View but were enthusiastically open to learning from stakeholders. These leaders created a Virtuous Teaching Cycle in which everyone learns and teaches.

Use the judgment process flow below to identify which stakeholders could contribute to a key judgment you are facing:

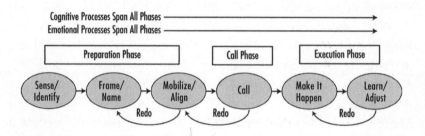

Stakeholder	How I Could Learn During the Preparation Phase	How I Could Learn During the Call Phase	How I Could Learn from the Execution Phase
Customer			
Supplier			
Partner			
Investor			
Labor Union			
Industry Association			
Regulatory Agency			
Interest Groups			
Community Groups			
Other?			

THE ROLE OF BUSINESS IN COMMUNITY

There is one stakeholder who we believe deserves special attention in today's environment. We have written elsewhere that corporate scandals, antiglobalization backlash, and global warming have put more pressure than ever on corporations to be good citizens. Likewise, the next generation entering the workforce places more emphasis on participating in their communities. As Jeff Immelt summed up, "More than ever before, people want to win, but they want to do it with heart."[9]

The case for engaging in the community can be made in moral terms or economic terms. We argue for a serious look at how leaders think about their organization's role in the community on the basic premise of this handbook: communities are key stakeholders in virtually all of an organization's big judgment calls. Consider, for example, the backlash that Walmart has faced regarding its pay policies, economic effect on small shopkeepers, and environmental impact. Alongside other retailers, the company has been prevented from entering certain markets in California and Illinois as a result of community lobbying for "big box" laws that prevent retailers over a given size from entering certain markets. Meanwhile, Wal-Mart has engaged in one of the biggest corporate environmental campaigns in history. Its headquarters in Bentonville has notices seemingly everywhere reminding people to turn off lights and avoid wasting paper or other resources unnecessarily. The company has put enormous pressure on its suppliers, such as PepsiCo and P&G, to change packaging to make it more environmentally friendly and improve recyclables.

During a session we were running with another client, a manager of a retail store said he could see the importance of community involvement for his CEO but wondered how it could impact him. We took a detour in our talk and used him as a live case example. We started with the question: What impacts the quality of life in your community for your customers and employees? After asking about a number of factors, we discovered that the manager was working in an urban community whose residents did not have a lot of disposable income. His customers and employees often used the bus to get to work but the bus stop was a quarter mile down the street across from a mega-retailer.

Whenever the store across from the bus stop was hiring, he would lose some of his best employees because the bus didn't stop in his shopping center. People liked the work environment but didn't like to walk the quarter mile in the winter. One of the other participants in our session, who also ran a store, asked whether the manager had ever worked with the city to have a bus stop installed. The store manager said he hadn't, so several participants with successful experience in other cities offered to help him work with city government and community boards. Those with experience noted that, when deciding whether to approve a request, the various governing bodies would likely want to see not only his store's positive economic contribution to the community but also its civic contribution.

Another aspect of community engagement is that community leaders

Quality of Life Factors

Economics
- Avg. Income
- Employment Rates
- Local Standards of Rich/Poor
- Distribution of Wealth
- Socioeconomic segregation

Business
- Industries
- Large vs. Small Bus
- Employment
- Concentration
- Local Partnership

Community Agencies
- Significant Church or Community Affiliations
- Meeting Locations/Times
- Degree of Organization/informality

Demographics
- Ethnicity
- Age
- Gender
- Marital Status
- Languages
- Population Growth

Quality of Life in My Community

Government
- Degree of Regulation
- Involvement in Community Affairs/Bodies

Housing & Infrastructure
- Housing
- Availability/Quality
- Housing Density
- Transportation System
- Parks and Public Recreation

Health Care
- Accessibility
- Nutritional Standards
- Public Health Care
- Standards

Education
- Avg. Education Level
- System Strength/Local School Variance
- Traditional/Vocational

often have rich local networks. For example, we explored the personal network of the head of a Boys and Girls Club in a major metro area, where we brought a business group for volunteer activities. His personal network was remarkable: he had the heads of several major corporations on his board, interacted frequently with the city's mayor and the state's governor, was friendly with the heads of other major not-for-profit organizations, was connected with the press, and had negotiated with the leaders of several street gangs. Building a personal relationship with this individual would put any person in this community one step away from most of the city's most powerful brokers.

Kathy Ligocki, former CEO of Tower Automotive, had an opportunity to not only engage the community but also partner with key stakeholders in her judgment network when she was running Ford of Mexico. Prior to becoming CEO of Tower in 2003, Ligocki spent five years at Ford in various senior management positions. While in Mexico, Ligocki was approached by several wives of Ford's key dealers. For nearly thirty years before Ligocki took the helm of Ford of Mexico, the company had agreed with its dealer network to contribute a percentage of every sale to an educational and environmental fund. Much of the proceeds had gone into building schools but, Ligocki said, "some of the activist dealer wives had adopted their schools and had gone in to see that they weren't being kept up." Additionally, the wives told Ligocki that critical family issues such as family violence and lack of family structure weren't being addressed. "Building the building," they explained to Ligocki, "wasn't enough to support education."

When the dealers' wives approached her, they may not have known that Ligocki's twenty-plus years of business experience was accompanied by a strong track record of personal involvement in community and women's issues. She saw that the dealers' wives were offering more than a good works project. Working with this constituent group enabled Ford to reap a better return on its community investment and positively impact the lives and economic well-being of its customer base, while simultaneously enhancing Ford's position and visibility in the community. Equally important, Ligocki had an opportunity to partner with one of Ford's key stakeholder groups. There was no doubt that Ford needed to maintain its strong relationship with its dealer network to be successful. How Ligocki reacted to the dealers' wives, who undoubtedly held considerable influence on their husbands' perceptions of Ford, would determine whether she alienated them or built a positive relationship.

Ligocki chose to involve the dealers' wives in a radical way. She gathered both Ford leadership and the dealers' network, and proposed transferring the responsibility for how the community funds were spent to an organized group of dealers' wives. While others at Ford initially objected on the basis that the dealers' wives were not Ford employees, Ligocki recognized that many of these women had been "part of the family for several generations because many times the wives' families originally owned the dealership." As Ligocki said, "we sometimes put narrow bounds around issues because people are not technically in our organization."

The result of Ligocki's judgment was "training courses for principals and teachers, accredited programs through the state, a national soccer and basketball team for both boys and girls, and computer centers in schools across the country." Building on the legitimacy of the Ford partnership, the dealers' wives negotiated a joint venture with a leading nonprofit organization to build the computer centers. The reallocation of funds also supported evening classes for adults to deal with domestic violence. Although the target audience was initially women, Ligocki said "about thirty percent of the people in the classes are the husbands who want to better handle the stress and violence than they have."

Ligocki has also mobilized a network to help support future judgment calls that will impact Ford's business success. More than 70 percent of the 120 dealers' wives have been involved in the various activities. Representatives of the wives' organization have touted their joint accomplishments in presentations across the company and even in Madrid.

Ligocki may not have had the dealers' wives on her list as a key stakeholder group when she took over as head of Ford of Mexico. However, her ability to see the power of this network and the importance of community engagement helped her build partnerships that continue to benefit Ford.

Despite the many benefits of community involvement, how to engage the community is often a blind spot for leaders. They equate it with charity rather than thinking seriously about how community forces may impact them. In today's society, we argue, every business leader must have his or her point of view on the matter.

Use the space below to outline your point of view:

My Teachable Point of View on My Organization's Role in the Community:

Significant Issues Facing My Community:

Impact on Customers/Employees:

How My Organization Can Better Engage in Our Community:

SECTION SEVEN

MAKE THE RIGHT CALL

The preceding pages of this handbook have asked you to consider the many facets of the judgment process. We hope that they have helped you to "sense and identify" and "name and frame" some of the challenges that may be facing you, your team, or your organization as you make judgment calls.

No judgment process is ever perfect. Although we have interviewed, observed, and worked side by side with outstanding leaders, we have yet to find one who gets it right every time. The attributes of leaders who make successful judgments include some of the items below:

- *Scanning the Environment.* They have a desire to find best practices, competitive drive, and paranoia about competitors that helps them to sense and identify impending issues.
- *Build Good Relationships.* They foster camaraderie and can internally and externally network.
- *Have Character and Courage.* They aren't afraid to make a call and do so based on values.
- *Measure Results.* They focus on the outcome of their judgment calls and feel accountable for driving execution.
- *Create Virtuous Teaching Cycles.* They create an environment in which people will tell the truth and teach others.
- *Have Self-Confidence to Be Wrong.* They know that they will make mistakes so they seek feedback, admit error, and "redo" judgment call phases as needed to drive execution.

Throughout this handbook, we have asked you to look at the knowledge bases that help you make successful judgment calls. The exercises have asked you to look in the mirror as a leader, evaluate how your team helps you to make judgment calls, how you engage your organization in the judgment process, and how you can better leverage your stakeholder relationships. You have hopefully identified many things that you are doing well and some that require action.

As you finish, there is one last judgment call you can make. You must make the call to act on what you have learned about yourself and others. As with any judgment call, your ability to identify the issue and your personal desire to improve are meaningless without a tenacious drive for execution. What is your next step to make it happen?

Issue:	What I Will Do:	By When:

Acknowledgments

We started the journey to write this book because we realized in our combined many years as academics and authors that neither of us had written on this topic. We soon learned that neither had our colleagues in the field. This started our work over the past five years to tackle an understanding of leadership judgment.

Without the tough love of Nancy Cardwell this book would not have been written. She was there throughout the research phase, helping with the many interviews and analysis of the interviews as well as helping us clarify our voices in writing. We are deeply grateful for her significant contributions and her good judgment to stay the course with us.

Early on in the judgment journey we spent a morning with Jack and Suzy Welch in their home in Boston. We had a free-ranging discussion on leadership and judgment, which gave us insight and concern. Jack was very open about his judgments as a leader of GE, both good ones and bad ones that he had made. He was very open about how he approached making judgments, which gave us the first real glimpse of the challenges we would have in conceptually framing this important aspect of leadership. As we engaged in a far-ranging conversation with Suzy and Jack we realized that we had to develop a conceptual framework that furthered the field of study among serious students of leadership and was simultaneously of pragmatic use to world-class leaders like Jack Welch. Several years later, after many interviews with leaders and many drafts of our conceptual work, we felt we could go back to Jack and Suzy with our framework; many thanks to them for their invaluable help.

Every one of the leaders we interviewed and worked with on the judgment journey are major contributors to the book. We give special thanks to A. G. Lafley, who provided us deep insight into people judgments and how he has made some great ones at P&G to drive a world-class transformation. Jeff Immelt is taking the world's most complex enterprise through a massive transformation for the twenty-first century and has given us insight and access to these important leadership judgments. Jim McNerney took over at Boeing as the third CEO in three years. He has done a remarkable job of revitalizing leadership at Boeing. Bob Knowling and Joel Klein have shown us that leadership judgment in the New York City public school system is the key to shaping future generations of good citizens. We thank all of the leaders who worked with us; they are the true authors of the book.

Warren gives special thanks to the support of Pat Biederman for her editorial judgment; David Cannom, M.D., John Mazziotta, M.D., and David Stein, M.D., for the opportunity to observe, firsthand, the practice of clinical judgment.

One of our academic colleagues, Michael Brimm, professor at INSEAD, was there throughout the journey. He had the courage to tell us, in his no-nonsense way, when we were down a blind alley. He would always help us find a new way forward. We are grateful for his substantial contribution to this book.

Our team at the University of Michigan, headed by my colleague Ida Faye Webster, are the unsung heroes of this project. From day one, the interviews, the research, and the production of this book were not possible without Ida's leadership and dedication. Janet Sherman was a key member of the team who supported us every step along the way, as did Marie Doolittle at USC.

Finally, we are deeply indebted to the team of Jeffrey Krames and Courtney Young, who joined us in the last leg of the journey to bring the book across the finish line. Courtney was extraordinary and tireless in her efforts to bring out the best in finishing the book and the handbook. Many thanks.

Sources

1. JUDGMENT AND LEADERSHIP

Notes

1. Colvin, Geoffrey. "The Ultimate Manager." *Fortune,* November 22, 1999.

2. Byrne, John A. "How Jack Welch Runs GE: A Close-up Look at How America's #1 Manager Runs GE." *BusinessWeek,* June 8, 1998.

3. Rossetti, William Michael. *Life of John Keats.* London: Walter Scott, 1887.

4. Kennedy, John F. Address to the Massachusetts Legislature, January 9, 1961.

5. Sorenson, Ted. "Judgment and Responsibility: John F. Kennedy and the Cuban Missile Crisis" in *Presidential Judgment: Foreign Policy Decision Making in the White House.* Aaron Lobel, ed. Hollis, New Hampshire: Hollis Publishing Company, 2000.

6. Lobel, Aaron, ed. *Presidential Judgment: Foreign Policy Decision Making in the White House.* New Hampshire: Hollis Publishing Company, 2000.

7. Kahneman, Daniel. "New Challenges to the Rationality Assumption," *Journal of Institutional and Theoretical Economics,* 150, no. 1(1994): 18–36.

8. Auden, W. H. "For the Time Being." In *For the Time Being.* New York: Random House, 1944.

9. Lukacs, John. *Five Days in London: May 1940.* New Haven: Yale University Press, 1999.

10. Tedlow, Richard S. "The Education of Andy Grove." *Fortune,* December 12, 2005.

11. Shakespeare, William. *Henry IV, Part 1.* act 3, scene 1. London: Oxford University Press, 1914.

12. Drucker, Peter. *The Effective Executive: The Definitive Guide to Getting the Right Things Done.* New York: HarperCollins, 2003.

Interviews
- Immelt, Jeffrey, General Electric. Interview by Noel Tichy, October 2001.

2. FRAMEWORK FOR LEADERSHIP JUDGMENT

Notes
1. Immelt, Jeffrey, General Electric. Presentation at the University of Michigan, Stephan M. Ross School of Business, September 2004.
2. Maney, Kevin. "Chambers, Cisco Born Again." *USA Today*, January 21, 2004.
3. Ibid.
4. Andrew Grove. *Only The Paranoid Survive: How to Exploit Crisis Points that Challenge Every Company and Career.* New York: Currency, 1996.
5. Tuchman, Barbara W. *The March of Folly: From Troy to Vietnam.* New York: Ballantine Books, 1985.
6. Hewlett-Packard 2004 Annual Report.
7. Krames. *What the Best CEOs Know.* New York: McGraw-Hill, 2003.
8. Larry Bossidy and Ram Charan. *Execution: The Discipline of Getting Things Done.* New York: Crown Business, 2002.
9. Immelt, Jeffrey, General Electric. Presentation at the University of Michigan, Stephan M. Ross School of Business, August 2003.
10. Ibid.
11. Gladwell, Malcolm. *Blink: The Power of Thinking Without Thinking.* Boston: Back Bay Books, 2007.
12. Groopman, Jerome. *How Doctors Think.* Boston: Houghton Mifflin Company, 2007.

Interviews
- Downing, Wayne, U.S. Army. Interview by Noel Tichy, May 2005.
- Immelt, Jeffrey, General Electric. Interview by Noel Tichy, October 2001.
- Welch, Jack, General Electric. Personal discussion with Noel Tichy, March 2001.
- Downing, Wayne, U.S. Army. Series of interviews by Noel Tichy, 2003–2005.
- Welch, Jack, General Electric. Personal discussion with Noel Tichy, March 2001.
- Personal discussion between Noel Tichy and a Best Buy Westminster, California, store associate, August 2004.

3. HAVING A STORYLINE

Notes
1. Congressional hearings. "Senate Armed Services Committee Holds Hearing on Boeing Company Global Settlement Agreement." August 1, 2006.
2. Pasztor, Andy. "Boeing to Settle Federal Probes for $615 Million." *Wall Street Journal*, May 15, 2006.

3. Congressional hearings. "Senate Armed Services Committee Holds Hearing on Boeing Company Global Settlement Agreement." August 1, 2006.

4. Ibid.

5. Teachable Point of View. Copyright Noel Tichy and Eli Cohen, 1997.

6. Tichy, Noel, and Chris DeRose. "Roger Enrico's Master Class." *Fortune,* November 1995.

7. Tichy, Noel, with Eli Cohen. *The Leadership Engine: How Winning Companies Build Leaders at Every Level.* New York: HarperCollins, 1997.

8. "Analyst Report: The Boeing Company Earnings Conference Call." Thompson Street Events, July 26, 2006.

9. The Boeing Company 2005 Annual Report.

10. *I Have a Dream: the Story of Martin Luther King in Text and Pictures,* New York: Time Life Books, 1968.

11. Congressional hearings. "Senate Armed Services Committee Holds Hearing on Boeing Company Global Settlement Agreement." August 1, 2006.

Interviews
• McNerney, Jim, Boeing. Interview by Noel Tichy, June 2006.

4. CHARACTER AND COURAGE

Notes
1. Focus: HOPE mission statement, www.focushope.edu/about.htm.

2. Drucker, Peter. *The Effective Executive: The Definitive Guide to Getting the Right Things Done.* New York: HarperCollins, 2003.

3. Immelt, Jeffrey, General Electric. Presentation at the University of Michigan, Stephen M. Ross School of Business, August 2003.

4. Hackett, James, Steelcase. Presentation at the University of Michigan, Stephen M. Ross School of Business, August 2002.

5. Ibid.

6. Ibid.

7. Ibid.

8. Ibid.

9. Peters, Tom, and Robert Waterman. *In Search of Excellence.* New York: Harper & Row, 1982.

10. Greenblatt Stephen, et al. *The Norton Shakespeare.* New York: W.W. Norton, 1997.

11. Focus: HOPE mission statement, www.focushope.edu/about.htm.

12. Josaitis, Eleanor. "Strive to Build a World that Embraces Diversity." *Detroit Free Press,* September 24, 2001.

13. Gergen, David. Foreword to *Geeks & Geezers.* Warren Bennis and Robert J. Thomas. Boston: Harvard Business School Press, 2002.

14. Grove, Andrew. *Only the Paranoid Survive: How to Exploit the Crisis Points that Challenge Every Company and Career.* New York: Currency, 1996.

15. George, Bill. *Authentic Leadership: Rediscovering the Secrets to Creating Lasting Value.* San Francisco: Jossey-Bass, 2003.

16. Ibid.

17. Carlyle, Thomas. *Sartor Resartus: The Life and Opinions of Herr Teufelsdrockh.* Oxford: Oxford University Press, 1987.

18. Leaf, Clifton. "Temptation Is All Around Us: Daniel Vasella of Novartis Talks About Making the Numbers, Self-Deception, and the Danger of Craving Success." *Fortune,* November 18, 2002.

19. Focus: HOPE mission statement, www.focushope.edu/about.htm.

Interviews

- Welch, Jack, General Electric. Personal discussion with Noel Tichy, March 2001.
- Hackett, James, Steelcase. Interview by Noel Tichy, August 2002.
- Liemandt, Joseph, Trilogy Software. Interview by Noel Tichy, November 2003.
- Gardner, John, Common Cause. Interview by Warren Bennis, August 2001.

5. PEOPLE JUDGMENT CALLS

Notes

1. Holstein, William J. "Best Companies for Leaders." *Chief Executive,* November 2005.

Interviews

- Bennett, Steve, Intuit. Interview by Noel Tichy, July 2003.
- Lafley, A. G., Procter & Gamble. Interview by Noel Tichy, January 2006.
- Downing, Wayne, U.S. Army. Interview by Noel Tichy, May 2005.
- Liemandt, Joseph, Trilogy Software. Interview by Noel Tichy, November 2003.
- McNerney, James, Boeing. Interview by Noel Tichy, October 2005.

6. PEOPLE JUDGMENT: CEO SUCCESSION

Notes

1. "Most Admired Companies." *Fortune,* January 1984–1990, February 1992–1993.

2. Colvin, Geoffrey. "The Ultimate Manager." *Fortune,* November 1, 1999.

3. Byrne, John A. "How Jack Welch Runs GE: A Close-up Look at How America's #1 Manager Runs GE." *BusinessWeek,* June 8, 1998.

4. Tichy, Noel, with Stratford Sherman. *Control Your Destiny or Someone Else Will.* New York: Doubleday, Currency, 1993.

5. From a whitepaper by Don Kane, Noel Tichy, and Gene Anderson.

Interviews

- Welch, Jack, General Electric. Internal meeting, November 1985.
- Weiss, Bill, General Electric. Internal meeting, March 1993.
- Welch, Jack, General Electric. Personal meeting with Noel Tichy, 1986.

7. STRATEGY JUDGMENTS

Notes

1. Immelt, Jeffrey, General Electric. Presentation at the University of Michigan, Stephen M. Ross School of Business, September 2005.
2. Deutsch, Claudia H. "At G.E., Whither the House Jack Built? His Successor Faces Skeptics and a Market Less in Awe." *The New York Times,* September 6, 2001.
3. Immelt, Jeffrey, General Electric. Presentation at the University of Michigan, Stephen M. Ross School of Business, September 2004.
4. Etzioni, Amitai. "Humble Decision Making." *Harvard Business Review,* July–August 1989.
5. Janis, Irving L. *Groupthink: Psychological Studies of Policy Decisions and Fiascoes.* Boston: Houghton Mifflin, 1983.
6. Lindblom, Charles, "The Science of 'Muddling Through'." *Public Administration Review* 19, no. 2, 79–88, 1959.
7. Etzioni, Amitai. "Humble Decision Making." Harvard Business Review, July–August 1989.
8. Ibid.
9. Selden, Larry, and Geoff Colvin. *Angel Customers and Demon Customers: Discover Which Is Which and Turbo-Charge Your Stock.* New York: Portfolio, 2003.
10. Fetterman, Mindy. "Best Buy Gets In Touch With Its Feminine Side." *USA Today,* December 20, 2006.
11. Owens, Jim. "Global Trade Galvanizes Caterpillar." *The Wall Street Journal,* February 26, 2007.
12. Ibid.

Interviews

- Immelt, Jeffrey, General Electric. Interview by Noel Tichy, October 2001.
- Gilbert, Julie, Best Buy. Personal interview, March 2005.
- Novak, David, Yum! Brands. Interview by Noel Tichy, August 2005.
- McNerney, Jim, Boeing. Interview by Noel Tichy, October 2005.

8. STRATEGY JUDGMENTS AT G.E.

Notes

1. Immelt, Jeffrey, General Electric. Presentation at University of Michigan, Stephen M. Ross School of Business, September 2004.
2. General Electric Annual Report letter by Jeffrey Immelt, 2005.
3. Immelt, Jeffrey, General Electric. Presentation at University of Michigan, Stephen M. Ross School of Business, September 2004.
4. General Electric Annual Report letter by Jeffrey Immelt, 2001.
5. Immelt, Jeffrey, General Electric. Presentation at University of Michigan, Stephen M. Ross School of Business, September 2004.
6. Ibid.

7. General Electric Annual Report 2005.

8. Immelt, Jeffrey, General Electric. Presentation at University of Michigan, Stephen M. Ross School of Business, September 2005.

9. Stewart, Thomas A. "Growth as a Process: An Interview with Jeffrey R. Immelt." *Harvard Business Review,* June 2006.

10. *GE Growth Tools.* GE internal document.

11. Charan, Ram. *Know-How.* New York: Crown Business, 2007.

12. Immelt, Jeffrey, General Electric. Presentation at University of Michigan, Stephen M. Ross School of Business, September 2005.

13. General Electric Annual Report letter by John Welch, 2000.

14. General Electric Annual Report 2005.

15. Guerrera, Francesco. "Companies International: Share Price Prevents Immelt Emerging from Welch's Shadow." *Financial Times,* February 26, 2007.

16. Immelt, Jeffrey, General Electric. Presentation at University of Michigan, Stephen M. Ross School of Business, September 2005.

Interviews
• Little, Mark, General Electric. Personal interview by Noel M. Tichy, October 2006.

9. CRISIS JUDGMENTS

Notes
1. Lafley, A. G., Procter & Gamble. Presentation at the American Institute for Contemporary German Studies, January 13, 2005.

2. Lafley, A. G., Proctor & Gamble. Presentation at University of Michigan Stephen M. Ross School of Business, January 2006.

3. Young, N. Refugees and Asylum Seekers: Implications for ED Care in Auckland, New Zealand. *Journal of Emergency Nursing,* August 2003

4. Zimmerman, P., Herr. *Triage Secrets.* St. Louis, MO: Mosby, Elsevier, 2005.

5. Blunt, James and John Blaire. *Leadership On the Future Battlefield.* Washington, D.C.: Pergamon-Brassey, 1985.

6. Ibid.

7. Smith, Ron, Buffalo State College. Web site: faculty.buffalostate.edu/smithrd/PR/Exxon.htm.

8. Tuchman, Barbara. *The March of Folly: From Troy to Vietnam.* New York: Ballantine Books, 1984.

9. Personal correspondence to Jac Nasser from Noel Tichy. May 30, 2001.

10. Wetlaufer, Suzy. "Driving Change: An Interview with Ford Motor Company's Jacques Nasser." *Harvard Business Review,* March–April 1999.

11. Ibid.

Interviews
• Gallo, Kathy, North Shore–Long Island Jewish Health System. Interview by Noel Tichy, January 2006.
• Downing, Wayne, U.S. Army. Interview by Noel Tichy, May 2005.

10. CRISIS AS A LEADERSHIP DEVELOPMENT OPPORTUNITY

Notes

1. Drucker, Peter. *Managing the Non-Profit Organization: Principles and Practices*. New York: HarperCollins, 1990.

2. Kelley, Jeffrey. "Circuit City Enters New Phase: Struggling Retailer Hopes a Shift in Strategy Brings a Change in its Fortunes." *Richmond Times,* May 20, 2007. This material is copyrighted by the *Times-Dispatch* and is used with permission.

3. Yum! Brands Annual Report letter by David Novak, 2006.

Interviews

• Novak, David, Yum! Brands. Interview by Noel Tichy, August 2005.

11. KNOWLEDGE CREATION

Notes

1. Lafley, A. G., Procter & Gamble. Presentation at University of Michigan, Stephen M. Ross School of Business, January 2006.

2. Immelt, Jeffrey, General Electric. Presentation at University of Michigan, Stephen M. Ross School of Business, August 2003.

3. Lafley, A. G., Procter & Gamble. Presentation at University of Michigan, Stephen M. Ross School of Business, January 2006.

4. Stewart, Thomas A. "Growth as a Processs: An Interview with Jeffrey R. Immelt." *Harvard Business Review,* June 2006.

5. Lafley, A. G., Procter & Gamble. Presentation at University of Michigan, Stephen M. Ross School of Business, January 2006.

6. Ibid.

7. Ibid.

8. Ibid.

9. Charan, Ram. *Know-How*. New York: Crown Business, 2007.

Interviews

• George, Bill, Medtronic. Interview by Noel Tichy, May 2003.

12. JUDGMENT FOR FUTURE GENERATIONS

Notes

1. Mayor Michael Bloomberg Presentation at the University of Chicago Convocation Address, June 2006.

2. Ibid.

3. New York City Leadership Academy Web page: www.newyorkcityleadershipacademy.org.

4. General Electric Annual Report letter by John F. Welch, 2000.

Interviews

- Klein, Joel, NYC Leadership Academy. Interview by Noel Tichy, September 2006.
- Knowling, Bob, NYC Leadership Academy. Interview by Noel Tichy and Nancy Cardwell, September 2006.

HANDBOOK

Notes

1. George, Bill. *True North: Discover Your Authentic Leadership*. San Francisco: Jossey-Bass, 2007.

2. Miles, Rufus, *The Origin and Meaning of Miles' Law* Public Administration Review, vol. 38, no. 5 (Sep.–Oct., 1978), 399–403.

3. Granovetter, Mark. "The Strength of Weak Ties: A Network Theory Revisited." *Sociological Theory* 1, 201–233, 1983.

4. Tichy, Noel. *The Cycle of Leadership: How Great Leaders Teach Their Companies to Win*. New York: HarperCollins, 2002.

5. Byrne, John. "The Fast Company Interview: Jeff Immelt." *Fast Company*, July 2005.

6. Granovetter, op. cit.

7. Jeffrey Immelt, General Electric. Address to University of Michigan, Stephen M. Ross School of Business, August 2004.

8. Byrne, op. cit.

Interviews

- George, William, Medtronic. Interviewed by Warren Bennis and Noel Tichy, May 2003.
- Downing, Wayne, U.S. Army. Series of interviews by Noel Tichy, 2003–2005.
- Gallo, Kathy, North Shore–Long Island Jewish Health System. Interview by Noel Tichy, January 2006.
- Owens, James, Caterpillar. Interview by Noel Tichy, August 2006.
- Schoonover, Philip, Circuit City. Personal discussions with Noel Tichy, 2006.
- Lafley, A. G., Procter & Gamble. Interview by Noel Tichy, September 2005.
- Immelt, Jeffrey, General Electric. Interview by Noel Tichy, September 2003.
- Novak, David, Yum! Brands. Interview by Noel Tichy, August 2005.
- Ligocki, Kathy, Tower Automotive. Interview by Noel Tichy, August 2005.

Index

Academic study
  of decision making, 10–12
  of strategy, 132–36
Accountability, lack of, negative effects,
    354
Adjustments to judgment
  CEO succession, 125–26
  crisis judgment calls, 220–22
  examples of, 37–39
  in execution phase, 37
  people judgment calls, 101–2
  strategy judgment calls, 40,
    167–69
  See also Redo loop
Akers, John, IBM crisis, 28, 108
Allen, Barry, 121
Allen, Bob, 108, 114
Allison, Graham, 11
Ameritech. See Notebaert, Dick; Weiss,
    Bill
Amersham, 131, 159, 170–71
Anderson, Brad
  Best Buy growth under, 139
  customer-centric strategy, 34, 37,
    40–41, 139–48, 252, 255–56,
    261, 345–47, 362
  framing/naming call, 34
  frontline leaders, 142–43, 254–57,
    347–49
  key lessons from, 65
  operating mechanism of, 348
  organizational knowledge, use of,
    40–41
  strategy judgment calls, 37, 139–48,
    252, 345–47
  TPOV of, 345

WOLF (Women's Leadership Forum),
    143–48
Antoine, Dick, 95–96, 98, 325
Armstrong, John, 114
Armstrong, Lance, 13
Armstrong, Michael, AT&T failure
    under, 1–2, 108
Avian flu scare, 216–17

Baker, James, 9
Barnard, Jesse, 82
Behavioral economics, 12
Beller, Ron, 269
Bennett, Steve
  board of directors, participation of, 260
  community outreach, 262
  frontline leaders, 253–54, 257–60,
    348–49
  key lessons from, 65
  stakeholder knowledge, use of, 41–42
Best Buy. See Anderson, Brad
Bhopal explosion, 202
Bloomberg, Michael
  judgment calls of, 265–66
  New York City schools transforma-
    tion, 263–69
  TPOV of, 265
  See also Klein, Joel; Knowling, Bob
Board of directors, and knowledge
    creation, 261
Boeing. See McNerney, Jim
Boiled frog phenomenon, 30, 328
Bossidy, Larry, 37, 114, 117, 205
Boston Consulting Group (BCG), 132
Brent Spar incident, 198, 203
Brimm, Michael, 269–70

Brown, Dick, 121–22
Brown, Greg, 109
Buffett, Warren, 156
Burke, Jim, Tylenol crisis, 28, 200–1
Burlingame, John, 116
Bush, George H. W., 6, 9–10
Bush, George W., 9–10

Call phase
    CEO succession, 112–13, 125
    crisis judgment calls, 217, 234–35
    elements of, 36–37
    people judgment calls, 99–100
    team members, 330–32
Capability building and making
        judgments, 292
Carlyle, Thomas, 81
Carnap, Rudolf, 11
Caterpillar. See Owens, Jim
CEO succession, 105–26
    good choices, examples of, 107, 115–20
    Immelt, selection as CEO, 117–20
    importance of, 108
    internal versus external candidates,
        106–10, 124
    judgment calls, phases of, 112–14,
        123–25
    and leadership pipeline, 111, 117–19
    poor choices, examples of, 106–15
    preparation phase, 114, 121
    transformation plus succession
        actions, 120–23
    Welch, selection as CEO, 115–17
Challenger, 74
Chambers, John, Cisco crisis, 28–29
Chaos, reality of, 71
Character, 70–74
    and courage, 75, 83
    elements of, 70–71, 74–75
    leadership judgment, examples of,
        71–74, 83–84
    self-assessment, 305–7
    and trust of others, 84
    and TPOVs, 312–13
Charan, Ram, 164
Chen, Steve, 82
Churchill, Winston, 7, 11
Circuit City. See Schoonover, Phil
Cisco crisis, 28–29
Clark, Richard, 114
Clinton, Bill, 5
Coaching, and CEO succession, 125

Coffin, Charles, 155
Cognitive maps, 34
Commitment, positive impact of, 356
Community, 364–68
    engaging, benefits of, 364–65
    partnerships, 261–62, 366–67
    quality of life factors, 365
Conaty, Bill, 119
Condit, Phil, 49
Constituencies
    and judgment calls, 20, 288
    knowledge of, 323
Contextual knowledge
    defined, 41, 260, 293
    and judgment calls, 41–42
    questions to ask, 21
    See also Stakeholder knowledge;
        Teamwork and judgment
Courage, 74–84
    and character, 75, 83
    examples of, 76–84
    and obstacles, 76–81
    self-assessment, 305–7
    and taking action, 75, 78
Creative solutions, 323
Credibility, data-based, negative
        impact of, 354
Crisis
    leader anticipation of, 180, 212
    leadership crisis, 191–92
    poor people judgments as cause,
        192–96, 208–10
Crisis judgment calls, 26–29, 178–210
    call phase, 217, 234
    components of, 26–27, 33, 178, 211
    execution phase, 217, 235
    framing/naming call, 216, 236
    good choices, examples of, 27–29,
        47–50, 62–64, 200–1, 204–7,
        212–19
    leadership actions, 207–8, 212–13, 234
    leadership capacity, enhancing, 190
    military. See Downing, Wayne
    mobilizing/aligning people, 217,
        219–20, 224
    poor choices, examples of, 196–99,
        202–203
    self-assessment, 305
    sensing/identifying need for, 216
    storyline for, 222–24
    triage nurse, 180–85
    and TPOVs, 181–82, 199–201, 219–24

Csikszentmihalyi, Mihaly, 12
Cuban missile crisis, 6–7, 134
Cunningham, Father William, Focus:
  HOPE, 67–69
Customer-centric strategy, 34, 37,
  40–41, 139–48, 252, 255–56, 261,
  345–47, 362

Damasio, Antonio, 12
Daschle, Tom, 172
Decision-making
  academic study of, 10–12
  compared to judgment, 287, 292
Dell, Michael, 5
  poor strategy judgment of, 138–39, 236
Dimon, Jamie, 30
Discrimination, racial, 83–84
Domains, judgment-making. *See*
  Judgment calls
Downing, Wayne
  on call phase, 36
  on crisis judgment calls, 27, 34–35, 37
  crisis judgment calls of, 185–88, 90
  key lessons from, 66
  Noriega, capture of, 186–88, 291
  on people judgment calls, 89
  redo loop, use of, 290–92
  on sure instinct, 17–18
  on timing and judgment, 318–19
Dream sessions, 164, 241, 260, 362
Drook, Gary, 121
Drucker, Peter, 5–6, 15, 25, 33, 70, 211,
  252–53
Dulles, John Foster, 8
Dunlap, Al, 83
Dunn, Brian, 40

Ebbers, Bernie, 70
Ecomagination, 159–60
Edge
  defined, 56
  Welch on, 33
Edison, Thomas, 155
80/20 Rule, 10
Eisenhower, Dwight, 8–9
Emotional factors
  energy, positive, generating, 56, 312–13
  and judgment calls, 33
  people judgment calls, 88–90
Enrico, Roger, leadership development
  program, 107
Etzioni, Amitai, 133–35

Execution phase
  CEO succession, 113, 125
  crisis judgment calls, 215, 233
  elements of, 37
  people judgment calls, 100–101
  strategy judgment calls, 142–43, 151,
    165–68
  team members, 332–35
Experience, judgment from, 297–303
  examples of, 297–98
  judgment journeyline, 299
  self-assessment, 297–303
ExxonMobil
  CEO succession, 114
  Exxon Valdez, 192, 199–200,
    202, 219
  leadership pipeline, 110

Fastow, Andy, 32, 70
Festinger, Leon, 11
Fingerspitzengefühl (sure instinct), 17–18
Fiorina, Carly, 30
  firing of, 103, 105–6
  hiring, poor judgment call, 106–7,
    124
  HP failure under, 2, 5, 22–24, 30,
    103, 195
Firestone tire crisis, 36, 102–3, 196,
  201, 207–8
Firing people, 23, 29, 32, 82, 83
Focus
  importance of, 15
  and making judgments, 292
Focus: HOPE. *See* Cunningham, Father
  William; Josaitis, Eleanor
Ford, Bill, 109, 196
Ford, Gerald, 8–9
Ford Motors. *See* Nasser, Jac
Forrester, Jay W., 11
Framing/naming call
  CEO succession, 124
  crisis judgment calls, 216, 225
  judgment calls, 33–35, 197
  people judgment calls, 95
Frist, Bill, 172
Frontline leaders, 253–60
  Anderson/Best Buy, 142–43, 254–57,
    347–49
  Bennett/Intuit, 253–54, 257–60,
    348–49
  development of, 142–43, 255–56,
    258–60

Frontline leaders (*cont.*)
  Liemandt/Trilogy, 253
  skills of, 255
  as teachers, 258

Gallo, Kathy
  crisis judgment calls of, 182–85
  on judgment from experience, 297–98
  sensing/identifying, need for judgment
    call, 317–18
Galvin, Christopher, 109
Gardner, John, 81–82
Geek Squad, 139, 146–48
General Electric (GE). *See* Immelt, Jeff;
    Welch, Jack
George, Alexander, 11
George, Bill
  on authentic leadership, 306
  on pressure to succeed, 80–81
  self-assessment, 289–90, 297
  on team work, 245, 321–22
Gerstner, Lou
  framing/naming call, 34
  hiring of, 108, 114
  IBM success under, 28, 34
Gilbert, Daniel, 12
Gilbert, Julie, 143–49
Gilmartin, Ray
  hiring of, 108–9, 111–14
  Merck failure under, 112
  Vioxx crisis, 7, 23–25, 35, 78, 103,
    109, 113, 195
Gladwell, Malcolm, 44
Global Business Partnership (GBP)
    crisis, 192–94
Globalization, GE, 252, 262
Goizueta, Roberto, 5
Greed, and judgment calls, 83
Greenstein, Fred, 11
Groopman, Jerome, 44
Group think, 11, 134
Grove, Andy
  courage of, 78
  Intel success under, 13
  on strategic inflection points, 30, 32
Grupo Salinas. *See* Salinas, Ricardo

Hackett, Jim
  on character/values, 71–74, 84
  key lessons from, 66
  wall panel recall decision, 73–74
Hamlet (Shakespeare), 75–76

Hardek, Moria, 147
Henretta, Deb, as leader, selection of,
    92, 96–102, 124–25, 325–26
Henry IV (Shakespeare), 14
Henry V (Shakespeare), 12
Herkstroter, Cor, 192, 196–99
Hewlett-Packard (HP). *See* Fiorina,
    Carly; Hurd, Mark
Human resources
  judgment capability, creating, 357
  system, assessment of, 358
Hurd, Mark
  framing/naming call, 34
  HP success under, 22–24, 30, 34, 107
  key lessons from, 65
  people judgment calls of, 22–23

IBM crisis, 28, 34
Immelt, Jeff
  Amersham purchase, 131, 159, 170–71
  on courage, 72
  cross-business applications, 174
  Crotonville leadership institute, 156,
    164–65, 260
  on decision-making, 13, 18, 36–37,
    39–40, 44, 330
  dream sessions, 164, 241, 260, 362
  economic recession, 177
  GE growth under, 3, 26, 176
  GE Health Advisory Board, 172
  GE values under, 166
  Growth Process at GE, 162
  growth tools, use of, 163–64
  healthymagination initiative, 171–72
  key lessons from, 65
  leadership tasks, scope of, 156–57
  nanotechnology strategy, 172–73
  R&D strategy, 164–71, 174
  selection as CEO, 117–20, 125
  self-knowledge, 72, 241–43
  stakeholder knowledge, use of, 41–42,
    362–63
  storyline of, 131–32, 157–60, 176
  strategic judgment calls of, 26, 36–37,
    128–32, 156–57, 160–76
  TPOV of, 160–61
Innovation
  GE R&D strategy, 164–71, 174
  requirements for, 165
Instinct, importance of, 17–18, 89
Integrity. *See* Character
Intuit. *See* Bennett, Steve

Jager, Durk, P&G failure under, 3, 86–87, 91, 110, 179
Janis, Irving, 11, 134
Jett, Joe, 195, 203
Jobs, Steven, 138–39
John E. Welsh Leadership Center, 155, 274
Johnson, Lyndon Baines, 8
Jones, Reg, 115–16
Josaitis, Eleanor
  courage of, 67–68, 76–77
  Focus: HOPE, building, 67–69
  key lessons from, 65
Judgment
  academic study of, 10–12
  compared to decision-making, 287, 292
  emotional factors, 33
  self-assessment, 294
  and thinking process, 30–31, 33, 34, 44
Judgment and leadership
  character/courage, 67–84
  contextual aspects, 1, 20, 21
  decision-making framework, 20–21
  domains. *See* Judgment calls
  and edge, 33, 56
  framing process of, 292
  good judgment, hallmarks of, 6, 15, 19, 290
  importance of, 4–8
  and instinct, 17–18, 89
  judgment process (chart), 42, 138, 289
  and knowledge creation, 237–62
  phases in judgment process. *See* Judgment calls
  stakeholders, participation of, 14–15
  storyline, 45–66
  and Teachable Points of View (TPOVs), 51–53
  and touch, 14
  and U.S. presidents, 6–10
Judgment calls, 21–43
  adjustments to, 29, 37–39
  call phase, 36–37
  crisis judgment calls, 26–28, 33
  execution phase, 37
  and experience, 297–303
  as flow of events, 29–31
  framing/naming call, 33–35
  judgment calls matrix, 21
  knowledge required for. *See* Knowledge creation

  mobilizing/aligning people in, 35–36
  negative behaviors affecting, 354–55
  people judgment calls, 22–24, 31–32
  preparation phase of, 31–36
  sensing/identifying need for, 31–33, 316–19
  strategy judgment calls, 24–26, 32–33
  and thinking process, 50
  and timing, 318–20
Judgment matrix
  judgment calls, 21
  people judgment calls, 93–99, 101

Kadushin, Charles, 352
Kahneman, Daniel, 10–11
Keats, John, 5
Kennedy, Carolyn, 268, 281
Kennedy, John F., 6–8, 134, 189
Ketchum, Mark, 95–96, 98
Kidder Peabody, GE purchase, 203
King, Martin Luther, Jr.
  assassination, 189
  TPOV of, 58
Klein, Gary, 12
Klein, Joel
  and Bob Knowling, 84
  challenges to job, 275
  key lessons from, 65
  New York City schools transformation, 263–76, 281–82
  people judgment calls, 268–72, 275–76
Knowledge creation, 237–62
  by board of directors, 261
  challenges to job, 275
  community, 261–62
  components of, 237–38
  contextual knowledge, 260, 293
  and good leadership, 238
  and judgment, scope of, 20–21, 293
  organizational knowledge, 40–41, 247–52, 293
  self-knowledge, 39, 238–45, 243–45, 293
  social network knowledge, 40, 245–47, 293
  stakeholder knowledge, 41–42
  team members, knowledge of, 323
  See also specific types of knowledge
Knowledge workers. *See* Frontline leaders
Knowling, Bob, 263, 269–81
  character/courage of, 83–84

Knowling (*cont.*)
  crisis judgment, teaching of, 280–81
  judgment calls of, 272–73, 276
  key lessons from, 65
  leadership development program,
    278–81
  New York City Leadership Academy,
    270, 270–82
  people blind spot of, 195–96
  and racial discrimination, 83
  TPOV of, 277–78
  Welch/Crotonville leadership
    institute, 274
Kozlowski, Dennis, 70

Lafley, A. G.
  crisis judgment calls, 179–80
  Henretta, selection of, 92, 96–102,
    124–25
  key lessons from, 65
  P&G crisis, 86–87, 178–79
  P&G growth under, 2–3, 90, 179
  people judgment calls, 92–102
  and redo loop, 43, 124–25, 326
  selection as CEO, 85–87
  self-knowledge, 237–38, 242
  storyline of, 91–92
  team engagement, 325–26
Lay, Ken, 32
Leadership
  crises of, 191–92
  selecting. *See* CEO succession
  teacher role of leader, 51–53, 238
  transformational, 51, 120–23
  winning leaders, traits of, 50–51
  See also Judgment and leadership
Leadership pipeline, and CEO
    succession, 109–11, 117–19, 124
LeVino, Ted, 116
Lewin, Kurt, 11
Licklider, J. C. R., 11
Liemandt, Joe
  key lessons from, 66
  on people judgment calls, 89–90
  on self-doubt, 78–80
  Trilogy University, 253
Ligocki, Kathy, community
    partnerships, 366–67
Little, Grady, 6
Little, Mark, 167–70
Loewenstein, George, 12
Lukacs, John, 11

McCain, John, 64
McNerney, Jim
  crisis judgment calls, 45–50, 62–64
  versus Immelt as GE CEO, 117,
    119–20
  key lessons from, 65
  outside hiring of, 109
  on people judgment calls, 103–4
  and planful opportunism, 61–64
  storyline of, 52–61, 151
  strategy judgment calls, 151–52
  TPOV of, 52–58, 151
Markham, Richard, 23, 108, 111–12
Marriott, Bill, 71–72
Martinez, Pedro, 6
Matrix
  strategic decision-making, 132
  See also Judgment matrix
May, Ernest, 11
Medtronic. *See* George, Bill
Miles, Rufus, 337
Milgram, Stanley, 338
Military decisions. *See* Downing, Wayne
Milton, Jim, 103
Mixed scanning model
  elements of, 135
  physician's use of, 136–37
Mobilizing/aligning people
  CEO succession, 124
  crisis judgment calls, 215, 217–18,
    222, 230–33
  strategy judgment calls, 141–42
  team members, 325–29
Moore, Gordon, 13
Mulally, Alan, 109

Nanotechology, Immelt/GE, 172–74
Nardelli, Robert, 117, 119, 125
Nasser, Jac, 36
  business leadership initiative, 207
  and Firestone tire crisis, 36, 102–3,
    192, 196, 201–10
  storyline of, 206, 208
  TPOV of, 209
Nepotism, 109
Network, 337–40
  assessment of, 339–40
  positive impact of, 356
Neustadt, Richard, 11
New City, 224–25
New York City Leadership Academy,
    84, 195–96, 268, 270–82

New York City schools. *See*
    Bloomberg, Michael; Klein,
    Joel; Knowling, Bob
Nixon, Richard, 5, 9
Nooyi, Indra Krisnamurthy, 107
Noriega, Manuel, 186–88, 291
North Shore-LIJ Hospital. *See* Gallo,
    Kathy
Notebaert, Dick
    Ameritech growth under, 123
    hiring of, 121–23
    Weiss as coach, 126
Novak, David
    adjustments to judgment, 43
    avian flu scare, 216–17
    crisis judgment calls of, 212–13,
        215–20, 235, 359
    key lessons from, 66
    operating mechanism of, 344
    poor strategy judgment of, 149–51
    red food dye crisis, 217–18
    stakeholder knowledge, use of, 362
    Taco Bell *E. coli* outbreak, 213,
        218–19, 359
    TPOV of, 219–20
Novartis, 81

Obstacles
    and courage, 77–78
    direct threats, 76–77
    disagreement from others,
        78, 82–83, 98–99
    discrimination, 83–84
    greed, 83
    pressure to succeed, 80–81
    self-doubt as, 78–80
Olsen, Ken
    Digital failure under, 31
Operating systems
    GE Operating System, 249–51
    and organizational knowledge, 249–51
Organizational knowledge, 247–52,
        337–58
    defined, 40, 293
    and frontline associates, 347–49
    frontline leaders, 253–60
    and judgment building process, 350–51
    and judgment calls, 40–41, 344–47
    and network, 337–40
    operating mechanism for gaining,
        340–43
    and operating systems, 249–51

questions to ask, 21
    sources of information, 248
Osler, Sir William, 7
Othello (Shakespeare)
Owens, Jim
    on judgment from experience, 297–98
    key lessons from, 65
    operating mechanism of, 342
    on self-knowledge, 300
    stakeholder knowledge, use of, 360–61
    strategy judgment calls, 152–53

Pareto, Vilfredo, 10
Parsons, Dick, 268, 281
People judgment calls, 22–24, 85–104
    adjustments to, 101–2
    call phase, 99–100, 112–13
    choosing CEO. *See* CEO succession
    components of, 24, 31–32, 85, 88
    emotional factors, 88–90
    execution phase, 100–101
    framing/naming call, 95
    good choices, examples of, 22–24,
        92–102, 268–72
    importance of, 87–88
    judgment matrix, 88, 93–99, 101
    judgment process in, 87–88, 93
    Lafley/P&G example, 92–102, 124–25
    mobilizing/aligning people, 95–99
    people blind spot, 194–96, 208–10
    poor choices, examples of, 192–96,
        208–10, 275–76
    preparation phase, 112
    self-assessment, 304
    sensing/identifying need for, 93–94
    team, selection of, 90–92, 102–3
    and team participation, 98–101
Pepper, John, 86–87
PepsiCo., 107, 110
Peters, Tom, 75
Phases in judgment process. *See*
    Judgment calls
Physicians, mixed scanning model, use
    of, 136–37
PIMS (Profit Impact of Market
    Strategy), 132
Planful opportunism
    defined, 61–62
    McNerney/Boeing example, 61–64
    and storyline, 53
    Welch and Honeywell acquisition, 38
Polaris. *See* Tiller, Tom

Preparation phase
   CEO succession, 112, 114, 121
   elements of, 31–36
   strategy judgment calls, 140–42
Presidents, U. S., judgment calls,
   examples of, 6–10
Procter & Gamble. See Lafley, A.G.
Purposeful abandonment, 33

Quine, W. V., 11

Rawls, Lawrence
   CEO succession, 114
   poor judgment calls, 192, 199–200,
      202, 219
Raymond, Lee, 114, 192, 200
Reagan, Ronald, 9
Red food dye crisis, 217–18
Redo loop
   defined, 43
   Downing/military example, 290–92
   Lafley/P&G example, 43, 124–25, 326
   and stakeholders, 360–61
   strategy judgment calls, 143–48
Reinemund, Steve, 107
Risk-aversion, negative impact of, 354
Risk-taking
   and courage, 78
   and self-confidence, 356
Rollins, Kevin
   poor strategy judgment of, 138–39
Rorsted, Kasper, 103
Rumsfeld, Donald, 82

Salinas, Ricardo
   Banco Azteca, 226, 232–33
   bear in the woods story, 226
   Grupo Elektra transformation
      process, 226–33
      current practices & processes, 227
      model stores, 233
      strategic judgments, 227, 247
      team projects, 227–33
   Grupo Salinas and global recession,
      212, 225–36
   strategy judgment calls, 234–36
   TPOV of, 234
Saro-Wiwa, Ken, 198–99
Scandals, corporate, 32, 70–71, 261
Schein, Edgar, 11
Schoeffler, Sidney, 132
Schoonover, Phil

Acceleration Initiative New Concept
   Team, 224–25
Circuit City downturn, 213–15,
   220–22, 317
crisis judgment calls of, 212–15,
   220–25, 247
key lessons from, 65
leadership development activities, 214
sensing/identifying, need for judgment
   call, 316–17
storyline, 214, 220–24
TPOV of, 214, 220–24
Schumpeter, Joseph, 32
Scientific management, 132
Scowcroft, Brent, 9
Selden, Larry, 140, 256, 345
Self-assessment, 297–308
   of character/courage, 305–7
   example of, 289–90
   of judgment experience, 297–303
   of past judgments, 302–8
   and self-knowledge, 307–8
Self-confidence, and risk-taking, 356
Self-doubt, as obstacle, 78–80
Self-knowledge, 238–45, 297–320
   defined, 39, 293
   Immelt/GE example, 72, 241–43
   and judgment calls, 39, 243–45
   Lafley/P&G example, 237–38, 243–44
   questions to ask, 20, 39
   and self-assessment, 307–8
   Welch/GE example, 238–41
Sensing/identifying
   CEO succession, 123
   crisis judgment calls, 214, 222–23,
      316–17
   judgment calls, 31–33, 316–19
   people judgment calls, 93–94
   strategy judgment calls, 139, 140–41
September 11 terrorist attacks, 74, 76,
   129, 183–84
Shakespeare, 5, 12, 14, 75–76
Shell Oil, poor crisis judgment at,
   194–99, 200, 203
Shin, Young, 82
Shinseki, General Eric, 82
Short-term, avoiding, 34–35
Simon, Herbert, 10
Skilling, Jeff, 32
Smale, John, 114
Smith, Ron, 200
Social network knowledge

building of, 245–47
defined, 40, 293
and judgment calls, 40
questions to ask, 20–21
See also Teamwork and judgment
Sorenson, Ted, 8, 9
Special Operations Forces. *See*
Downing, Wayne
Springer, Bill, 121–22
Stacey, Patti, 120–21, 272, 274, 345
Stakeholder(s)
impact on storyline, 359–61
types of, 41, 260, 293, 361
Stakeholder knowledge, 359–68
community as stakeholder, 364–68
defined, 41
Immelt/GE example, 362–63
and judgment process, 362–63
Owens/Catepillar example, 360–61
See also Contextual knowledge
Steelcase. *See* Hackett, Jim
Stein, Sandra, 271–73
Stemple, Bob, 114
Sternberg, Robert, 12
Stonecipher, Harry, 47, 48, 151
Storyline, 45–66
and crisis judgment calls, 199, 222–24
development of, 52–53, 315–16
elements of, 45, 53, 62, 310
Immelt/GE example, 131–32, 157–60
Lafley/P&G example, 91–92
McNerney/Boeing example, 52–61, 151
Nasser/Ford example, 209
and planful opportunism, 53
questions addressed in, 59–61, 157–59
Schoonover/Circuit City, 222–24
stakeholder, impact on, 359–61
and TPOVs, 52–53, 58, 160, 199,
310–14
Strategic inflection points, 30
Strategy judgment calls, 24–26, 127–53
academic study of, 132–36
adjustments to, 40, 167–69
components of, 25, 32–33, 127
execution phase, 142–43, 151, 165–68
good choices, examples of, 25–26,
139–48, 151–53, 160–76
mobilizing/aligning people, 141–42
negative behaviors affecting, 355
poor choices, examples of, 24–25,
138–39, 148–50
preparation phase, 140–42

redo loop, 143–48
self-assessment, 305
sensing/identifying need for, 139,
140–41
Success
and good judgment, 5–6, 290
leader traits related to, 369
pressure to succeed, 80–81
Sunbeam, 83
Swope, Gerard, 155

Taco Bell E. coli outbreak, 213, 218–19
Teachable Points of View (TPOVs), 51–53
Anderson/Best Buy, 345
Bloomberg/NY City schools, 265
and crisis judgment calls, 181–82,
191, 199–201, 212, 219–22
defined, 51, 310–12
implementing, factors in, 313–14
Knowling/NY City Leadership
Academy, 277–78
McNerney/Boeing example, 52–58, 151
and mixed scanning model, 135
Nasser/Ford example, 209–10
Novak/Yum!, 219–20
Schoonover/Circuit City, 222–24
and storyline, 52–53, 58, 160, 199,
209, 212, 310–14
Teaching
by frontline leaders, 258, 348
judgment building process, steps in,
350–51
role of leader, 51–52, 238
virtuous teaching cycles, 239–40,
257, 341–42, 363
See also Teachable Points of View
(TPOVs)
Teamwork and judgment, 321–36
assessment of, 322–35
call phase, 330–32
as context for decision-making, 21
errors/corrective action, 328–29, 331–35
execution phase, 332–35
frontline leaders, 253–60, 347–49
knowledge sources of team, 323
members, skills/assets of, 246–47
mobilizing/aligning people, 36, 325–29
and organizational knowledge, 40–41
and people judgment calls, 98–101
stakeholder knowledge, use of,
14–15, 41–42
team, selection of, 90–92

Teamwork and judgment (*cont.*)
  team first/strategy second concept,
    102–3
  team judgment knowledge capacity
    building (chart), 248
  transformation team, 121
  trust of team, 84
Thain, John, 31
Thinking process, and making judg-
    ments, 30–31, 33–34, 44, 50, 292
Tichy, Noel, 51, 56, 75, 111, 115,
    120–21, 180, 191–94, 196–98,
    201–9, 241, 272, 274, 341
Tiller, Tom, key lessons from, 65
Tillerson, Rex, 114
Timing, and judgment calls, 318–20
TPOVs. *See* Teachable Points of View
    (TPOVs)
Trani, John, 119
Transformational leadership
  defined, 51
  and TPOVs, 51
  Weiss/Ameritech example, 120–23
Transparency, and making judgments, 292
Triage nurse. *See* Gallo, Kathy
Trilogy. *See* Liemandt, Joe
Truman, Harry, 5
  courage of, 77
  unpopular decisions, 82
Trust
  in leader with character, 84
  untrustworthy leader, example of,
    192–94
Tuchman, Barbara, 31, 200
Tversky, Amos, 11
Tylenol crisis, 27–28, 200–1

Union Carbide crisis, 202
Urgency, lack of, negative impact of, 354

Vagelos, Roy
  Gilmartin, hiring of, 23–24, 108, 111–14
Values. *See* Character
Vasella, Daniel, on character of leader, 81
Vioxx crisis, 7, 23–25, 33, 35, 109, 113,
    195
Virtuous teaching cycles, 239–40, 257,
    341–42, 363

Walmart, 140, 213, 224, 247, 317, 364
Walters, John, 108, 114
Warner, John, 47

Waterman, Robert, 75
Way, Al, 116
Weick, Karl, 12, 188–91
Weiner, Norbert, 11
Weiss, Bill
  CEO succession/transformational
    tasks of, 120–23
  as coach, 126
  Notebaert, hiring of, 121–23
Welch, Jack
  on chaos, 71
  as coach, 125
  crisis judgment calls, 204–6
  Crotonville leadership institute, 26,
    117, 155, 205, 209, 239–42, 269, 274
  on the "edge," 33
  execution of plan, 38–39
  on focus, 15
  framing/naming call, 33
  GE growth under, 3, 25–26, 128
  GE Operating System, 249–51
  GE values under, 166
  Honeywell acquisition decision, 3,
    37–39, 43
  Immelt, selection as CEO, 117–20, 125
  leadership pipeline, design of, 117–19,
    124
  and New York schools
    transformation, 269, 274–76
  operating mechanism of, 341
  on people judgment calls, 89
  and Peter Drucker, 25–26
  poor judgment calls, 35–36, 195
  selection as CEO, 115–17
  self-knowledge, 238–41
  strategic judgment calls of, 25–26
  strategic planners, firing of, 132–33
  on team work, 14
  time card scandal, 204–5
Wendt, Gary, 119
Whybrow, Peter, 12
Winkler, Mike, 103
Wittgenstein, Ludwig, 11
WOLF (Women's Leadership Forum),
    143–48
Wood, Dr. Susan, 82
Wriston, Walter, 116

Young, Owen, 155
Yum!. *See* Novak, David

Zander, Ed, 109